# INFORMATIONAL DISPERSAL
# AND PARALLEL PROCESSING

# Cambridge International Series on Parallel Computation

Managing Editor:

W.F. McColl, *Programming Research Group, University of Oxford*

Editorial Board:

Cambridge International Series on Parallel Computation: 3

# INFORMATION DISPERSAL AND PARALLEL COMPUTATION

YUH-DAUH LYUU

*NEC Research Institute*
*Princeton, New Jersey*

**CAMBRIDGE**
UNIVERSITY PRESS

PUBLISHED BY THE PRESS SYNDICATE OF THE UNIVERSITY OF CAMBRIDGE
The Pitt Building, Trumpington Street, Cambridge, United Kingdom

CAMBRIDGE UNIVERSITY PRESS
The Edinburgh Building, Cambridge CB2 2RU, UK
40 West 20th Street, New York NY 10011–4211, USA
477 Williamstown Road, Port Melbourne, VIC 3207, Australia
Ruiz de Alarcón 13, 28014 Madrid, Spain
Dock House, The Waterfront, Cape Town 8001, South Africa

http://www.cambridge.org

First published 1992
First paperback edition 2004

*A catalogue record for this book is available from the British Library*

*Library of Congress Cataloguing-in-Publication Data*
Lyuu, Yuh-Dauh.
Information dispersal and parallel computation / Yuh-Dauh Lyuu.
p.  cm. – (Cambridge international series on parallel
computation : 3)
Includes bibliographical references (p.  ) and index.
ISBN 0 521 43226 X hardback
1. Parallel processing (Electronic computers)  2. Computer
algorithms.  3. Fault-tolerant computing.  I. Title.  II. Series.
QA76.58.L98   1992
004´.35–dc20                                       92-29635
                                                      CIP

ISBN 0 521 43226 X hardback
ISBN 0 521 60279 3 paperback

To the memory of CHRISTINE LYUU

# Contents

List of Figures                                                            xi

Preface                                                                   xiii

Acknowledgments                                                            xv

Glossary of Notations                                                    xvii

1  Introduction                                                             1
   1.1  The von Neumann Machine Paradigm  . . . . . . . . . . . . . . . .   2
   1.2  Issues in Parallel Processing  . . . . . . . . . . . . . . . . .    3
   1.3  Overview of the Book  . . . . . . . . . . . . . . . . . . . . . .   6

2  Information Dispersal                                                     8
   2.1  Introduction  . . . . . . . . . . . . . . . . . . . . . . . . . .   9
   2.2  Results from Algebra and Number Theory  . . . . . . . . . . . .    11
   2.3  The Vandermonde Matrix  . . . . . . . . . . . . . . . . . . . .    12
        2.3.1  Relation with polynomial interpolation  . . . . . . . . .   12
        2.3.2  Methods for interpolating polynomials  . . . . . . . . .    13
        2.3.3  The discrete Fourier transform  . . . . . . . . . . . . .   13
   2.4  An IDA Schema  . . . . . . . . . . . . . . . . . . . . . . . . .    14
   2.5  Fast Information Dispersal Algorithms  . . . . . . . . . . . . .    16
        2.5.1  Choosing a commutative ring  . . . . . . . . . . . . . .    18
        2.5.2  Comparison with Rabin's IDA  . . . . . . . . . . . . . .    19
        2.5.3  Variations on a theme  . . . . . . . . . . . . . . . . .    20
        2.5.4  Related work  . . . . . . . . . . . . . . . . . . . . . .   22
   2.6  Application to Voting  . . . . . . . . . . . . . . . . . . . . .    22

**3  Interconnection Networks**                                                          **26**

   3.1  Introduction . . . . . . . . . . . . . . . . . . . . . . . . . . .   27

   3.2  Basic Terminology for Networks . . . . . . . . . . . . . . . . .   27

       3.2.1  Interconnection and node structures . . . . . . . . . . . .   27

       3.2.2  Switching . . . . . . . . . . . . . . . . . . . . . . . .   30

       3.2.3  Universality . . . . . . . . . . . . . . . . . . . . . .   31

   3.3  Graph-Theoretical Modeling . . . . . . . . . . . . . . . . . .   32

   3.4  Sample Networks . . . . . . . . . . . . . . . . . . . . . . . .   32

       3.4.1  The hypercube network  . . . . . . . . . . . . . . . . .   32

       3.4.2  The de Bruijn network . . . . . . . . . . . . . . . . .   33

       3.4.3  The butterfly network . . . . . . . . . . . . . . . . .   33

       3.4.4  Other networks . . . . . . . . . . . . . . . . . . . . .   34

   3.5  Some Desirable Properties for Networks . . . . . . . . . . . . .   36

**4  Introduction to Parallel Routing**                                                 **41**

   4.1  Introduction . . . . . . . . . . . . . . . . . . . . . . . . . . .   42

   4.2  The Parallel Routing Problem . . . . . . . . . . . . . . . . . .   42

   4.3  Outline of Approach  . . . . . . . . . . . . . . . . . . . . . .   44

   4.4  Summary of Results . . . . . . . . . . . . . . . . . . . . . . .   45

   4.5  Other Work on IDA-Based Routing Schemes  . . . . . . . . . .   47

   4.6  Previous Work on Parallel Routing  . . . . . . . . . . . . . . .   47

**5  Fault-Tolerant Routing Schemes and Analysis**                                      **50**

   5.1  Parallel Communication Scheme . . . . . . . . . . . . . . . . .   51

   5.2  Basic Terminology and Conventions . . . . . . . . . . . . . . .   52

   5.3  Routing on the Fault-Free Hypercube . . . . . . . . . . . . . .   55

       5.3.1  Definitions . . . . . . . . . . . . . . . . . . . . . . .   55

       5.3.2  SRA: description and preliminary analysis  . . . . . . . .   56

       5.3.3  Analysis of SRA . . . . . . . . . . . . . . . . . . . . .   58

       5.3.4  Remarks on the tightness of bounds . . . . . . . . . . .   61

   5.4  Routing on the Hypercube with Faults . . . . . . . . . . . . .   62

       5.4.1  Definitions . . . . . . . . . . . . . . . . . . . . . . .   62

       5.4.2  Description of FSRA . . . . . . . . . . . . . . . . . . .   63

       5.4.3  Analysis of FSRA under the fault-free model  . . . . . . .   64

       5.4.4  Analysis of FSRA under random fault models . . . . . . .   67

   5.5  Routing on the de Bruijn Network . . . . . . . . . . . . . . . .   71

       5.5.1  Definitions . . . . . . . . . . . . . . . . . . . . . . .   71

       5.5.2  RABN: description and preliminary analysis  . . . . . . .   72

       5.5.3  Analysis of RABN under the fault-free model . . . . . . .   74

        5.5.4   Analysis of RABN under a random fault model . . . . . . . . 78

  5.6  On Time Bounds and Models . . . . . . . . . . . . . . . . . 81

  5.7  A General Framework for IDA-Based Schemes . . . . . . . . 82

  5.8  FSRA under a More Realistic Fault Model . . . . . . . . . . 83

**6  Simulation of the PRAM                             86**

  6.1  Introduction . . . . . . . . . . . . . . . . . . . . . . . . . . 87

  6.2  The PRAM model . . . . . . . . . . . . . . . . . . . . . . . 88

        6.2.1   Simulation of the PRAM . . . . . . . . . . . . . . . 89

        6.2.2   Previous work on simulation of PRAMs . . . . . . . . 90

        6.2.3   Combining in the priority model . . . . . . . . . . . 91

        6.2.4   A digression on "hot spot" contention . . . . . . . . . 92

  6.3  Special Case Simulation . . . . . . . . . . . . . . . . . . . 94

        6.3.1   The simulation algorithm and results . . . . . . . . . 95

        6.3.2   Analysis of size of regular buffers . . . . . . . . . . . 96

        6.3.3   Analysis of size of wait buffers . . . . . . . . . . . . 100

        6.3.4   Analysis of slowdown . . . . . . . . . . . . . . . . . 106

  Appendix: A Universal Simulation Scheme . . . . . . . . . . . . . 107

**7  Asynchronism and Sensitivity                   110**

  7.1  Introduction . . . . . . . . . . . . . . . . . . . . . . . . . . 111

  7.2  Terminology and Definitions . . . . . . . . . . . . . . . . . 112

  7.3  Asynchronous Routing Using Local Synchronization . . . . . 112

  7.4  Run-Time Sensitivity to Component Speeds . . . . . . . . . 116

        7.4.1   A general theorem . . . . . . . . . . . . . . . . . . . 117

        7.4.2   Sensitivity analysis of FSRA . . . . . . . . . . . . . 119

  7.5  Communication Complexity and Sensitivity . . . . . . . . . 121

**8  On-Line Maintenance                       123**

  8.1  Introduction . . . . . . . . . . . . . . . . . . . . . . . . . . 124

  8.2  On-Line Wire Maintenance on Hypercubes with FSRA . . . . 124

        8.2.1   Definitions and outline of approach . . . . . . . . . . 125

        8.2.2   Partition $\mathcal{P}$ . . . . . . . . . . . . . . . . . . . . . 126

        8.2.3   Analysis of partition $\mathcal{P}$ . . . . . . . . . . . . . . 127

**9  A Fault-Tolerant Parallel Computer           130**

  9.1  Introduction . . . . . . . . . . . . . . . . . . . . . . . . . . 131

  9.2  Introductory Fault-Tolerant Computing . . . . . . . . . . . 131

        9.2.1   Techniques . . . . . . . . . . . . . . . . . . . . . . . 131

      9.2.2   Samples . . . . . . . . . . . . . . . . . . . . . . . . . . . .  133

  9.3  HPC: Approach and Building Blocks  . . . . . . . . . . . . . . . .  134

      9.3.1   Cluster: fault containment and communication . . . . . . .  135

      9.3.2   HPC-Routing: analysis of run-time  . . . . . . . . . . . .  139

  9.4  Conclusions . . . . . . . . . . . . . . . . . . . . . . . . . . . . .  139

**Bibliography**                                                                                     **141**

**Index**                                                                                               **171**

# List of Figures

2.1   The Working of IDA. . . . . . . . . . . . . . . . . . . . . .   9
2.2   Idea of Voting. . . . . . . . . . . . . . . . . . . . . . . .   23
2.3   An IDA-Based Voting Scheme FILTERING. . . . . . . . . . . .   23

3.1   Two Ways to Organize Processors and Memory Modules. . . . . .   28
3.2   Direct (Communication) Network Architecture. . . . . . . . .   29
3.3   Sample Networks. . . . . . . . . . . . . . . . . . . . . . .   38
3.4   Sample Networks (continued). . . . . . . . . . . . . . . . .   39
3.5   Sample Networks (continued). . . . . . . . . . . . . . . . .   40

4.1   Routing in a Direct Network. . . . . . . . . . . . . . . . .   43

5.1   SRA ("Subcube Routing Algorithm"). . . . . . . . . . . . . .   57
5.2   The Working of SRA on $C_4$. . . . . . . . . . . . . . . . .   59
5.3   A Routing Scheme without the Subcube Concept. . . . . . . .   61
5.4   FSRA ("Fault-Tolerant Subcube Routing Algorithm"). . . . . .   63
5.5   The Working of FSRA on $C_6$. . . . . . . . . . . . . . . . .   65
5.6   RABN ("Routing Algorithm for the de Bruijn Network"). . . . .   73
5.7   The Working of RABN on $N_{3,3}$. . . . . . . . . . . . . . .   75
5.8   Rabin's Paradigm. . . . . . . . . . . . . . . . . . . . . . .   83
5.9   Unsuccessful Routing Under $O(1)$ Link Failure Probability. .   85

6.1   The PRAM Model of Computation. . . . . . . . . . . . . . . .   88
6.2   Tree Saturation. . . . . . . . . . . . . . . . . . . . . . .   93
6.3   How Pieces Got Combined in Subphase 2.1. . . . . . . . . . .   98
6.4   Combining and Wait Buffers in Subphase 2.1. . . . . . . . .   102

7.1   How SA Works. . . . . . . . . . . . . . . . . . . . . . . . .   114
7.2   Properties of the $l$-Graph. . . . . . . . . . . . . . . . .   118
7.3   Sensitivity of SRA on $C_2$. . . . . . . . . . . . . . . . . .   120

9.1   The Clusters. . . . . . . . . . . . . . . . . . . . . . . . 136
9.2   How HPC-Routing Works. . . . . . . . . . . . . . . . . 137
9.3   The HPC-Routing Algorithm. . . . . . . . . . . . . . . 138

# Preface

It has long been recognized that computer design utilizing more than one processor is one promising approach — some say the only approach — toward more powerful computing machines. Once one adopts this view, several issues immediately emerge: how to connect processors and memories, how do processors communicate efficiently, how to tolerate faults, how to exploit the redundancy inherent in multiprocessors to perform on-line maintenance and repair, and so forth.

This book confronts the above-mentioned issues with two keys insights. There exist error-correcting codes that generate redundancy which is efficient in terms of the number of bits. Such redundancy is used to correct errors and erasures caused by component failures and resource limitations (such as limited buffer size). This insight comes from Michael Rabin. The next insight, due to Leslie Valiant, demonstrates the criticality of randomization in achieving communication efficiency.

We intend to make this book an up-to-date account of the information dispersal approach as it is applied to parallel computation. We also discuss related work in the general area of parallel communication and computation and provide an extensive bibliography in the hope that either might be helpful for researchers and students who want to explore any particular topic. Although materials in this book extend across several disciplines (algebra, coding theory, number theory, arithmetics, algorithms, graph theory, combinatorics, and probability), it is, the author believes, a self-contained book; adequate introduction is given and every proof is complete.

## Technical Summary

Efficient schemes are presented for the following problems: fast parallel communication, low congestion, fault tolerance, simulation of ideal parallel computation models, synchronization in asynchronous networks with low sensitivity to variations in component speed, and on-line maintenance. All of the schemes either employ, or have inspirations from, Rabin's information dispersal idea. We also describe efficient information dispersal algorithms (IDAs) and their application to the enforcement of regions of fault containment.

Let $N$ denote the size of the hypercube network. We present a randomized communication scheme, FSRA ("Fault-Tolerant Subcube Routing Algorithm"), that routes in $2 \log N + 1$ time using only constant size buffers and with probability of success $1 - N^{-\Theta(\log N)}$. FSRA furthermore tolerates $O(N)$ random link failures with high probability. Similar results are also proved for the de Bruijn network. A general framework for fault-tolerant routing is described for the large class of node-symmetric networks (such as the hypercube).

FSRA is employed to simulate, without using hashing, a class of CRCW PRAM ("Concurrent-Read Concurrent-Write Parallel Random Access Machine") programs with a slowdown of $O(\log N)$ with almost certainty if combining is used. Fault-tolerant simulation schemes for general CRCW programs are also presented.

A simple acknowledgment synchronizer can make the routing schemes in this book run on asynchronous networks without loss of efficiency. We further show that speed of any component — be it a processor or a link — has only linear impact on the run-time of FSRA; that is, the extra delay in its run-time is only proportional to the drift in the component's delay and is independent of the size of the network.

On-line maintainability makes the machine more available to the user. We show that, under FSRA, a constant fraction of the links can be disabled with essentially no impact on the routing performance. This result immediately suggests several efficient maintenance and repair procedures.

Based on the above results, a fault-tolerant parallel computing system, called HPC ("hypercube parallel computer"), is sketched at the end of this book.

# Acknowledgments

The study of information dispersal and its various applications was initiated by my thesis advisor at Harvard University, Prof. Michael Rabin, under whose supervision and encouragement I completed my thesis *An Information Dispersal Approach to Issues in Parallel Processing* and several other papers [233, 234, 235, 236, 237]. The architecture of that thesis is largely preserved in this book. His ability to approach seemingly difficult problems with clear but at first not so obvious insights compels me to strive for simplicity and precision. He also raised the sensitivity issue for asynchronous algorithms.

I thank Prof. Meichun Hsu and Prof. Les Valiant for serving on my thesis committee. Prof. Valiant's seminal work on parallel routing also strongly influences the direction of my research.

This book benefits from several people's comments, knowledge, and generosity. Prof. Rabin contributed to the proof of Theorem 7.1. Satish Rao first suggested the possibility of an information dispersal algorithm (IDA) based on the Fourier transform. After such an IDA had been developed (see Chapter 2), Prof. Krizanc of Rochester University pointed out that the scheme had largely been anticipated by Preparata [280]. Prof. Beaver of Pennsylvania State University also pointed out the connection between my scheme and Shamir's secret-sharing algorithm and subsequent idea advanced by Ben-Or, Goldwasser, and Wigderson [46] in that setting. (It turns out that all of them are Reed-Solomon codes.) Joe Kilian and Prof. Rabin improved the phrasing of Theorem 8.3. Prof. Tsantilas of Columbia University has always been a generous source on the literature of, and ideas about, routing. With the help of Bill Gear of NEC Research Institute, we showed that a global minimum is indeed produced by Eq. (6.8), correcting an error in the original proof of Lemma 6.15. Harry Bochner and Joanne Klys of Aiken Computation Laboratory, Harvard University, provided valuable assistance on the use of graphical tools and subtle features of LaTeX. Part of Chapter 3 was written at the Department of Computer Science and Information Engineering, National Taiwan University, under Kuo-Liang Chung's computer account. Jehoshua Bruck of IBM, Yonatan Aumann of the Hebrew University of Jerusalem, and Peter Mysliwietz of the University of Paderborn suggested relevant literature. Prof. McColl of Oxford University not only suggested the title, but also made the publication possible.

I am indebted to NEC Research Institute for the unmatched generosity and the vision that autonomy is essential to scientific inquiry. The research reported in my original dissertation was generously supported by National Science Foundation Grant MCS-8121431 at Harvard University.

It has been a pleasure to work with Dr. Alan Harvey, Editor of Mathematical Sciences, and Lauren Cowles, Editor of Mathematics and Computer Science, both at Cambridge University Press. My thanks are due to them and their staff.

The constant supports from my wife, Chih-Lan, made the writing experience a pleasant one. Although my son, Raymond, has increased in age since his birth when I was writing my thesis *with* him, I again had to write this book with him. Fortunately, now, as before, the computer has made the destruction of manuscripts much less life-threatening.

# Glossary of Notations

| notation | page number | notation | page number |
|---|---|---|---|
| $\approx$ | 13 | $D$ | 96 |
| $|A|$ | 11 | $D_1$ | 97 |
| $A_{ij}$ | 11 | $D_2$ | 99 |
| $A_t(y)$ | 97 | $dim(i)$ | 126 |
| $A^T$ | 11 | $E(G)$ | 52 |
| $A^*$ | 11 | $E(i, l, t)$ | 126 |
| $A^{-1}$ | 11 | $F$ | 14 |
| $\mathcal{A}$ | 14 | $|F|$ | 9 |
| $\tilde{\mathcal{A}}$ | 15 | $F_{n,n}$ | 13 |
| $\mathcal{A}_{\mathrm{FFT}}$ | 16 | $G_1 \subseteq G_2$ | 52 |
| $\mathcal{A}_{\mathrm{V}}$ | 16 | $G_1 \cap G_2 = \emptyset$ | 52 |
| $a_t$ | 97 | $GF(p)$ | 11 |
| $\bar{a}$ | 34 | $G(V, E)$ | 32 |
| $[a_{ij}]_{\substack{1 \le i \le n \\ 1 \le j \le m}}$ | 11 | $I$ | 11 |
| $B$ | 14 | $\mathcal{I}_x$ | 135 |
| $BF(x)$ | 52 | $IDA(n, m)$ | 14 |
| $B(m, N, q)$ | 54 | $L$ | 14 and 53 |
| $B_t(y)$ | 97 | $L(i, j)$ | 117 |
| $B_t^i(y)$ | 100 | $L_{i,l}$ | 126 |
| $bits_k(i)$ | 56 | $M$ | 90 |
| $bits_3(i)$ | 126 | $M_i$ | 14 |
| $\beta_x(l)$ | 96 | $m_0$ | 53 |
| $C_n$ | 55 | $N_{d,n}$ | 71 |
| $C_{n-k}(y)$ | 56 | $N_{d,n}(i : l)$ | 72 |
| $C_{n-k-1}(i : l)$ | 62 | $nodes(l)$ | 126 |
| $\mathcal{C}(x)$ | 135 | $n_0$ | 53 |
| $\gamma_t$ | 103 | $n_x$ | 96 |

| notation | page number |
|---|---|
| $P_{\bar{a}}(x)$ | 12 |
| $\mathcal{P}$ | 127 |
| $P(i)$ | 73 |
| $P_x$ | 53 |
| $P_x(i)$ | 53 |
| $P_x(i) \in V$ | 53 |
| $p_0$ | 60 |
| $\pi$ | 42 |
| $R(+, \cdot, 0, 1)$ | 11 |
| $T(i)$ | 117 |
| $\Delta t$ | 116 |
| $(u, v)$ | 32 |
| $V(G)$ | 52 |
| $v_x(i)$ | 96 |
| $x[i:j]$ | 55 |
| $x(i:l)$ | 63 |
| $x^{(i)}$ | 63 and 135 |
| $x//i$ | 55 |
| $x \circ y$ | 56 |
| $X^*(t)$ | 103 |
| $\mathbf{Z}_q$ | 11 |
| $Z_{t,x,l}$ | 101 |
| $\omega$ | 13 |

# Chapter 1

# Introduction

> It takes all the running *you* can do,
>
> to keep in the same place.
>
> If you want to get somewhere else,
>
> you must run at least twice as fast as that!
>
> —Lewis Carroll

After briefly examining the challenges facing designing ever more powerful computers, we discuss the important issues in parallel processing and outline solutions. An overview of the book is also given.

# 1.1   The von Neumann Machine Paradigm

The past five decades have witnessed the birth of the first electronic computer [257] and the rapid growth of the computing industry to exceed $1,000 billion (annual revenue) in the U.S. alone [162]. The demand for high-performance machines is further powered by the advent of many crucial problems whose solutions require enormous computing power: environmental issues, search for cures for diseases, accurate and timely weather forecasting, to mention just a few [271]. Moreover, although unrelenting decrease in the feature size continues to improve the computing capability per chip, turning that into a corresponding increase in computing performance is a major challenge [152, 316]. All these factors point toward the necessity of sustained innovation in the design of computers.

That the **von Neumann machine paradigm** [37], the conceptual framework for most computers, considered at the system level will impede further performance gains is not hard to see. Input and output excluded, the von Neumann machine conceptually consists of a processing unit, a memory storing both programs and data, and a wire that connects the two. In an execution cycle the processing unit fetches from memory an instruction, and decodes and executes it, which may cause additional data movements in the wire, all in *serial* manner. Clearly, no matter how fast the processor and the memory are, the wire connecting the two sets the limit to the overall performance, as the machine can be only as fast as the wire can deliver information. The von Neumann machine moreover makes inefficient use of its resources, since only *one* location in memory is accessible in a cycle with the rest remaining idle [155]. Backus called this wire the **von Neumann bottleneck** [36].

The von Neumann bottleneck is of architectural origin [11]. With the cost of processing logic dropping rapidly, the advent of VLSI, and the development of automated design tools, the von Neumann machine paradigm becomes outdated for designing high-speed computers [43, 151], and major performance improvements must now come from architectural designs capable of **parallel processing**. Today, all high-performance computers use some kind of parallel processing, and their designs are extremely diverse to satisfy their equally diverse goals [43]. They include pipelining (superscalar and superpipeline), VLIW ("Very Long Instruction Word"), and so forth [152, 342]. But parallelism in improving uniprocessor performance is restricted by such factors as fundamental physical limits, diminishing returns, source level parallelism, and compiler technology, whereas parallel architectures promise an essentially open-ended scope of performance [316].

## 1.2  Issues in Parallel Processing

Six important issues in parallel processing are identified and discussed in this book: (i) network topology, (ii) interprocessor communication, (iii) fault tolerance, (iv) simulation of ideal parallel computation models, (v) asynchronism without compromising efficiency and with low sensitivity to variations in component speed, and (vi) on-line maintenance. They are treated briefly in the following paragraphs.

### Issue 1: network topology

All physical devices have natural limits imposed by the speed of light and materials, and they have to be extremely tiny to be fast (as it takes a signal at least $10^{-9}$ second to travel one foot), which is expensive and has serious reliability problems to tackle [316, 347]. Instead of relying solely on fast gates and small dimensions to reduce delays, parallel processing attempts to speed up computation by replicating the logic [186, 340]. With more than one processor, the immediate question is how to connect them to achieve the desired speed-up in a way that is both economical and physically feasible, since the network can easily dominate the hardware cost and program execution time.

Interconnection networks for parallel computers are surveyed in Chapter 3. Discussed there are important issues such as diameter, easiness of control, routing, tolerance for faults, and cost considerations. Concise as the coverage necessarily is, it is relatively complete and many important concepts are defined.

### Issue 2: fast interprocessor communication

Once connected to become a parallel computer, processors communicate *via* routing messages through wires or their equivalents. [1] Since signal-propagation time between widely separated modules can easily dominate the delay due to device-switching time, even if logic signals travel at the speed of light [340], the paramount issue here is how to minimize such delays, which is formalized as the **parallel routing problem**.

We first summarize our approach to, our results for, and previous work on, the parallel routing problem in Chapter 4. Then, in Chapter 5, fast, space-efficient ran-

---

[1] If processors do not communicate between themselves, they do not need to be connected in the first place. For example, today, 500 microprocessors together can easily carry out more than 2,500 million floating point operations per second (Mflops). But, that alone does not a Cray Y-MP make; Cray Y-MP's total peak performance is rated at 2,670 Mflops [163] (peak performance, cynics say, is nothing but "the maximum performance that the manufacturer guarantees no program will exceed" [44, 153] or the "speed of a computer when not running any software" [334, p. 40]). See [129, Table 1] and [163, Tables 1 and 2] for the (claimed) performance of several supercomputers from the U.S. and Japan. See also [312] for a brief history of supercomputers and [44, 247, 251, 327, 334, 355, 386] for an up-to-date account of fast computers.

domized routing algorithms for the hypercube and the de Bruijn networks are described and analyzed. Although these are randomized algorithms, each fails to route successfully with extremely small probability. Take the algorithm for the hypercube network, FSRA ("Fault-Tolerant Subcube Routing Algorithm"), as an example. Let $N$ denote the size of the network. This algorithm runs in $2 \log N + 1$ time[2] without queueing delay and uses only constant size buffers. Its probability of unsuccessful routing is at most $N^{-2.419 \log N + 1.5}$, which for all practical purposes is zero. This result also solves Rabin's conjecture [285].

Two numerical examples can illustrate how improbable FSRA may fail to route successfully. The probability of unsuccessful routing in a $1,024$-node hypercube network is less than $4.9 \cdot 10^{-69}$. As another example, a $2^{16}$-node hypercube network, the size of a full-size Connection Machine CM-2 [349], would have an unsuccessful routing with probability at most $6.4 \cdot 10^{-180}$.

## Issue 3: fault tolerance without high cost

There are no fault-free devices in the real world [326]. Even highly reliable components make transient faults due to reasons such as thermal fluctuations [245]. With large numbers of components, as parallel computers almost by definition must be, some component will go wrong with non-negligible probability according to simple statistical principles. Indeed, it has been surmised that "the practical size limit of [parallel] machines may well depend on reliability — the mean time between failure and mean time to repair must be small enough to permit the system to compute for a useful fraction of the time" [316]. This has serious consequences for parallel computers. To save a computation from errors, not only the processor that experienced faults has to take actions, *all* other processors receiving data from it must also take actions, then processors that received data from these processors, too, etc. This wave of corrective actions was dubbed the "**domino effect**" by Randell [292]. Since this effect can occur even if there is only one transient fault at only one site during the whole computation, clearly it is important to confine all errors to their originating places [382].

We will show that the fast routing schemes developed in Chapter 5 for the hypercube and the de Bruijn networks tolerate random link failures. For example, the one for the hypercube network (FSRA, that is) tolerates $\Theta(N)$ random link failures with high probability. A voting scheme is also developed in Subsection 2.6 to mask out node failures. This scheme can be easily incorporated into FSRA to create regions of fault containment, as shown in the final chapter.

---

[2]All logs are to the base 2 throughout this book unless noted otherwise.

## Issue 4: simulation of ideal parallel computation models by feasible parallel computers

Communication has long been abstracted out of computation models, which traditionally focus on *logical* operations. The research on parallel processing, however, demonstrates clearly that communication is an inseparable part of computation [245].

In Chapter 6 parallel computation models are surveyed. At the end of that chapter, we briefly show how the PRAM ("Parallel Random Access Machine") model — the most popular theoretical model — can be simulated on the hypercube network with a slowdown of $O(\log N)$ with probability tending to one as $N$, the number of processors, or the number of PRAM instructions approaches infinity. Our main focus there is a class of PRAM programs whose efficient simulation does not require the expensive hashing of the address space. We show that such PRAM programs can be simulated with a slowdown of $8 \log N$ with almost certainty. Both simulation schemes are IDA-based and fault-tolerant.

## Issue 5: asynchronism without compromising speed and low communication complexity, but with low sensitivity to variations in link or processor speed

It is desirable that a parallel computer has no global control, which may become a communication bottleneck and a single point of failure. Global clocks in particular are also difficult to implement due to the problem of clock skews and delays in large systems [119]. It is moreover desirable that the execution time is not too sensitive to variations in component speeds, which may be caused by a wide variety of reasons such as differences in wire length or computing power (as in heterogeneous systems [192]), statistical phenomena, variations in electrical characteristics, and processors diverted to run diagnostics.

In Chapter 7 we address both problems. First we show that our routing schemes can run on asynchronous networks without loss of efficiency in either time or communication complexity, defined as the number of **synchronization messages** used to simulate the global clock pulses. Then we show that FSRA is not sensitive to variations in component speed in that if a link or a processor is slowed by an amount of $\Delta t > 0$, the run-time of FSRA will skew by only $O(\Delta t)$, which is *linear* in $\Delta t$ and *independent* of the size of the network. As a consequence, increase in the machine size will not affect the sensitivity to component speed.

## Issue 6: efficient, on-line maintenance

With fault tolerance comes redundancy [326], which should be exploitable to make maintenance less disrupting to the user. We hence propose a novel on-line maintenance and repair concept.

In Chapter 8 we show that wires of the hypercube network can be partitioned into 352 sets of roughly equal sizes such that those in the same set can be disabled simultaneously *without* disrupting the ongoing computation or degrading the routing performance much, if FSRA is used. This partition can also be computed locally and efficiently. As a result, efficient, on-line wire testing and replacement on the hypercube network can be realized. Furthermore, the maintenance procedure can be completed in 352 cycles, *independent* of the number of processors.

The idea of space-efficient **information dispersal**, pioneered by Rabin [285], is vital to results in this book. An information dispersal algorithm (IDA), parametrized by $n$ and $m$ for $m \leq n$, is an algorithm which breaks any given piece of information $F$ into $n$ pieces, each only one $m^{\text{th}}$ the length of $F$, so that any $m$ of them suffice to reconstruct $F$. Efficient IDAs with ideas from the theory of error-correcting codes, especially those related to Reed-Solomon codes, are presented in Chapter 2.

With these results, we are only a step shy of a parallel computing system design. We take that extra step in Chapter 9, where a fault-tolerant hypercube parallel computer is sketched. That design, called the **hypercube parallel computer** (HPC), uses replication of program execution and employs FSRA as the routing scheme.

Fault-tolerant IDA-based routing schemes depend heavily on finding node-disjoint paths in the network. The classic result of Menger [72], linking connectivity with the number of node-disjoint paths, is not strong enough because the *lengths* of these paths — which determine the efficiency of routing — are left out. Such motivations lead to graph-theoretical concepts that take into account path lengths. The performance of the standard two-phase fault-tolerant IDA-based routing scheme due to Rabin [285] can now be expressed in a general form when applied to **node-symmetric** graphs, to whose class the hypercube belongs.

## 1.3   Overview of the Book

The concepts of information dispersal and an efficient FFT-based IDA are presented in Chapter 2. The application of IDA to voting is also developed there. Chapter 3 briefly surveys interconnection networks (**Issue 1**). From there on, our main focus will be the hypercube network, though routing schemes for the de Bruijn network will also be presented. We present fast, fault-tolerant routing algorithms for these two networks in Chapter 5 (**Issues 2** and **3**), after the preview in Chapter 4. A general formulation of two-phase IDA-based routing and its connection to graph theory are also covered. The simulation of PRAMs is addressed in Chapter 6 (**Issue 4**), where a class of PRAM programs is treated in detail since such programs may be more amiable to general-purpose simulation in practice. In Chapter 7 we prove that our routing schemes can run on asynchronous networks without loss of efficiency. Furthermore, we show that FSRA has low sensitivity to variations in link and processor speeds (**Issue 5**). In Chapter 8 it is proved that FSRA allows efficient on-line maintenance (**Issue 6**). Finally, we propose a fault-tolerant parallel computer in Chapter 9. We remark that **Issues 5** and **6** have not been addressed analytically before, to the author's best knowledge. A more technical summary of this book can be found in the preface.

Due to limited space, this book cannot discuss all relevant issues concerning parallel processing. Fortunately, there are excellent papers and books to fill that void: architecture [11, 110, 120, 127, 153, 341], memory hierarchy [161], program transformation [185, 341], synchronization [35, 103, 104, 109, 128, 196, 293], VLSI [194, 210, 221, 245, 331, 352, 360], cache coherence [19, 109, 383], experience of using and building parallel computers [22, 91, 123, 167, 168, 315, 382], data flow architecture [96], limitation in speedup [13, 121, 144, 180], performance analysis [60, 86, 98, 99, 182, 204, 264, 311], and the possible impact of optical technology [54, 107, 113, 141, 154].

Finally, some words on history. John von Neumann is himself a pioneer in parallel processing [21, pp. 30, 41, and 275]; the suffix "bottleneck" applies only to the von Neumann machine paradigm. On the other hand, some prominent researchers like Hennessy and Patterson believe the term, von Neumann machine, "gives too much credit to von Neumann, who wrote up the ideas, and too little to the engineers, Eckert and Mauchly, who worked on the machines" [153, pp. 23–24]. There are also disputes about whether Atanasoff at Iowa State University in the early 1940s built the first electronic computer before Eckert and Mauchly [153, 257].

# Chapter 2

# Information Dispersal

> Ten times thyself were happier than you are,
>
> If ten of thine ten times reconfigured thee.
>
> —Shakespeare

The concept of information dispersal is introduced, and an information dispersal algorithm (IDA) based on polynomial evaluation and interpolation is described. This scheme can take advantage of the Fast Fourier Transform (FFT) algorithm under certain circumstances. Several variations on this algorithm are also explored. An IDA-based software voting method is presented as an application and analyzed under a random fault model.

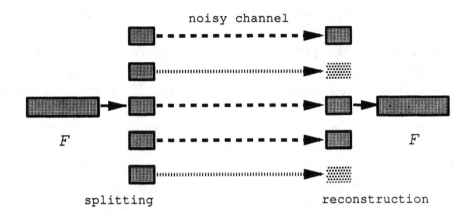

Figure 2.1: THE WORKING OF IDA WITH $n = 5$ AND $m = 3$. The original information $F$ is first split into five pieces and two of them are subsequently unavailable. However, as long as at least three pieces are accessible, as in the case above, $F$ can be reconstructed.

## 2.1   Introduction

An **information dispersal algorithm** (IDA) is any efficient method that can split a given string of bits $F$ into $n$ **pieces** in such a way that any $m$ of them suffice to reconstruct the original $F$. Each piece, moreover, is of size $|F|/m$, where $|F|$ is the size — measured as the number of characters throughout this book — of $F$; the pieces, therefore, total $(n/m)|F|$ characters. The two parameters $n$ and $m$ can be any two integers as long as $m \leq n$. See Figure 2.1 for illustration. The study of space-efficient information dispersal with application to fault-tolerant interprocessor communication is due to Rabin [285]. Subsection 2.5.4 reviews related work.

The value of $m$ can be adjusted to meet the desired combination of the reliability level and the total space used by the $n$ pieces. With $m$ approaching $n$, less space is consumed by the pieces; on the other hand, with $m$ approaching one, more pieces can afford to be lost since less of them are needed to reconstruct $F$. Hence, given $n$, we can fine-tune $m$ to strike a balance between two seemingly diametrically opposed goals: efficient use of space and high degree of reconstructibility.

In this chapter we introduce an efficient IDA based on the Vandermonde matrix where the splitting operation is **polynomial evaluation** and the reconstruction operation **polynomial interpolation**. When certain conditions are satisfied, we can even apply the **Fast Fourier Transform** (FFT). Our scheme is asymptotically more efficient than Rabin's original IDA [285] (see Subsection 2.5.2).

Information dispersal can be viewed from the error-correcting codes standpoint [63, 228, 238, 272]: one wants to decode the code words from errors [285]. As we are mainly concerned with a particular kind of errors, **erasures**, our approach takes the more limited *interpolation* standpoint: one wants enough sample values to interpolate the function representing the original information. The error-correcting codes viewpoint is explored in Subsection 2.5.3.

One natural application of IDA is the dispersal of files in a computer system such as the Redundant Arrays of Inexpensive Disks (RAID) systems [58, 153, 265, 372]. Instead of keeping only one copy, we may use IDA to split a file into smaller files and disperse them across the network. This increases the availability of a file, since it is accessible as long as at least $m$ of the deposit sites are up. This IDA-based scheme, furthermore, saves disk space in comparison with the more common replication scheme where each file is copied in its entirety. Other applications can be found in [286].

In this book, IDA is employed to achieve fast, fault-tolerant parallel routing, where packets are first split into pieces by IDA before being routed in parallel to their destinations (see Chapter 5). Since each packet can afford to lose up to $n - m$ of its pieces during routing, loss of information due to buffer overflow and/or link failures can be tolerated. Allowing pieces to be lost also eliminates queueing delay.

IDA can also be used to **filter** out polluted data, thus erecting some defense against error propagation and the "domino effect" (see Chapter 9). The algorithm FILTERING for this purpose and its analysis is presented in Section 2.6. In FILTERING, voting is applied to *pieces* instead of the complete results; hence, messages are shorter, implying faster communication. FILTERING works roughly as follows. If a processor detects that its own pieces do not agree with, say, the majority of the received pieces, it may safely declare that its result is wrong and then take corrective steps. On the other hand, a processor whose pieces are supported by the majority of the received pieces can treat as **suspects** those processors having sent conflicting pieces. This voting process can be invoked before each communication round to prevent innocent processors from accepting invalid data, thus creating regions of fault containment (see Chapter 9).

This chapter is organized as follows. First we introduce basic concepts from number theory and algebra needed for later developments. Polynomial evaluation and interpolation, the cornerstone of our IDA, are then discussed as well as their relation with the FFT. The general approach for IDA is presented in Section 2.4, and our specific implementation as well as its variations in Section 2.5. Application to voting is covered in Section 2.6.

## 2.2 Results from Algebra and Number Theory

Let $R\,(+,\cdot,0,1)$ — or simply $R$ — denote a **commutative ring** with **unit element** 1 throughout this chapter, where "+" is addition and "." multiplication [61]. For our purpose, we just mention the following as examples: the complex numbers, $\mathbf{Z}_q$ of integers modulo $q$, the finite field (or Galois field) $GF(p)$ with $p$ being prime, and the finite field $GF(p^m)$ which is the set of all polynomials in $x$ of degree at most $m-1$ and coefficients from $GF(p)$ with calculations performed modulo an irreducible polynomial over $GF(p)$ with degree $m$. A polynomial is **irreducible** over $GF(p)$ if it is not the product of two polynomials of lower degree with coefficients from $GF(p)$.

By an $n \times m$ **matrix** we mean a doubly indexed family of elements of $R$, $[\,a_{ij}\,]_{\substack{1 \le i \le n \\ 1 \le j \le m}}$, also written in the form

$$\begin{bmatrix} a_{11} & \cdots & a_{1m} \\ \vdots & \ddots & \vdots \\ a_{n1} & \cdots & a_{nm} \end{bmatrix}.$$

We adopt several notations regarding matrices.

**Definition 2.1** *Let* $A = [\,a_{ij}\,]_{i,j}$ *be an* $n \times n$ *matrix. We denote by* $|A|$ *the* **determinant** *of* $A$ *and* $A^T = [\,a_{ji}\,]_{i,j}$ *the* **transpose** *of* $A$. *The* $(n-1) \times (n-1)$ *matrix* $A_{ij}$ *is obtained from* $A$ *by deleting its* $i^{\text{th}}$ *row and* $j^{\text{th}}$ *column. The* $n \times n$ *matrix* $A^* = [\,a_{ij}^*\,]_{i,j}$ *is defined by*

$$a_{ij}^* = (-1)^{i+j} \cdot |A_{ji}|.$$

*The* **(multiplicative) inverse** *of* $A$, *if it exists, is denoted by* $A^{-1}$, *and the* **identity matrix** *by* $I$.

The following fact is well-known [198, Proposition 4.16].

**Theorem 2.2** $AA^* = A^*A = |A|\,I$. *The determinant* $|A|$ *is* **invertible** — *has a multiplicative inverse in* $R$ — *if and only if* $A$ *is invertible, and then*

$$A^{-1} = \frac{1}{|A|}A^*.$$

**Comment 2.3** The inverse of $A$, if it exists, is unique. Suppose $AA^* = I$ and $AB = I$. Then $B = (AA^*)\,B = (A^*A)\,B = A^*I = A^*$.

Finally, we state a result from number theory.

**Theorem 2.4** ([147, Theorem 57]) _If_ $gcd(k, m) = d$, _then the congruence_

$$k \cdot x \equiv l \bmod m$$

_is soluble for_ $x$ _if and only if_ $d \,|\, l$, _and then it has_ $d$ _solutions._

## 2.3   The Vandermonde Matrix

The **Vandermonde matrix** is of the form [145]

$$A = \begin{bmatrix} 1 & x_1 & x_1^2 & x_1^3 & \cdots & x_1^{n-1} \\ 1 & x_2 & x_2^2 & x_2^3 & \cdots & x_2^{n-1} \\ \vdots & \vdots & \vdots & \vdots & \ddots & \vdots \\ 1 & x_n & x_n^2 & x_n^3 & \cdots & x_n^{n-1} \end{bmatrix} = [\, x_i^{j-1} \,]_{1 \leq i,j \leq n}, \tag{2.1}$$

where $x_i \in R$ and $x_i - x_j$ is invertible for $i \neq j$ (hence, the $x_i$'s are distinct).

We now turn to the inverse of the Vandermonde matrix.

**Theorem 2.5** _The Vandermonde matrix is invertible._

**Proof:** Let $A$ be the Vandermonde matrix of (2.1). That $|A| = \pm \prod_{i<j} (x_i - x_j)$ is well-known [61, p. 323]. Since each $x_i - x_j$ is invertible for $i \neq j$, $|A|$ is invertible. Theorem 2.2 then implies that $A$ is invertible. Q.E.D.

### 2.3.1   Relation with polynomial interpolation

Let $\vec{a} = [\, a_1 \, a_2 \, \cdots \, a_n \,]^T$ and $\vec{f} = [\, f_1 \, f_2 \, \cdots \, f_n \,]^T$ be two column vectors satisfying $\vec{f} = A\,\vec{a}$, where $A = [\, x_i^{j-1} \,]_{1 \leq i,j \leq n}$ is a Vandermonde matrix. Then,

$$f_i = \sum_{j=1}^{n} a_j \cdot x_i^{j-1}, \qquad 1 \leq i \leq n,$$

are exactly the **sample values** of the polynomial $P_{\vec{a}}(x) \overset{\text{def}}{=} \sum_{j=1}^{n} a_j \cdot x^{j-1}$ at $n$ **sample points**, $x_1, \ldots, x_n$. To solve $\vec{a}$ given $\vec{f}$ amounts to interpolating the unknown $P_{\vec{a}}(x)$, given its sample values at $x_1, \ldots, x_n$.

## 2.3.2 Methods for interpolating polynomials

Polynomial interpolation can be achieved using $\approx 2.5\,n^2$ arithmetic operations by the standard technique of **divided-differences table** [89] (throughout this book, by $A(n) \approx B(n)$ we shall mean $A(n)/B(n) \to c$ for some constant $c$ as $n$ goes to infinity). We list one such algorithm from [136, pp. 119–121] below, where $f_i$ is the sample value at $x_i$ for $1 \leq i \leq n$.

1. **For** $k = 1$ **To** $n - 1$
    **For** $i = n$ **To** $k + 1$
    $f_i \leftarrow (f_i - f_{i-1})/(x_i - x_{i-k-1});$
2. **For** $k = n$ **To** 1
    **For** $i = k$ **To** $n - 1$
    $f_i \leftarrow f_i - f_{i+1} \cdot x_k;$

Steps **1** and **2** take $\approx 1.5\,n^2$ and $\approx 2\,n^2$ arithmetic operations, respectively. If we invert the $(x_i - x_j)$'s once and for all, the total number of arithmetic operations can be reduced to $\approx 2\,n^2$. Since all the sample points are pre-determined in our scheme, such preconditioning is always applicable.

Asymptotically faster algorithms for interpolating polynomials exist. Horowitz [159, pp. 453–455] shows that polynomial interpolation can be done using $O(n \log^3 n)$ arithmetic operations. Preconditioning can reduce the complexity to $O(n \log^2 n)$ [76, pp. 103–104]. These FFT-based methods can be competitive only when $n$ is large enough, however [176].

## 2.3.3 The discrete Fourier transform

The discrete Fourier transform can be seen as polynomial evaluation at specific sample points. We shall see later in Subsection 2.5.3 that, with a suitable ring, evaluating polynomials at well-chosen sample points, as is done by the discrete Fourier transform, leads to fast interpolation.

An element $\omega \in R$ is said to be a **principal $n^{\text{th}}$ root of unity** [5] if

1. $\omega \neq 1$,

2. $\omega^n = 1$, and

3. $\displaystyle\sum_{j=0}^{n-1} \omega^{jl} = 0,$ for $1 \leq l < n$.

**Definition 2.6** *Assume the commutative ring $R$ has a principal $n^{\text{th}}$ root of unity $\omega$. Define the $n \times n$ **Fourier transform matrix** $F_{n,n}$ as $[\omega^{(i-1)(j-1)}]_{1 \leq i,j \leq n}$. Let*

$\vec{a}$ *be a column vector of length* $n$ *with elements from* $R$. *The* (**discrete**) **Fourier transform** *of* $\vec{a}$ *is defined by* $F_{n,n}\,\vec{a}$.

**Comment 2.7** Letting $x_i = \omega^{i-1}$, we can see that $F_{n,n} = [\,x_i^{j-1}\,]_{1 \le i,j \le n}$ is a Vandermonde matrix.

**Comment 2.8** If $n$ is a power of 2, it is a classic result that the Fourier transform can be solved by the FFT algorithm using only $\approx 1.5\,n \log n = O(n \log n)$ arithmetic operations (see, for example, [5]), among which roughly $n \log n$ are additions and $0.5\,n \log n$ are multiplications. We also mention in passing that FFT also exists for arbitrary $n$, and significant time savings are possible when $n$ is highly composite [80, p. 190].

Brigham's book [80] contains a clear and in-depth presentation of the FFT. Pollard [278] discusses FFT in finite fields. See also [267, 328] for implementing the FFT in $O(\log N)$ parallel steps and [353] for the VLSI complexity of the FFT.

## 2.4   An IDA Schema

Some conventions for matrices will greatly aid the presentation. The $i^{\text{th}}$ row of a matrix $M$ is denoted by $M_i$. Let $A_1, \ldots, A_l$ be column vectors of equal length. Then $[A_1\,|\,A_2\,|\,\cdots\,|\,A_l]$ denotes the matrix whose $j^{\text{th}}$ column is $A_j$ for $1 \le j \le l$. Similarly, if $A_1, \ldots, A_l$ are row vectors, then

$$\begin{bmatrix} A_1 \\ \vdots \\ A_l \end{bmatrix}$$

denotes the matrix whose $j^{\text{th}}$ row is $A_j$, where $1 \le j \le l$.

Let $F = (\,b_1\,b_2\,\cdots\,b_L\,)$ be a string of characters, represented by integers within the range $[\,0, B\,]$, to be split by IDA. Let $n$ and $m$ be two integers and $m \le n$. Assume $m \,|\, L$ for simplicity. We want to find a commutative ring $R$ and an $n \times m$ matrix $\mathcal{A}$ such that the following two operations — **splitting** and **reconstruction** — can be done efficiently. Denote by $IDA(n, m)$ any efficient scheme that implements splitting and reconstruction according to the following schema due to Rabin [285].

### The Splitting Operation

Segment $F$ into sequences of integers of length $m$,

$$F = (\,b_1 \cdots b_m\,)(\,b_{m+1} \cdots b_{2m}\,) \cdots (\,b_{L-m+1} \cdots b_L\,) = S_1\,S_2 \cdots S_{L/m}.$$

The splitting operation transforms $F$ into $n$ **pieces**, $F_1, \ldots, F_n$, by

$$
\begin{bmatrix} F_1 \\ \hline \vdots \\ \hline F_n \end{bmatrix} \stackrel{\text{def}}{=} \mathcal{A}
\begin{bmatrix}
b_1 & b_{m+1} & \cdots & b_{L-m+1} \\
b_2 & b_{m+2} & \cdots & b_{L-m+2} \\
\vdots & \vdots & \ddots & \vdots \\
b_m & b_{2m} & \cdots & b_L
\end{bmatrix}
$$

$$
= \mathcal{A} \left[ S_1^T \mid S_2^T \mid \cdots \mid S_{L/m}^T \right] = \left[ \mathcal{A} S_1^T \mid \mathcal{A} S_2^T \mid \cdots \mid \mathcal{A} S_{L/m}^T \right]. \tag{2.2}
$$

Obviously, $|F_i| = |F|/m$, independent of $n$.

**Comment 2.9** The splitting operation can be implemented as a sequence of $L/m$ matrix-vector multiplications (call it the "**standard method**"), which totally uses $\approx 2\,n\,L$ arithmetic operations (among which half are additions and half multiplications), *independent* of $m$. More efficient splitting operations can be obtained if we choose $\mathcal{A}$ wisely (see Section 2.5).

## The Reconstruction Operation

Let $F_{k_1}, \ldots, F_{k_m}$ be any $m$ (received) pieces produced by (2.2) and $1 \le k_1 < k_2 < \cdots < k_m \le n$. Let the $m \times m$ matrix $\tilde{A}(k_1, k_2, \ldots, k_m) \stackrel{\text{def}}{=} \tilde{A}$ be such that $\tilde{A}_j = A_{k_j}$ for $1 \le j \le m$. That is, $\tilde{A}$'s $j^{\text{th}}$ row is equal to $\mathcal{A}$'s $k_j^{\text{th}}$ row. We then have the following identity from (2.2)

$$
\begin{bmatrix} F_{k_1} \\ \hline \vdots \\ \hline F_{k_m} \end{bmatrix} = \tilde{A}
\begin{bmatrix}
b_1 & b_{m+1} & \cdots & b_{L-m+1} \\
b_2 & b_{m+2} & \cdots & b_{L-m+2} \\
\vdots & \vdots & \ddots & \vdots \\
b_m & b_{2m} & \cdots & b_L
\end{bmatrix}
$$

$$
= \tilde{A} \left[ S_1^T \mid S_2^T \mid \cdots \mid S_{L/m}^T \right] = \left[ \tilde{A} S_1^T \mid \tilde{A} S_2^T \mid \cdots \mid \tilde{A} S_{L/m}^T \right]. \tag{2.3}
$$

Now, $F$ can be reconstructed from $F_{k_1}, \ldots, F_{k_m}$ by

$$
\left[ S_1^T \mid S_2^T \mid \cdots \mid S_{L/m}^T \right] = \left( \tilde{A} \right)^{-1}
\begin{bmatrix} F_{k_1} \\ \hline \vdots \\ \hline F_{k_m} \end{bmatrix}. \tag{2.4}
$$

To realize the above two operations, splitting and reconstruction, we have two tasks before us. The first is to find a commutative ring $R$ in which all the elementary operations can be carried out efficiently. The second task is to find an $n \times m$ matrix $\mathcal{A}$ such that: (1) the splitting operation can be done efficiently; (2) $\tilde{\mathcal{A}}(k_1, k_2, \ldots, k_m)$ is invertible for *any* $m$ numbers $1 \leq k_1 < \cdots < k_m \leq n$; and (3) now that $\tilde{\mathcal{A}}$ is invertible, the reconstruction operation (2.4) can be carried out efficiently.

## 2.5  Fast Information Dispersal Algorithms

We choose $\mathcal{A}$ of (2.2) to be $\mathcal{A}_V = [\, x_i^{j-1} \,]_{\substack{1 \leq i \leq n \\ 1 \leq j \leq m}}$, a submatrix of the Vandermonde matrix $[\, x_i^{j-1} \,]_{1 \leq i,j \leq n}$. In particular, when $n$ is a power of 2 and $R$ is a commutative ring with a principal $n^{\text{th}}$ root of unity $\omega$, we can further pick $x_i = \omega^{i-1}$ in $\mathcal{A}_V$ to get $\mathcal{A}_{\text{FFT}} = [\, \omega^{(i-1)(j-1)} \,]_{\substack{1 \leq i \leq n \\ 1 \leq j \leq m}}$, which consists of the first $m$ columns of $F_{n,n}$.

### The Splitting Operation

**Theorem 2.10** *With* $\mathcal{A} = \mathcal{A}_{\text{FFT}}$, *the splitting operation can be achieved using* $\approx$ $1.5\,L\,n \log m/m$ *arithmetic operations, among which roughly* $L\,n \log m/m$ *are additions and roughly* $0.5\,L\,n \log m/m$ *are multiplications.*

**Proof:** To calculate $\mathcal{A}\,S_i^T$ of (2.2) for $1 \leq i \leq L/m$, we can pad $S_i^T$ with $n-m$ zeros to obtain $S_i'^T$, a vector of length $n$. It is easy to see that $\mathcal{A}\,S_i^T = F_{n,n}\,S_i'^T$, the Fourier transform of $S_i'^T$. Hence $\approx 1.5\,n \log n$ arithmetic operations are needed for each $\mathcal{A}\,S_i^T$ (Comment 2.8).

This bound can be improved. Since those arithmetic operations involving the zero elements in $S_i'^T$ need not be carried out, a more careful analysis of the FFT reduces the complexity to $\approx 1.5\,n \log m$, among which roughly $n \log m$ are additions and $0.5\,n \log m$ are multiplications. There being $L/m$ $S_i$'s, the total number of arithmetic operations is thus as claimed.
Q.E.D.

The condition that $n$ — the number of pieces to be split into — be a power of 2 for the FFT to be applicable can be relaxed. Assume $R$ has a principal $n'^{\text{th}}$ root of unity where $n' = 2^k \geq n$. Now, to implement the splitting part of $IDA(n, m)$, we can choose $\mathcal{A}$ to be the $n' \times m$ $\mathcal{A}_{\text{FFT}}$ but keep only $n$ of the produced pieces. Observe that, in doing so, we do not sacrifice *space* efficiency since, each piece being of size $|F|/m$, the adopted pieces still total $(n/m)\,|F|$ characters.

**Comment 2.11** We can compare the number of arithmetic operations used by the FFT-based IDA and that by the "standard method" in Comment 2.9, i.e., compare

$1.5\,L\,n\,\log m/m$ and $2\,L\,n$. Simple calculations show that, for the splitting operation, the "standard method" uses 2.66 times, 3.55 times, and 5.33 times as many arithmetic operations as our FFT-based scheme for $m = 4, 8, 16$, respectively. Since multiplication is more expensive than addition and our scheme uses *proportionally* less multiplications, the above favorable comparison is an understatement.

**Comment 2.12** In general, when $\mathcal{A}_V$ is chosen for $\mathcal{A}$, Horner's rule can be used for the splitting operation, as each matrix-vector multiplication $A\,S_i^T$ of (2.2) is simply evaluation of an $(m-1)$-degree polynomial at $x_1, \ldots, x_n$ (see Subsection 2.3.1). Hence, the total number of arithmetic operations used is $\approx 2\,n\,m\,(L/m) = 2\,L\,n$, the same as the "standard method" in Comment 2.9. We note that evaluation of an $(m-1)$-degree polynomial at $n$ points can be achieved in $O(n\log^2 m)$ arithmetic operations [159, pp. 451–452]; consequently, the splitting operation can be achieved using $O(L\,n\,\log^2 m/m)$ arithmetic operations. Again, this approach is practical only if $n$ is large enough to cover the overhead.

## The Reconstruction Operation

Let $1 \leq k_1 < k_2 < \ldots < k_m \leq n$. The matrix

$$\tilde{\mathcal{A}} \stackrel{\text{def}}{=} \tilde{\mathcal{A}}\,(k_1, k_2, \ldots, k_m) = [\,x_{k_i}^{j-1}\,]_{1 \leq i,j \leq m}$$

is an $m \times m$ Vandermonde matrix and is invertible by Theorem 2.5. So, from the discussion in Subsection 2.3.1 and (2.4), we have the following $L/m$ polynomial interpolations to solve

$$\begin{bmatrix} f_{1,i} \\ \vdots \\ f_{m,i} \end{bmatrix} = \tilde{\mathcal{A}}S_i^T, \qquad \text{for} \quad 1 \leq i \leq L/m,$$

where $[\,f_{1,i}\,f_{2,i}\cdots f_{m,i}\,]^T$ denotes the $i^{\text{th}}$ column of $[\,F_{k_1}^T\,|\,F_{k_2}^T\,|\,\cdots\,|\,F_{k_m}^T\,]^T$ in (2.3). In Subsection 2.3.2 we saw that each interpolation can be solved using $\approx 2\,m^2$ arithmetic operations by the divided-differences table method. So the total number of arithmetic operations for this reconstruction method is approximately $2\,m^2\,(L/m) = 2\,m\,L$, independent of $n$.

Alternatively, we can use FFT-based polynomial interpolation techniques. Since there exist algorithms that require only $O(m\log^2 m)$ arithmetic operations to interpolate polynomials, as discussed at the end of Subsection 2.3.2, the total number of arithmetic operations for the reconstruction operation can be reduced to $O(L\log^2 m)$. Again, this is practical only if $m$ is large enough to cover the overhead. Finally, we mention that, if $n - m = \Theta(\log n)$, the complexity of the reconstruction operation can be reduced to $O(L \log m)$ [280].[1]

## 2.5.1   Choosing a commutative ring

The requirements for $R$, if $\mathcal{A}_{\mathrm{FFT}}$ is to be chosen for $\mathcal{A}$ so that the FFT is applicable, are summarized below:

$< \mathcal{C}.\alpha >$. $n$ is a power of 2,

$< \mathcal{C}.\beta >$. There exists a principal $n^{\mathrm{th}}$ root of unity $\omega$, and

$< \mathcal{C}.\gamma >$. $\omega^i - \omega^j$ is invertible for $0 \le i \ne j < n$.

Below, we list four candidate rings. $\mathcal{A}_{\mathrm{FFT}}$ can be chosen in the first three and $\mathcal{A}_{\mathrm{V}}$ the fourth, for $\mathcal{A}$.

**1. The Complex Numbers.**   Choose $\omega = e^{2\pi i/n}$ where $i = \sqrt{-1}$. This $\omega$ is a principal $n^{\mathrm{th}}$ root of unity in the ring of complex numbers. IDA's arithmetic operations are carried out in the ring of complex numbers.

One disadvantage of this ring is that more computer memory may be needed for enough precisions to get exact results. Another one is that floating point operations are expensive.

**2. The Galois Field $GF(p)$ ($p$ is prime).**   Assume $n = 2^k$ and $B < p$. Recall that each character is from $[0, B]$. From [147, Theorem 88], it is not hard to show that a principal $n^{\mathrm{th}}$ root of unity in $GF(p)$ exists if and only if $n \mid (p-1)$. So primes of the form $2^e \cdot l + 1$ where $k \le e$ have to be found. Lipson has shown that there are more than $x/(2^{e-1} \ln x)$ such primes less than $x$ with exponent $e$ [230].

One problem with $GF(p)$ is that a number modulo $p$ most likely would not fit into the standard unit in computer memory, typically some multiples of 8 bits; so some bits will be "wasted." Another minor problem is that we do not have total control over $p$ as $n$ grows.

**3. Ring of Integers Modulo $q$: $\mathbf{Z}_q$.**   We first state a theorem.

**Theorem 2.13** ([5, p. 266]) *Let $n$ and $\omega$ be positive powers of 2 and let $q = \omega^{n/2} + 1$. Then in $\mathbf{Z}_q$, both $n$ and $\omega$ have multiplicative inverses modulo $q$ and $\omega$ is a principal $n^{\mathrm{th}}$ root of unity.*

---

[1]It is mentioned in [213, p. 611] that the same complexity holds for $m = \Theta(n)$ as well, but this claim seems to be erroneously deduced.

Fix $n$, $q$, and $\omega$ as described in Theorem 2.13. Now, we only have Condition $< \mathcal{C}.\gamma >$ to satisfy, and we have to prove that every $\omega^i - \omega^j$ for $0 \leq i \neq j < n$ has a multiplicative inverse.

First note that $-1$ is invertible; its inverse is simply $-1$. Also note that 2 is invertible: since $gcd\,(2, q) \,|\, 1$, Theorem 2.4 implies that $2 \cdot x \equiv 1 \bmod q$ has a unique solution, which is 2's inverse. We proceed to show that $\alpha = \omega^i - \omega^j$ is invertible for $0 \leq i \neq j < n$. Assume $i > j$ without loss of generality because $-1$ is invertible. Since $\alpha = \omega^j \cdot (\omega^{i-j} - 1)$ and $w^j$ is invertible by Theorem 2.13, we only have to show that $\omega^{i-j} - 1$ is invertible.

Let $c > 0$ be such that $(i - j) \cdot c \equiv n/2 \bmod n$. Since $gcd\,(n, i - j) \,|\, \frac{n}{2}$, such $c$ exists by Theorem 2.4. Let $\beta = (\omega^{i-j})^{c-1} + (\omega^{i-j})^{c-2} + \cdots + 1$. Then,

$$(\omega^{i-j} - 1) \cdot \beta = \omega^{(i-j)c} - 1 \equiv \omega^{n/2} - 1 \equiv -2 \bmod q.$$

Since $-2 = (-1) \cdot 2$ is invertible, $(\omega^{i-j} - 1) \cdot \beta \cdot (-2)^{-1} \equiv 1 \bmod q$, proving the invertibility of $w^i - w^j$.

We may choose $\omega$ such that $B < q = \omega^{n/2} + 1$. Multiplication modulo $q$ can be carried out on a binary computer without using expensive divisions [79, p. 282]. Of course, as computers usually use byte as memory unit, at least one bit is "wasted."

**4. The Finite Field $GF(2^s)$.** We may pick $GF(2^s)$ as in [285]. This finite field allows complete utilization of the currently universal byte-based memory systems. We remark that arithmetics in $GF(2^s)$ are easy to implement (see [284] for details and [57] for a possible VLSI implementation).

Since $GF(2^s)$ has no principal $n^{\text{th}}$ root of unity with $n$ being a power of two,[2] we can no longer choose $\mathcal{A} = \mathcal{A}_{\text{FFT}}$. Instead, we take $n$ distinct numbers $x_1, \ldots, x_n$ for $\mathcal{A} = \mathcal{A}_{\text{V}}$. Note that $x_i - x_j$ is invertible for $i \neq j$ since $GF(2^s)$ is a field.

## 2.5.2 Comparison with Rabin's IDA

Rabin [285] chooses the Cauchy matrix [175, 238, 248] $\left[\frac{1}{x_i + y_j}\right]_{i,j}$ for $\mathcal{A}$. For the splitting part, Rabin's IDA uses $\approx 2\,n\,L$ arithmetic operations if the "standard method" is used. Comment 2.11 shows that our FFT-based scheme requires less arithmetic operations. Even when the FFT is not applicable, our scheme can still achieve the same bound as Rabin's by using Horner's rule (Comment 2.12); moreover, it has a more

---

[2]It is known that, for an element $x$ from a finite field to satisfy $x^n = 1$, its **order** $d$, defined as the minimum positive integer such that $x^d = 1$, must divide $n$ [238, Problem 7(i), p. 98]. Hence, if there exists an element $x \in GF(2^s)$ for which $x^n = 1$, its order $d$ would divide $n$. The Fermat-Euler Theorem [61, Corollary 1, p. 148] also implies $x^{2^s - 1} = 1$; hence $d$ divides $2^s - 1$. Since $n$ is a power of two, $x$ must be 1 and, thus, cannot be a principal root of unity.

compact representation and uses less working space since at most $x_1, x_2, \ldots, x_n$, instead of all of $\mathcal{A}$'s $n\,m$ elements, have to be stored in memory when applying Horner's rule.

For the reconstruction part, Rabin's scheme calculates the inverse of $\mathcal{A}$, i.e., $[(-1)^{i+j}(x_j + y_j)/(c_j \cdot d_i \cdot e_j \cdot f_i)]_{1 \leq i,j \leq m}$, as follows (for simplicity, assume the *first* $m$ pieces survive; similar forms hold in other cases)

$$
\begin{aligned}
c_k &= \prod_{\substack{i<k \\ k<j}} (x_i - x_k) \cdot (x_k - x_j) \\
d_k &= \prod_{\substack{i<k \\ k<j}} (y_i - y_k) \cdot (y_k - y_j) \\
e_k &= \prod_j (x_k + y_j) \\
f_k &= \prod_j (x_j + y_k)
\end{aligned}
\qquad \text{for } 1 \leq k \leq m,
$$

and the $x_i$'s and $y_j$'s are chosen in a systematic way once and for all [285]. It is easy to see that the set-up of $\mathcal{A}^{-1}$ requires $\Theta(m^2)$ arithmetic operations. Once $\mathcal{A}^{-1}$ is available, the rest is just matrix-vector multiplications as in (2.4), which take $\approx 2\,m\,L$ arithmetic operations, the same as our IDA scheme using the divided-differences table method in Section 2.5. Our scheme thus uses $\Theta(m^2)$ fewer arithmetic operations, which reflect the fixed cost for setting up $\mathcal{A}^{-1}$.

### 2.5.3   Variations on a theme

It is not hard to see that our scheme of Section 2.5, besides tolerating $n - m$ erasures, is capable of correcting up to $\lfloor (n-m)/2 \rfloor$ errors (i.e., up to that many pieces can be erroneously transmitted). The argument goes as follows. Without loss of generality, consider the first column[3] of (2.2) and call it $\vec{f} = [\,f_1 \cdots f_n\,]^T$. Suppose $w$ errors have occurred and we receive $\vec{y} = [\,y_1 \cdots y_n\,]^T$. Let $\vec{e} = \vec{y} - \vec{f}$ be the error vector. Note that $\vec{e}$ has $w$ non-zero components. So we have

$$
y_i = e_i + f_i = e_i + \sum_{j=1}^m b_j \cdot x_i^{j-1}, \qquad 1 \leq i \leq n. \tag{2.5}
$$

Clearly, any $m$ of the above equations have exactly one solution since the $m \times m$ matrix denoting the linear equations is a Vandermonde matrix and hence invertible by Theorem 2.5. Among the $\binom{n}{m}$ sets of $m$ linear equations from (2.5), exactly $\binom{n-w}{m}$ will agree and give the correct $\vec{y}$. An incorrect $\vec{y}$ can be the solution of at most $w + m - 1$ equations, consisting of $w$ erroneous equations and $m - 1$ correct ones.

---

[3]We will do the same for the rest of this subsection when we are discussing the relationship between our IDA scheme and other coding methods. The computational complexity for IDAs based on such schemes will be $(L/m)\,f(n)$, where $f(n)$ is the complexity for the error-correction codes in question, since there are $L/m$ columns.

Thus an incorrect $\vec{y}$ can be the solution of at most $\binom{w+m-1}{m}$ sets of $m$ equations. Thus the message $\vec{y}$ will be obtained correctly if $\binom{n-w}{m} > \binom{w+m-1}{m}$, i.e., if

$$n - m + 1 > 2\,w.$$

Exactly the same argument can be used to combine the effects of errors and erasures to show that if

$$n - m + 1 > 2\,w + e,$$

then we can decode, where $e$ is the number of erasures.

The above chain of reasoning is due to Reed and Solomon in their seminal paper on Reed-Solomon codes [296], [238, p. 306], [272, pp. 262–263]. It also gives an (inefficient) algorithm based on voting. Reed-Solomon codes are widely used, for instance, in compact discs (2-byte error correction), the Voyager (16-byte error correction), military communications, mobile radio, magnetic tape and disk, deep-sea probes [64], the Digital Audio Tape (DAT), and the Digital Compact Cassette (DCC) [255, p. 43], [114]. The codes are independently discovered by Arimoto in Japan in 1961 [64].

Reed-Solomon codes can be derived from our IDA scheme in Section 2.5 as follows [238, Chapters 9 and 10]. Let $\mathcal{A}_V = [\,x_i^{j-1}\,]_{\substack{1 \leq i \leq n \\ 1 \leq j \leq m}}$ as before, $R = GF(q)$ for $q = p^r$, and $n = q - 1$. Hence the number of pieces is that of non-zero elements in the ground field $R$. Now, let $x_i = \omega^{(i-1)}$, where $\omega \in GF(q)$ is a **primitive** $(q-1)^{\text{th}}$ **root of unity** (i.e., $\omega^{q-1} = 1$ but $\omega^s \neq 1$ for $0 < s < q-1$). Such an $\omega$ always exists since we can pick a **generator** $\alpha$ of the set of non-zero elements of $R$ (i.e., $\alpha, \alpha^2, \alpha^3, \ldots, \alpha^{q-1}$ exhaust these $q-1$ non-zero elements) [238, Theorem 2, p. 96].

The computational complexity of decoding Reed-Solomon codes of block length $n$ with errors and erasures is $O(n \log^2 n)$ [310, Corollary 3]. The standard $O(n^2)$ algorithm is discussed in [50] and [272]. Attempts have also been made to replace costly multiplications and divisions with cyclic shifts by choosing a suitable ring for the Reed-Solomon codes under the erasure-only condition [66]. See also [238, p. 369] for a discussion of the computational complexity of various coding schemes.

We make some final remarks. Reed-Solomon codes are **maximum distance separable** (MDS), meaning they have the maximum possible distance between codewords [238, p. 317]. Reed-Solomon codes are a special case of the important BCH codes [228, 238, 272]. BCH codes can also be seen from the viewpoint of signal processing [62] instead of the more usual algebraic approach. Finally, BCH codes are a special case of the generalized Reed-Solomon codes [238, pp. 303–305], and we mention in passing that our IDA scheme with $\mathcal{A}_V$ is a generalized Reed-Solomon code.

### 2.5.4   Related work

We first review Shamir's scheme for secret sharing. Let $p$ be a prime and $0 \leq s < p$ a **secret**. Pick an $(m-1)$-degree polynomial $P(x) = \sum_{i=0}^{m-1} a_i \cdot x^i$ with $a_0 = s$ and $a_i$ chosen randomly from $[0, p-1]$ for $1 \leq i < m$. If we distribute $n$ pieces of information as $P(1), \ldots, P(n)$ where $m \leq n < p$, then any $m$ of them can unlock the secret by interpolating the polynomial $P(x)$, but any $m - 1$ of them give *no* knowledge about $s$ since any integer in $[0, p-1]$ is as likely [318]. We remark that Blakley [65] also independently arrives at a secret-sharing scheme. Shamir's scheme is used by Ben-Or, Goldwasser, and Wigderson's to compute a function without revealing any additional information other than the function value (they basically use $\mathcal{A}_{\mathrm{FFT}}$) [46].

Our scheme has much in common with Shamir's. Recall that the splitting operation with $\mathcal{A} = \mathcal{A}_{\mathrm{V}}$ is nothing but a sequence of multiplications of the matrix $[x_i^{j-1}]_{\substack{1 \leq i \leq n \\ 1 \leq j \leq m}}$ by some vector of length $m$, say $[a_0 \cdots a_{m-1}]^T$, but that is just evaluation of the polynomial $Q(x) = \sum_{i=0}^{m-1} a_i \cdot x^i$ at $x_1, x_2, \ldots, x_n$. Since all $Q(x)$'s coefficients together constitute the original information instead of only the constant term, our scheme leads to $(n/m)$-fold increase in space in comparison with Shamir's $n$-fold increase.

Preparata's IDA [280] is exactly $\mathcal{A}_{\mathrm{FFT}}$. He shows that when $n - m \ll n$, then reconstruction can be done in $O(L \log n)$ steps. In fact, our IDA scheme has been largely anticipated by McEliece and Sarwate [244] almost a decade ago when they pointed out the relation between Shamir's scheme and Reed-Solomon codes. The basic idea of information dispersal is also hinted in their paper.

## 2.6   Application to Voting

In this section, we apply IDA to voting to filter out bad data; see Figure 2.2. Consider $n$ processors, $p_1, \ldots, p_n$, and assume each processor $p_i$ computes a value $F^i \in [0, B]^L$ by executing the same program. Let $B = 2^8 - 1$ for the following analysis. In the presence of faults, the $F^i$'s may not be all identical. Figure 2.3 presents our IDA-based algorithm, FILTERING, to vote on the $F^i$'s in order to filter out polluted results.

FILTERING works as follows. Each processor $p_i$ compares its own $F^i$'s $j^{\mathrm{th}}$ piece with $F^j$'s $j^{\mathrm{th}}$ piece produced by node $p_j$, where $1 \leq j \leq n$ and $j \neq i$, and then takes a vote. If its $n$ pieces are supported by a safe majority of $m$ out of $n$ (its own

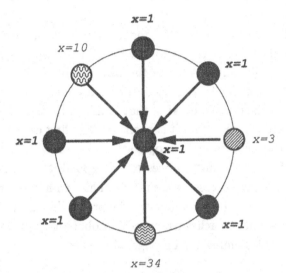

Figure 2.2: IDEA OF VOTING. The node in the center compares its $x$ value with its neighbors' $x$ values, and a majority of five agree with it. If the node were to have, say, $x = 49$, then it would have some confidence in abandoning 49.

Algorithm FILTERING $(n, m)$
**For** $p_i$, $1 \leq i \leq n$, **Do**:

1. Use $IDA(n, m)$ to split $F^i$ into $n$ pieces, $F^i_1, \ldots, F^i_n$.

2. Broadcast the $i^{\text{th}}$ piece $F^i_i$ to all the other processors.

3. If $\left| \{ j \mid F^i_j = F^j_j, j \neq i \} \right| \geq m - 1$, keep $F^i$ and mark those $p_j$ with $F^j_j \neq F^i_j$ as suspects.

4. Otherwise, suspend and run diagnostics.

Figure 2.3: AN IDA-BASED VOTING SCHEME: FILTERING.

$F_i^i$ is included in the vote count by default), it accepts $F^i$ and marks any $p_j$ with a different $j^{\text{th}}$ piece as a suspect. Otherwise, it suspends itself. If we had let the processors exchange their $F^i$ with everyone else, these messages would have used $m$ times as much space. FILTERING can be invoked when faulty processors are suspected to exist.

We shall analyze FILTERING under the model where each processor can fail independently with probability $1/2 > p > 0$ and, when faults occur, each bit of $F^i$ can be 0 or 1 with equal probability. Assume the IDA scheme with $\mathcal{A} = \mathcal{A}_{\text{V}}$ (Section 2.5) based on the finite field $GF(2^8)$ is used. There are two cases to consider: (i) a non-faulty processor is misled into thinking that it might be faulty, and (ii) a faulty processor is "misled" into thinking that it is healthy.[4] The first case wastes computing resources; the second may lead to error propagation. We show neither is likely.

Consider (i) first. For a non-faulty processor to suspend itself, it is necessary that more than $n-m$ of its fellow processors are faulty. This can happen with probability $B(n-m+1, n-1, p)$, where $B(a, b, q)$ denotes the probability that at least $a$ out of $b$ independent Bernoulli trials, each with success probability $q$, are successful. For $(n-1)p \le m \le (n+3)/2$, Lemma 5.7 on page 55 implies

$$B(n-m+1, n-1, p) \le B((n-1)/2, n-1, p) < 2^{n-1} p^{(n-1)/2},$$

a small number for small $p$ and independent of $m$. For example, if $p = 10^{-6}$, the probability for (i) to occur is less than $2^{n-1} 10^{-3(n-1)} \approx 10^{-2.7(n-1)}$.

We now consider (ii). Assume $L = m$ for the first analysis and let $F^i = (b_1^i \cdots b_L^i)$ with $b_l^i \in [0, B]$. We have seen in Subsection 2.3.1 that $F_j^i$ is evaluation of the $(m-1)$-degree polynomial

$$P_{F^i}(x) \stackrel{\text{def}}{=} \sum_{l=0}^{m-1} b_{l+1}^i \cdot x^l$$

at $x_j$ for $1 \le j \le n$. Suppose $p_f$ is faulty but it thinks it is *not* faulty after FILTERING. Then, it must be that at least $m-1$ of $F^f$'s pieces agree with the corresponding pieces of the $n-1$ *received* ones (note that its own $f^{\text{th}}$ piece is by default counted as supportive). In other words, there exist $1 \le i_1 < i_2 << i_{m-1} \le n$, where $i_1 \ne f, \ldots, i_{m-1} \ne f$, such that

$$F_{i_l}^f = P_{F^f}(x_{i_l}) = P_{F^{i_l}}(x_{i_l}) = F_{i_l}^{i_l} \tag{2.6}$$

---

[4]Here we assume FILTERING is always correctly executed for the analysis' sake. This assumption is useful when the fault is transient. A faulty processor will eventually be caught anyway since it produces non-consistent values.

for $1 \leq l \leq m-1$. There are at most $\binom{n-1}{m-1}$ choices of $i_1, \ldots, i_{m-1}$. Since any such set of agreements uniquely determines a polynomial of degree $m-1$, since any $m$ pieces of $F^f$ are independent [49, 376], and since any particular $P_{F^f}(x)$ occurs with equal probability $(B+1)^{-m}$, (2.6) holds with probability at most $\frac{\binom{n-1}{m-1}}{(B+1)^m}$. For example, the above probability is less than $1.25\,10^{-10}$ for $n=10$ and $m=5$. In the general case where $L \geq m$, the argument is similar except that, now, any agreement with $m-1$ other processors' pieces determines $L/m$ polynomials of degree $m-1$ each, with a total number of $L$ coefficients. Hence, the probability for (ii) to happen becomes at most

$$\frac{\binom{n-1}{m-1}}{(B+1)^L}.$$

In summary, any given processor makes a mistake with probability less than

$$(1-p)\,2^{n-1}\,p^{(n-1)/2} + p\,\frac{\binom{n-1}{m-1}}{(B+1)^L}.$$

We make some final remarks on our fault model. We have assumed independence of faults, random faults, no collusions, no malicious behaviors, and reasonably low probability of faults. The rationale is that faults at different sites are unlikely to produce identical results and that simultaneous faults are unlikely. These seemingly innocent beliefs may not be true in reality. In any case, fault tolerance analysis cannot start without a fault model.

# Chapter 3

# Interconnection Networks

> What is interesting is always interconnection.
>
> —Michel Foucault

We survey interconnection networks that link the processors in a parallel computer. Important terms and design issues pertaining to networks are also briefly discussed. This chapter is intended to be concise and sufficiently complete.

# 3.1   Introduction

The interconnection network in a multiprocessor specifies how the processors are tied together. The processors then communicate by sending information through the network. Since the interprocessor delay easily dominates the execution time [56] except where interprocessor communications are rare or only nearly processors exchange information, the choice of the network makes the difference between an efficient system and an inefficient one; clearly, a network where information has to traverse, say, 100 links on the average is less efficient than the one where only ten suffice, other things being equal. Besides the efficiency issue, the interconnection network also sets a limit to the number of faults a parallel computing system can sustain. For example, since a disconnected network that isolates some processors from the others makes joint computation impossible, the network should be able to withstand many faulty links.

This chapter surveys interconnection networks and related issues. In Section 3.2 some of the basic terms for networks are reviewed. A simple and useful graph-theoretical abstraction of networks is introduced in Section 3.3. Several popular networks are then briefly surveyed in Section 3.4, followed by Section 3.5, where some key issues in the choice of networks are summarized.

# 3.2   Basic Terminology for Networks

The selected terms below are grouped under three topics: (i) interconnection and node structures, (ii) switching, and (iii) universality.

## 3.2.1   Interconnection and node structures

Each node of a network contains a **switching element** (SE) responsible for interprocessor communications. Processors and/or memory modules are then attached either directly to the SE or to their input/output ports. If a processor wants to communicate with another processor or memory module, it injects a piece of information into its SE. This information then traverses a sequence of neighboring SEs until it reaches the SE to which the destination processor or memory module is attached. This process is called **routing**. The destination processor or memory module finally removes this information from the network.

There are basically two types of networks: **indirect** and **direct** [2, 314, 315]. Indirect networks are sometimes called **switching networks** and direct networks **communication networks** [363]. In indirect interconnection schemes, processors

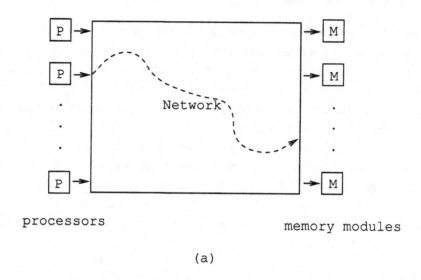

processors                              memory modules

(a)

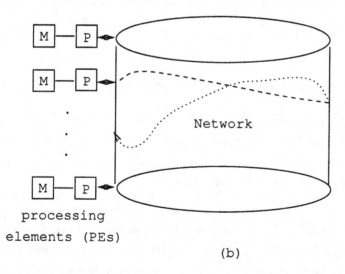

processing
elements (PEs)
(b)

Figure 3.1: TWO WAYS TO ORGANIZE PROCESSORS AND MEMORY MODULES:(a)
the processor-to-memory organization and (b) the PE-to-PE organization. The dotted lines
indicate the routing of information.

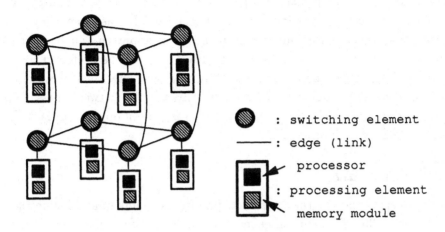

Figure 3.2: DIRECT (COMMUNICATION) NETWORK ARCHITECTURE. Each SE is attached to by a PE in direct interconnection schemes.

and memory modules are attached only to the input/output ports of the SE. There are two major configurations: **processor-to-memory** ("dance hall") and PE-to-PE ("boudoir"). In the processor-to-memory organization, the network is put *between* the array of processors and the array of memory modules, and interprocessor communications are achieved by processors' sending messages through the network to shared variables in the memory modules; see Figure 3.1a. This organization is used, for example, in the C.mmp/HYDRA machine [167, 381] and the NYU Ultracomputer [137]. The main advantage of this organization is the ability to share large blocks of data and to vary the amount of memory used by each processor [322, 323]. In the PE-to-PE configuration, in contrast, each processor is paired by a memory module, forming a **processing element** (PE), which is then attached to one of the input ports *and* one of the output ports of the network; see Figure 3.1b. This approach is taken by, for example, the BBN Butterfly™ computer [92]. The main advantage of this configuration is fast local memory references [322, 323].

In direct interconnection schemes, each node is attached to by a PE; see Figure 3.2. Hence, each PE is connected *directly* to a number of PEs *via* neighboring SEs. Communications may take advantage of locality under this organization since some communication patterns involve only nearby PEs. Direct networks appear in, for example, the Cosmic Cube multiprocessor [315], the Illiac IV [38], and the Connection Machine [349].

Historically speaking, indirect interconnection schemes have evolved under the shared-memory model of parallel computation, while the direct structures have been used mainly for message-passing architectures [258]. It has been conjectured, in [315] for example, that the indirect interconnection approach will be preferred for systems with tens of processors, while the direct one will be preferred for systems with hundreds or thousands of processors.[1] In any case, only the direct network has the notion of **neighborhood** for its PEs. Finally, the line between message-passing and shared-memory systems is often in reality a matter of opinion; in fact, they can be seen as duals of each other [202].

## 3.2.2   Switching

Switching refers to the way the SEs switch data from one link to another on the way to its destination [336]. There are three main approaches to switching: circuit switching, message switching, and packet switching [239, 321, 336]. In **circuit switching**, once a path is established the SEs on the path remain dedicated until the path is released. The Intel PSC/2 and iPSC/860 use circuit switching for long data [157]. In **message switching**, in contrast, a logical unit of data called **message** (telegrams, electronic mails, files, etc.) makes its way from SE to SE, releasing links and SEs immediately after using them. At each node, the entire message is stored briefly before being transmitted to the next node. This system is also known as **store-and-forward** message system [336], and the network as **store-and-forward/point-to-point** network [346].[2] Message switching has many advantages over circuit switching [239], greater line efficiency and no need for the simultaneous availability of sender and receiver being two of them.

**Packet switching** is very much like message switching, the principal difference being that the length of the units of data presented to the network is limited. The data units in the packet switching system are referred to as **packets**. Limiting the size of a data unit to a small length turns out to have a dramatic effect on performance [336]. We will consider *buffered, packet switching, direct* networks in later chapters.

---

[1]Though the BBN Monarch [299] shared-memory design with $2^{16}$ processors may have invalidated this claim, that machine was not built. The Stanford Dash cache-coherent shared-address multiprocessor with 64 RISC microprocessors is also challenging that conjecture — this machine is under construction [224]. Finally, Gordon Bell [44] believes the Kendall Square Research's KSR 1 Multiprocessor has disproved that conjecture. See also [179, 205] for comparisons.

[2]A point-to-point link is a physical circuit which connects exactly two nodes without passing through an intermediate one [102]. A **multipoint** link, a **bus** for example, is a single line which is shared by more than two nodes. We will not discuss bus networks.

### 3.2.3 Universality

**Universality** of indirect networks under, without loss of generality, the PE-to-PE configuration refers to the capability to realize *every* permutation on the PEs by a suitable setting of the SEs so that packets can traverse the network *simultaneously* without conflicts [262, 380]. Such networks are also called rearrangeable networks [117, 195, 240]. A celebrated example is the Beneš network [45], which is used in the IBM GF-11 parallel computer [11, 341] and proposed as a candidate for optical switching network [156]. Although the popular omega network (page 34) is not rearrangeable, a network formed by cascading three omega networks is [262, 380]; recently (1990), that number has been reduced to the optimal two [81]. These networks, however, all require relatively slow **control algorithms**, which set up the SEs so that packets reach their destinations without traversing the same link. The GF-11, for example, uses *pre*computed control data. As a consequence, fast, simple control algorithms which can realize only a useful subset of all permutations are often preferred [86, 253]. See also [345] for an analysis of the permutation power of networks.

Universality concerns only networks *without* buffers, and once the SEs have been set up to realize any particular permutation, the packets only have to follow the routes as determined by the SEs to reach their destinations without conflicts. In contrast, it is trivial for a buffered network to realize any permutation [199], as any conflicts due to packets demanding the same link can be resolved by simply forwarding only one packet and putting the rest in the buffer for the next time step. As complicated queueing patterns may develop, it is not hard to see that the central problem for buffered networks lies in the analysis of their performance.

A rearrangeable network is said to be **(strictly) non-blocking** if, after any partial permutation on the PEs has been realized, it can still realize communication between any new pair of PEs, by setting the SEs, without changing the paths taken by packets of those PEs involved in the above-mentioned partial permutation. Clos network [88] is an example of non-blocking network. A non-blocking network with $N$ PEs can be constructed such that it has depth $O(\log N)$ and size $O(N \log N)$ [240].

Another notion of universality is equally important. We say a network is universal if, loosely speaking, it can simulate any other network of comparable size with only a logarithmic factor slowdown [213, p. 439]. The hypercube network and its relatives form such a family of networks [214].

# 3.3   Graph-Theoretical Modeling

At the abstract level, it is helpful to view a network as a graph of nodes connected by edges. This graph constitutes the network's **topology**. To be more specific, a network is modeled as a **digraph** (directed graph) $G(V, E)$, where $V$ is the set of nodes and $E$ the set of edges. A node in $V$ corresponds to either a PE or an SE in the network. An edge $(u, v)$ is in $E$ if there is a link from $u$ to $v$ in the network. An edge $(u, v) \in E$ is said to be **incident from** $u$ and **to** $v$. The **in-degree** of a node is the number of edges that are incident *to* that node. Similarly, the **out-degree** of a node is the number of edges that are incident *from* that node. A **path** in $G$ is a sequence of nodes $v_0, \ldots, v_k$ such that $(v_i, v_{i+1}) \in E$ for $0 \leq i < k$. The **length** of such a path is $k$. The **connectivity** of $G$ is the minimum number of nodes (edges) which must be deleted in order to destroy all the paths between a pair of nodes. The **diameter** of $G$ is the maximum distance between any pair of nodes [72].

For instance, rearrangeability of networks can be stated as follows. Let $G(V, E)$ be the digraph corresponding to a network with some nodes in $V$ marked as PEs. A network is rearrangeable if, for any permutation $\pi$ on the PEs, there exist edge-disjoint paths from $p$ to $\pi(p)$ for all PEs $p$. The beauty of this type of presentation is that a lot of implementation details can be abstracted away without destroying the essential features of a network.

# 3.4   Sample Networks

Here we are interested in proposed network topologies, modeled as graphs, for multiprocessors. Illustrations appear in Figures 3.3, 3.4, and 3.5. References [4, 11, 117, 139, 178, 240, 250, 277, 321, 322, 378] contain more detailed surveys in specific areas.

## 3.4.1   The hypercube network

In the $n$-dimensional (binary) cube, each node is represented as an $n$-bit number and each edge connects two nodes which differ in exactly one position. This network has been extensively studied [146], receives early consideration for connecting large numbers of processors [335], and has been praised often ("For large systems the Boolean cube is best." [343]). The hypercube network is used in the Cosmic Cube multiprocessor [315], the Connection Machine CM-2 [155], the Intel PSC/2 and iPSC/860, the NCUBE [11], and many other machines.

The hypercube network has many derivatives. The **indirect binary cube network** of Pease [268] is its indirect version. Replacing each node of a hypercube network by a ring of $n$ nodes, one obtains the **cube-connected-cycles** (CCC) **network** of Preparata and Vuillemin [281]. If we let each node be a $d$-ary, instead of binary, $n$-tuple, then we obtain the **generalized hypercube network** [59].

It remains an open question if the hypercube network of dimension greater than three is rearrangeable in that edge-disjoint paths exist for any permutation on the nodes [333]. It is known that the Szymanski conjecture, which says the answer to the above question is affirmative, becomes false when we demand that the paths be shortest [232]. On the other hand, the hypercube network and many of its relatives are universal in their ability to simulate other networks efficiently [213, p. 439].

### 3.4.2   The de Bruijn network

In the de Bruijn network of dimension $n$, each node is an $n$-bit number and there is an edge between $x$ and $y$ if $x$'s last $n - 1$ bits equal $y$'s first $n - 1$ bits [94]. This kind of connection has been frequently rediscovered [289]. The above definition can be extended to the $d$-ary de Bruijn network, where each node is represented as a $d$-ary $n$-tuple [308]. The **Kautz network** is a de Bruijn network except that any consecutive tuples are distinct [52]. Both the de Bruijn and Kautz networks have very good connectivity properties; in fact, a recent (1991) study by Du, Lyuu, and Hsu shows one can connect any node to many other nodes using up to $c$ (the connectivity) node-disjoint paths (some of which can share destinations) of length no more than the network diameter plus one or two [108]. The concept **spread**, which subsumes the connectivity concept, is introduced as a result. Similar results are also obtained for the generalized hypercube network [160], the **loop network** (a generalization of the chordal ring network) [160], and the **star network** [101], but only for a more restricted case where paths cannot share destinations. The de Bruijn network shares, sometimes even surpasses, most of the good properties of the hypercube network and is championed by some researchers as an ideal network for parallel computers [53, 308, 329]. It is also an essential building block of universal MINs [118]. Liu has an optimal algorithm to find the shortest path on the directed and undirected de Bruijn network.

### 3.4.3   The butterfly network

The butterfly network of dimension $n$ is the graph where each node is represented as a pair $(x, i)$ in which $x$ is an $n$-bit number and $0 \leq i \leq n$. Edges connect $(x, i)$ with $(x, i + 1)$ and with $(x//i, i + 1)$, where $x//i$ is derived from $x$ by negating its $i^{\text{th}}$ bit. A wrap-around version is obtained if $(x, n)$ is identified with $(x, 0)$. Since each node $(x, i)$ is linked only to nodes with $i - 1$ or $i + 1$ as their second components, $i$ is called $(x,i)$'s **level** or **stage**. A leveled/staged network such as the butterfly network is called a **multistage interconnection network** (MIN). The indirect butterfly network and its topological equivalents are extremely popular; for example, they are used in the BBN Butterfly™ computer [92], the IBM RP3 [273], the NYU Ultracomputer [137], and the Cedar machine [187].

As with the de Bruijn network, the butterfly network can be extended to $d$-ary, called the **$d$-way digit-exchange network** [276, 361]. A recent (1989) extension of the butterfly network is Upfal's **multi-butterfly network** [363], constructed by superimposing $O(1)$ butterfly networks in a certain pattern to have the expansion property between levels. Building optical networks along this direction is also being explored [266]. An analysis of why edge replication has surprising increase in performance can be found in [177].

The butterfly network has several notable properties. There is a unique path from an **input node** $(x,0)$ to an **output node** $(y,n)$. An MIN with this **unique path property** (UPP) [178] is called a **banyan network** [132]. The second property is that the network is **digit-controlled (delta)**. Label an edge from $(x,i)$ to $(y,i+1)$ by 0 (1) if the $i^{\text{th}}$ bit of $y$ is 0 (1). Then the path from any input node to the output node $(y_0 y_1 \cdots y_{n-1}, n)$ will use edges with labels $y_0, y_1, \ldots, y_{n-1}$, in that order. In other words, this sequence of edge labels is completely determined by the destination output node, making routing easy. The performance of delta networks, introduced by Patel [264], has been extensively analyzed [98, 182, 274]. The third property is that a lot of networks have been shown to be topologically equivalent to the butterfly network (see [183, 262, 324] and especially Wu and Feng's [379]); they include the **omega**[3] [203], the **baseline** [379], the **reverse baseline** [379], the **(Staran) flip** [40, 41], the **modified data manipulator** (butterfly) [116], and the indirect binary cube networks [268].

### 3.4.4   Other networks

In the **shuffle-exchange network**, first discussed by Stone [339], each node is an $n$-bit number and $x_0 x_1 \cdots x_{n-1}$ is connected to $x_1 \cdots x_{n-1} x_0$ (*via* the **shuffle** edge) and $x_0 x_1 \cdots x_{n-2} \overline{x_{n-1}}$ (*via* the **exchange** edge), where $\bar{a}$ denotes the negation of the bit $a$. The shuffle interconnection scheme is ubiquitous among MINs; in fact, it is the building block of the omega network, hence all its topological equivalents. The shuffle-exchange network is actually a subgraph of the binary de Bruijn network [115].

The **mesh** is a two-dimensional grid and was used, for example, in the Illiac IV [38],

---

[3]The pioneering omega network, proposed by Lawrie [203], is an MIN where neighboring stages are connected by the ubiquitous shuffle connection scheme [201, 267, 268, 339, 340].

the Touchstone [227], and the Stanford Dash [224]. We obtain the **torus** network, adopted by the iWarp machine, if wrap-around edges are added. Higher-dimensional meshes can be easily envisioned. In fact, the $n$-dimensional cube network can be seen as a special case of $n$-dimensional mesh.

The **group-based graphs** are constructed using group theory [143]. A group is a set $G$ and an associative binary operation $\oplus$ on $G$ such that $G$ contains an identity element and every element has an inverse. Such graphs are generally quite symmetric. In a **Caley graph**, named after a prominent nineteenth-century mathematician and physicist, the nodes are elements of a group $G$ and there is an edge from $a$ to $b$ if $b = a \oplus g$ for some generator $g$ of $G$ [8, 125, 143]. Caley graphs are node-symmetric, which loosely means the graph "looks" the same from any node [295]. Caley graphs include the hypercube, the CCC, the wrap-around butterfly, the star, and the **pancake** networks [8, 15].

The **binary tree network** [47] has many variations, a tree with double roots being one. In the **fat-tree [222] network**, proposed by Leiserson, the PEs are attached to the leaves of the tree while the tree's internal nodes are SEs; furthermore, the closer an internal node is to the root, the more the number of edges is between it and its father. The Connection Machine CM-5 adopts this topology [223, 350]. The **x-tree network** [97] is a binary tree network with additional edges between neighboring nodes on the same level.

The **pyramid network** is composed of layers of meshes with dimensions of the meshes decreasing by one half as we go up the network. It is first proposed in [348] with applications mainly in multiresolution processing of images [302].

The **mesh-of-trees network** of Leighton [210, 211] contains an edge-less mesh and a binary tree on top of each row and column of the mesh.

The **tree-of-meshes** is formed by replacing each node of a complete binary tree with mesh and each edge by several edges which link the meshes together [210]. The fat-tree is based on the tree-of-meshes [222].

The **Beneš network** [45] can be seen as two butterfly networks tied back to back. Its relatives include the **Joel** and the **Waksman** networks [260].

The **crossbar** or the **completely connected network** has an edge between every pair of nodes.

Other common network topologies include **chordal ring** [52], **ring** (used mainly in local area networks), **linear array** [193, 194], and **star** (common among PBX — Private Branch Exchange — telephone networks [102]).

# 3.5  Some Desirable Properties for Networks

The desired properties for interconnection networks include [4, 11, 53]:

- **Small communication delay or latency.** As the diameter of a graph is the number of edges a packet has to traverse in the worst case, small diameter means low communication delay. However, this demand should be balanced against cost concerns. For example, although the crossbar network has the smallest diameter, its number of edges grows quadratically with the number of nodes, which is impractical even for networks of moderate sizes.

- **Small or fixed degree.** The physical fan-in and fan-out of a node generally cannot exceed certain upper bounds [313]. A fixed-degree network has the additional advantage that only one SE design has to be built.

- **Easy routing.** A network topology admitting distributed routing algorithms without requiring packets to carry much routing information is certainly desirable. In delta networks, for example, only the destination address is needed for routing.

- **"Regularity" in topology.** The complexity of the routing algorithm clearly depends upon the regularity of the network topology [279]. A highly unstructured interconnection pattern not only is hard to analyze, but also very likely requires extensive hardware/software support. The traffic pattern in regular networks may also be more easily balanced.

- **Fault tolerance.** The network should continue to function in the presence of failures. One measure commonly used in this regard is the network's connectivity. Diameter can also be a measure of fault tolerance, as the more edges a message has to traverse, the more likely it will be lost due to failures [70]. One measure that generalizes the two is the **spread** concept [108].

- **Extensibility.** This corresponds to how easy it is to construct large networks. Networks with recursive definition such as the hypercube network [305] are easy to construct from smaller ones.

- **Embeddability of other topologies.** This would allow one to use algorithms originally designed for another topology. See [213, 250, 301] for surveys and results. Efficient embedding also implies efficient simulation. Finally, embedding of a process structure graph into the network topology is important for locality of communication and load-balancing properties [51, 315].

- **Hardware cost.** The network should not be too costly to manufacture.

Choosing a network involves trade-offs. For example, although small degree implies low connectivity and large diameter, hence low fault tolerance, physical constraints limit the degree of a node. The Moore bound, which is an upper bound on the maximum number of nodes given a maximum degree and diameter, clearly shows there is a trade-off between degree and diameter [59].

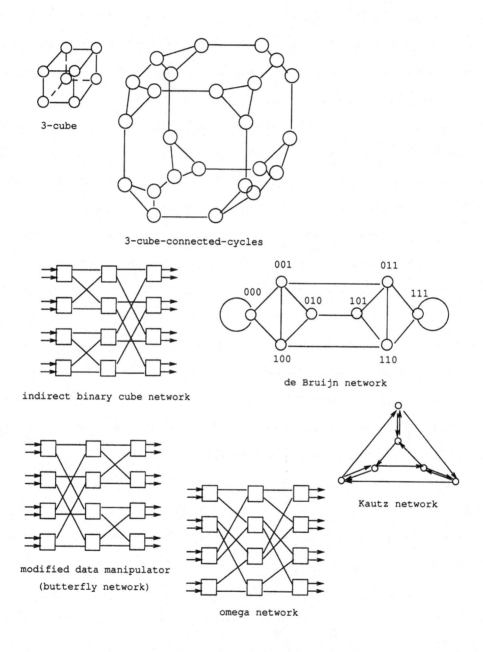

Figure 3.3: SAMPLE NETWORKS.

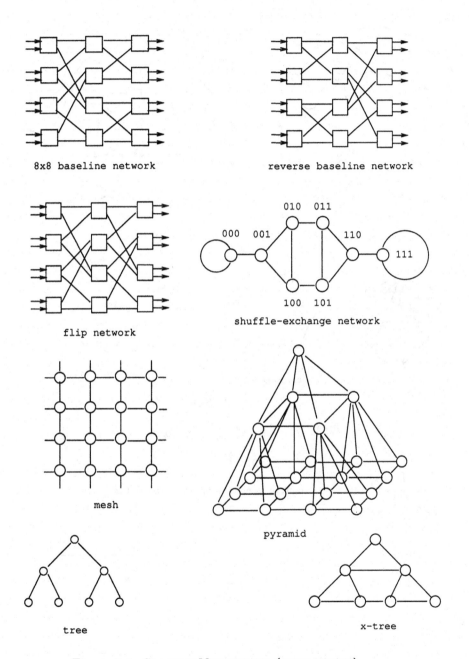

8x8 baseline network

reverse baseline network

flip network

shuffle-exchange network

mesh

pyramid

tree

x-tree

Figure 3.4: SAMPLE NETWORKS (CONTINUED).

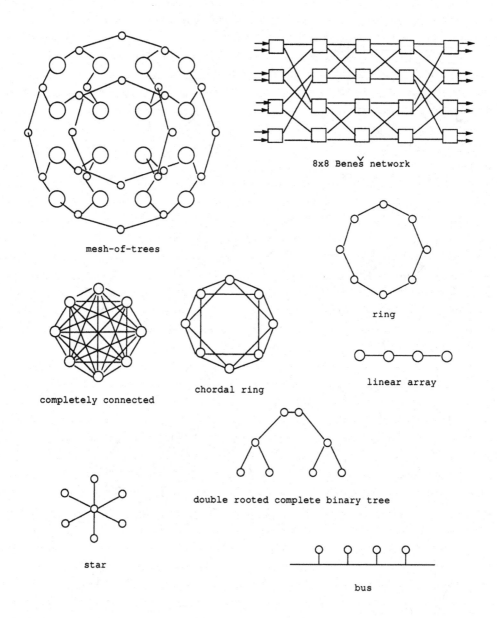

8x8 Benes̆ network

mesh-of-trees

ring

completely connected

chordal ring

linear array

double rooted complete binary tree

star

bus

Figure 3.5: SAMPLE NETWORKS (CONTINUED).

# Chapter 4

# Introduction to Parallel Routing

[E]very time that I went out for a walk

I used to be afraid that the house would

catch fire and the manuscript [ of

*Principia Mathematica* ] get burnt up.

—Bertrand Russell

This chapter serves two purposes: review of previous work and preview of our new results on the parallel routing problem. Our general approach to the problem is also outlined. The routing schemes and their analysis will appear in the next chapter.

# 4.1   Introduction

Perhaps the most important issue in parallel computers is interprocessor communication. Since processors are linked together by a relatively sparse network due to cost considerations, packets have to traverse many links and even be delayed by other packets due to conflicts or full buffers before reaching their destinations. Communication time, therefore, can easily dominate the total execution time, making designing fast communication schemes a primary concern. It is also preferable that the buffer size be a constant independent of the size of the network for the sake of scalability. Finally, as more components mean more faults [326], other things being equal, the issue of fault tolerance without loss of efficiency should be dealt with together.

We review previous work and preview our approach and results in this chapter. In the next chapter, it will be shown how the above-mentioned problems can be tackled simultaneously using information dispersal.

# 4.2   The Parallel Routing Problem

The **parallel routing problem** is an abstraction of the interprocessor communication problem [368]. Consider a buffered, packet switching, direct network modeled as a digraph. A set of packets are initially placed at their origins, and they must be routed *in parallel* to their destinations by a **(parallel) routing algorithm**. In other words, given the network topology and the destinations of the packets, the routing algorithm determines paths which the packets go after. The routing algorithm also ensures that only one packet traverses any link at each step (this is called **scheduling** [290]); see Figure 4.1 for illustration. A packet generally contains its origin, its destination, and the data, maybe plus some bookkeeping information.

In a **(full) permutation routing**, each node initially has, and is the destination of, one packet. In the next chapter, we will restrict ourselves to permutation routing and let $\pi$ denote the permutation on the set of nodes to be realized through routing. In a **(full) $h$-relation routing** [371], each node initially has, and is the destination of, $h$ packets.

A routing algorithm is **local** or **distributed** if each node decides locally on its next action [75]. There exist **global** strategies, where the actions of any node depend on the entire permutation, which can route using only $O(\log N)$ passes through the shuffle-exchange network [262, 380]. Global algorithms, however, are not suitable for parallel computers because the overhead for setting up the SEs is generally too expensive.

A routing algorithm is **oblivious** if the route taken by a packet depends, possibly

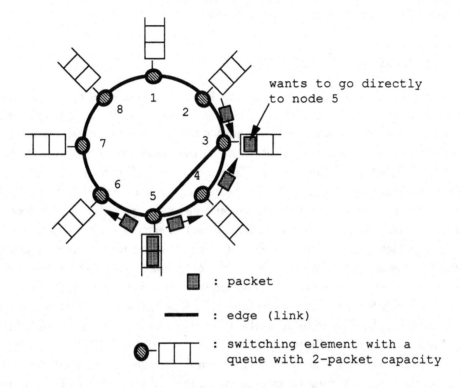

wants to go directly
to node 5

▦ : packet

— : edge (link)

⬤—▭▭ : switching element with a
queue with 2-packet capacity

Figure 4.1: ROUTING IN A DIRECT NETWORK. Here is a direct network consisting of eight nodes, each having a buffer with capacity for two packets. The processing elements are not shown. Observe that one of the two packets going to node 3 will be lost since only one position is available. Node 3 is blocked by node 5, which has a full buffer. Furthermore, the second packet in node 5 is delayed by its predecessor. We shall see that allowing loss of packets can get rid of both types of delay.

subject to some randomness, only upon its origin and destination [75, 366]. A fundamental result of Borodin and Hopcroft, later improved by Kaklamanis, Krizanc, and Tsantilas, states that any deterministic oblivious routing strategy runs in time $\Omega(\sqrt{N}/d)$ for any network having in-degree $d$, where $N$ is the number of nodes [75, 169]. Optimal deterministic oblivious routing algorithms exist for the shuffle-exchange [199] and the hypercube networks [169].

## 4.3   Outline of Approach

Our routing algorithms share the following form. First each packet is split into a number of pieces by IDA. Then, these pieces are routed in parallel to randomly chosen intermediate nodes, from which they are routed to their common destination, that is, the destination of the original packet. Some of the pieces may be lost due to buffer overflow or link failures in the process. The packets are finally reconstructed from the received pieces at their destinations. In the case of the hypercube and the de Bruijn networks, the routes followed by each packet's pieces are picked in such a way that a substantial proportion of them are node-disjoint in each of the three phases of the algorithms, which implies good tolerance of link and, albeit with some complications discussed in Section 9.3, node failures.[1] That only small buffers are needed follows IDA's space-efficiency property. All our schemes are oblivious and distributed.

Our approach follows Rabin's ideas in [285]. The major contribution here is — besides applying those ideas to networks other than the hypercube — improvement of the success probability of routing from $1 - N^{-\Theta(1)}$ to $1 - N^{-\Theta(\log N)}$ by choosing routes that are also much simpler than Rabin's. We remark that an interesting method using error-correcting codes is proposed in [226] for fault-tolerant routing in the omega network. That scheme can, to use our terminology, correct single-bit faults in every piece; hence, it shares some of our philosophy.

Since each piece is small in size, we assemble pieces competing for the same link into one packet instead of letting some pieces wait for the front ones to move. Furthermore, as a certain number of pieces can afford to be lost due to the redundancy provided by IDA, the algorithms send out pieces *regardless* of the status of the receiving buffers (such as, is there enough room for the incoming pieces?), thus avoiding

---

[1]The existence of more than one disjoint path in the interconnection network is often perceived as a necessary condition for good fault tolerance capability. The classic Menger's theorem [48, p. 167] states that a digraph has (node) connectivity at least $h$ if and only if any two distinct nodes can be joined by $h$ node-disjoint paths. But it does not bound the path lengths. The spread concept mentioned in the previous chapter generalizes the connectivity concept by, among other things, incorporating the lengths of such node-disjoint paths.

deadlock completely: a full buffer simply rejects any incoming packet, and its constituent pieces are lost. **Blocking** due to full buffers is hence not needed. As a consequence, there is no queueing delay and all our algorithms run *within* their said time bounds. In contrast, duplicating packets would take up too much buffer space and occupy too much space. Chopping each packet into smaller subpackets [191] of equal size solves the space problem; however, loss of any single subpacket would result in an unsuccessful routing.

The standard technique to achieve multiple paths in the case of MINs with UPP has been to add more hardware such as an extra stage plus the bypassing capability [3], more links [216, 263], larger SEs in terms of the number of fan-ins and fan-outs [259], etc. Extra hardware or not, multiple passes through the unique-path MIN, each pass realizing a partial permutation, may still be necessary [288, 373]. Redundant buses were also adopted by early fault-tolerant bus-based multiprocessor systems like the FTMP [158] and the SIFT computers [377]. Our approach, in contrast, "floods" a network of enough connectivity with small pieces created by IDA such that, with high probability, one run of the routing algorithm suffices.

## 4.4  Summary of Results

Let $N$ be the size of the network. For the hypercube network, we present in Section 5.3 a simple and efficient routing scheme SRA ("Subcube Routing Algorithm") that runs in $2 \log N$ time,[2] uses only constant size buffers, and has probability of successful routing at least $1 - N^{-2.419 \log N + 1.5}$. Our result proves Rabin's conjecture in [285], also independently arrived at by Giladi [131]. SRA, for all practical purposes, never fails to route successfully. As an example, a $2^{16}$-processor hypercube parallel computer such as the Connection Machine CM-2 would have an unsuccessful routing with probability at most $6.4 \cdot 10^{-180}$, as mentioned in Chapter 1.[3] SRA is extremely simple and it introduces the central idea of partitioning the network into disjoint subnetworks, a concept also exploited by our other IDA-based routing algorithms reported here and elsewhere [235].

SRA, however, is not fault-tolerant. In Section 5.4 we present a simple and efficient hypercube-based routing scheme, FSRA ("Fault-Tolerant Subcube Routing Algorithm"), that not only achieves the same bounds as SRA (Theorem 5.15) but

---

[2]Again, all logs are to the base 2 unless noted otherwise.

[3]This means, *hypothetically*, that a $2^{16}$-node hypercube computer that can achieve $10^6$ communications per second (a CM-2 machine typically achieves between $80 \cdot 10^6$ and $250 \cdot 10^6$ communications with 32-bit data per second [349]) would have a single unsuccessful routing since the Big Bang with probability at most $3.03 \cdot 10^{-156}$!

also tolerates: (i) $N/(12\,e\log N)$ random link failures with probability at least $1 - 2N(\log N)^{-\log N/12}$ (Theorem 5.21) and (ii) $\Theta(N)$ random link failures with probability $1 - O(N^{-1})$ (Theorem 5.22).

Routing algorithm on the de Bruijn network is presented in Section 5.5. Let $N$ be the size of the network. Our scheme RABN ("Routing Algorithm for the de Bruijn Network") with constant size buffers runs in $\approx 2\ln N/\ln\ln N$ time and with probability of successful routing at least $1 - N^{-\ln N/2}$ for a class of de Bruijn networks (Corollary 5.34). RABN also tolerates $N/12$ random link failures with probability at least $1 - N^{-\ln\ln\ln N/6}$ on the same class of networks (Theorem 5.38). Comparable results have also been derived for the $d$-way digit-exchange network [233, 237]. Routing algorithms for the butterfly network can be found in [213, 233].

We make some comments on the time bounds. In our schemes, pieces are bundled to form a super packet and sent across a link, all in *one* time step. Suppose each original packet has length $L$ and carries an additional $\Theta(\log N)$ addressing bits such as its destination. Although we guarantee in our schemes that a super packet has length $O(L)$, proportional to that of the original packet, a super packet carries $\Theta(c(N)\log N)$ addressing bits if it contains $c(N)$ constituent pieces, and $c(N)$ may not be a constant. In FSRA, SRA, and RABN, for example, we have $c(N) = \Theta(\log N)$. Since each super packet has length $\Theta(L + (c(N)\log N))$, while the original packet only has length $\Theta(L + \log N)$, one may object that we cannot charge only one time step to the sending of a super packet, as is commonly done when dealing with a packet, unless $L + (c(N)\log N)$ is proportional to $L + \log N$ as $N$ grows. This challenge will be met in Section 5.6 when SRA and FSRA are shown to run in their said time bounds even if we count as taking one time step a *piece* crossing a link and we do not allow bundling of pieces. Note that since a piece is only of length $o(L)$ due to IDA plus $\Theta(\log N)$ addressing bits, it is shorter than a packet.

A unified framework exists for many IDA-based routing schemes. For them, a single general theorem can account for their description and analysis. We discuss these ideas in Section 5.7.

All the above results regarding fault tolerance employ fault models where links fail with a probability *not* independent of the size of the network, because these models are used as approximations to fault models where up to a certain number of links can randomly fail. Hence, these models, *as such*, are not realistic. In Section 5.8 we consider a fault model where links fail with constant probability $p$. A bound on the probability of unsuccessful routing is derived under this fault model for FSRA (Theorem 5.42). Numerical calculations show that, given realistic values for $p$, hypercube networks of reasonable sizes can tolerate random link failures with high probability.

## 4.5 Other Work on IDA-Based Routing Schemes

SRA and FSRA improve Rabin's scheme RA ("Routing Algorithm"), which also works on the hypercube network [285]. RA runs in $2 \log N + 2$ time with probability of successful routing $1 - N^{-\Theta(1)}$. RA moreover tolerates $O(N/\log N)$ random link failures with probability $1 - N^{-\Theta(\log \log N)}$; however, this result holds by ignoring buffer overflow. In comparison, FSRA can achieve comparable bounds (see (i) above) without ignoring buffer overflow, since unsuccessful routing due to buffer overflow is a negligible $N^{-\Theta(\log N)}$.

Håstad, Leighton, and Newman [150] also have a simple scheme that tolerates $O(N)$ random link failures with high probability, as FSRA does. Without the subcube concept, however, their algorithm routes, under the fault-free model, with probability of successful routing $1 - N^{-\Theta(1)}$ instead of our sharper bound of $1 - N^{-\Theta(\log N)}$.

IDA is used in Aumann and Ben-Or's scheme of emulation of fault-free mesh network by faulty ones [25]. They also employ IDA to simulate the PRAM by faulty hypercube networks [24].

## 4.6 Previous Work on Parallel Routing

We first review previous work on randomized routing algorithms.[4] Let $N$ denote the size of the network. In the classic paper [365], Valiant proposes a two-phase communication scheme on the hypercube network with buffer size[5] $O(\log N)$ and shows that each phase runs in $O(\log N)$ time with overwhelming probability: in Phase 1, each packet is sent to a random node; then in Phase 2 it is sent to its destination. The general philosophy of two-phase routing will be implemented on the Inmos C104 routing chip [95, p. 200]. Analysis can be much simplified if packets traverse in order of dimension instead of in random order [371]. Routing in order of dimension is also deadlock-free [93]. Similar techniques are also applied to the de Bruijn network by Valiant and Brebner [371]. Then Aleliunas [10] and Upfal [361] independently improve the network degree to $O(1)$ by considering the de Bruijn and the $d$-way digit-exchange networks, respectively. Pippenger [276] further reduces the queue size to $O(1)$ by considering the $d$-way digit-exchange network. A small probability of deadlock is allowed in Pippenger's scheme, however. Ranade [291] extends Pippenger's result using a simple deadlock-free scheme on the butterfly network with **combining** mechanism, which allows requests to the same data to be combined into one. This scheme is used

---

[4]Algorithms are *randomized* in the sense of [283].

[5]Buffer size is measured as the number of packets in this section.

to simulate CRCW PRAMs[6] with a slowdown of $O(\log N)$ with probability tending to one as $N$ or the number of instructions approaches infinity. Ranade's proof is later simplified and his result generalized by Leighton, Maggs, and Rao [217].

None of the above schemes, however, have proven fault-tolerant quality without loss of efficiency. The loss of a single packet due to, say, link failures would immediately result in an unsuccessful routing. Furthermore, even if link failures are guaranteed not to occur, since not a single packet can be lost, a full buffer at one processor can cause its neighboring processors to wait. Hence, long delay or even deadlock might occur. Deadlock and long delay can surely be handled by stopping a routing if it has taken more than a predetermined time bound and then restarting it. Routing algorithms may also be run several times or packets duplicated to guarantee delivery. These suggestions, however, share one drawback: the amount of traffic in the network and/or the run-time must increase to make small the probability that all the packets are received.

Two approaches to fault-tolerant routing on the hypercube network are reported in [150]. One, called **offset routing**, tries to route around faults. The other, called **reconfiguration**, assigns nodes to working nodes and edges to working paths (this process is named **embedding**) in such a way that the faulty hypercube network can simulate a full hypercube network efficiently; this done, routing can be carried out on the reconfigured faulty hypercube. This second approach has also been improved in [6] and applied to the de Bruijn [14] and butterfly networks [218]. In both approaches, a different fault model from ours was assumed: faults are not allowed to occur dynamically during offset routing or reconfiguration — at least not when a packet is using the very resource. Lately, Leighton, Maggs, and Sitaraman [218] show that, if we allow a node to be simulated by possibly many nodes in the faulty butterfly network, then a faulty butterfly network with $N^{1-\epsilon}$ worst-case faults for any constant $\epsilon > 0$ can emulate a fault-free one of the same size with only constant slowdown. Note that this approach differs from the reconfiguration approach in that the embedding phase is avoided; therefore, dynamic faults can be tolerated.

Routing is related to sorting. A standard technique shows that if we can sort in time $r(N)$, then we can route in time $O(r(N))$ [75, 252, 320]. Batcher's $O(\log^2 N)$ sorting network [39] therefore implies a distributed routing strategy with a run-time of $O(\log^2 N)$. We can also use the sorting network of Ajtai, Komlós, and Szemerédi [7] to route in $O(\log N)$ time or use Leighton's result [212] in the case of direct networks. However, the large constant factor renders this latter approach impractical. All the above algorithms are deterministic. Sorting networks that sort with very

---

[6] CRCW PRAM stands for "Concurrent-Read Concurrent-Write Parallel Random Access Machine" (see Chapter 6). It is the most popular theoretical parallel computation model.

high probability using logarithmic depth with small constant are also available [220]. Leighton, Ma, and Plaxton also extend that work to networks which allow failures [215].

Two breakthroughs make $O(\log N)$-step deterministic permutation routing with $O(1)$ buffer size more competitive. Both use the multi-butterfly network and neither resorts to sorting. Upfal [363] is the first to achieve this. Through pipelining, $O(\log N)$ permutations can be routed in $O(\log N)$ steps as well. Leighton and Maggs [216], applying more careful analysis, improve the run-time in Upfal's scheme for the indirect multi-butterfly network to be at most $82 \log N$ steps using $14 \times 14$ crossbar switches. They also show that the multi-butterfly network is highly fault-tolerant in the sense that no matter how an adversary chooses $f$ faulty switches there are at least $N - O(f)$ inputs and $N - O(f)$ outputs between which $\log N$ permutations can be routed in $O(\log N)$ steps. For random faults, their scheme can tolerate $N^{\alpha}$ switch faults with high probability, where $1/2 < \alpha < 1$.

There is also rich literature on mesh network routing, culminating in Leighton, Makedon, and Tollis' optimal algorithm [219], whose run-time is exactly the diameter plus some smaller terms and the queue size is $O(1)$.

A short section certainly cannot do justice to a rich field. Leighton's comprehensive book [213] and survey paper [214] can be consulted for some of the details.

# Chapter 5

# Fault-Tolerant Routing Schemes and Analysis

Lee and Jackson were now separated,

and only victory would reunite them.

—Winston Churchill

Fast, fault-tolerant communication schemes using constant size buffers on the hypercube and the de Bruijn networks are presented. All our schemes run with probability of successful routing $1 - N^{-\Theta(\log N)}$, where $N$ denotes the number of processors. A summary of this chapter's results can be found in Section 4.4.

# 5.1  Parallel Communication Scheme

The notion of **symmetric parallel communication scheme** (SPCS) captures the essence, and facilitates the analysis, of our parallel routing algorithms.

**Definition 5.1** *In an* **epoched communication scheme** (ECS), *packets are sent in* **epochs**, *numbered from* 0. *In any epoch, packets that demand transmission to neighboring nodes in that epoch, as determined by the routing algorithm, are sent along the links as requested. A* **symmetric parallel communication scheme** (SPCS) *is an* ECS *that satisfies the following conditions.*

1. *Each node initially has* $h$ *packets.*

2. *All packets are routed* independently *by the routing algorithm; that is, in any epoch, a packet crosses an out-going link independently with equal probability.*

3. *The expected number of packets at each node is* $h$ *at the end of each epoch.*

*Such a scheme is called an* $h$-SPCS.

**Comment 5.2** Condition **3** implies that no packets can be lost. In all our schemes, however, pieces (that is, packets in the definition of ECS) can be lost due to buffer overflow. This is not a serious problem since we can analyze a scheme *as if* pieces over the capacity of the buffer were *not* lost. The probability of overflow for an SPCS is surely greater in this **non-destructive model** than in the original model, where pieces can be lost. The non-destructive model is assumed in the analysis of all our schemes. We also mention that, in our analysis, pieces would correspond to ECS packets in the above definition.

Networks using ECSs are globally synchronized since an epoch cannot start until the previous one has ended. Such synchronization can be easily implemented by an $O(\log N)$ depth combinational boolean circuit that makes sure all the nodes and links have been cleared of packets that demand transmission and broadcasts the result to every node to start the next epoch. Global synchronization, actually, is not needed; local synchronization through message passing is all we need (see Section 7.3 for details). In fact, the above implementation is highly vulnerable to faults.

The following bound will be useful for analyzing SPCSs.

**Fact 5.3** ([287]) *Let* $Y_1, \ldots, Y_M$ *be independent Bernoulli trials with the expected value of their sum being* $E\left(\sum_j Y_j\right) = n$. *Let* $\delta > 0$. *Then*

$$Pr\left(\sum_j Y_j \geq (1+\delta)\,n\right) \leq \left(\frac{e^\delta}{(1+\delta)^{(1+\delta)}}\right)^n. \tag{5.1}$$

**Theorem 5.4** *Under an* $h$-SPCS, *the probability that a node has at least* $(1+\delta)\,h$ *packets at the end of any given epoch is at most* $\left(e^\delta/(1+\delta)^{(1+\delta)}\right)^h$.

**Proof:** Label the packets in the network by $0, 1, \ldots$ and consider node $y$ and epoch $t$. Let $Y_i$ be the random variable that is 1 if packet $i$ arrives at $y$ in epoch $t$ and 0 otherwise. The probability that $y$ has at least $(1+\delta)\,h$ packets at the end of epoch $t$ becomes $Pr\left(\sum_j Y_j \geq (1+\delta)\,h\right)$.

Obviously, the $Y_i$'s denote Bernoulli trials and are independent by Condition **2** of SPCS. Finally, Condition **3** of SPCS says $h$ is the expected value of $\sum_j Y_j$. This theorem can now be proved by applying Fact 5.3.
Q.E.D.

Note that Theorem 5.4 does not involve the size of the network. The following corollary can be proved from Theorem 5.4 with $h = 4$.

**Corollary 5.5** *Under an* $h$-SPCS, *the probability that a node has at least* $5\,h$ *packets at the end of any given epoch is at most* $(e^4/5^5)^h$.

Recall that packets *during* routing in all our schemes are assembled from pieces and exist only for one epoch (see Sections 4.3 and 5.2). These (super-)packets should not be confused with the packets that the routing algorithm starts with.

## 5.2    Basic Terminology and Conventions

As in Section 3.3, a network is represented as a digraph $G$. Each node has a PE and an SE with buffer. $BF(x)$ denotes the buffer at node $x$. $V(G)$ denotes $G$'s nodes and $E(G)$ its directed edges. $G_1 \subseteq G_2$ means graph $G_1$ is a subgraph of $G_2$. $G_1 \cap G_2 = \emptyset$ says $G_1$ and $G_2$ are subgraphs of a given graph — which will always be clear by context — and they have no *nodes* in common. Recall that $\pi$ is a permutation on $V(G)$.

Let $n_0$ and $m_0$ be two integers and $m_0 \leq n_0$. $P_x$ denotes the packet originally at node $x$. It is split by $IDA(n_0, m_0)$ into $n_0$ **pieces**, $P_x(0), \ldots, P_x(n_0 - 1)$, each of length $L/m_0$ such that any $m_0$ of the pieces suffice to reconstruct $P_x$, where $L = |P_x|$. The route any piece traverses is called a **path**. The **paths of a packet** are the collected paths of its pieces. $P_x$'s $i^{\text{th}}$ **path** is the path taken by $P_x(i)$. A path **fails** if any of its links fails. To save notations, $P_x(i)$ will also denote the *node* the piece $P_x(i)$ currently resides in; for example, "$P_x(i) \in V$" means "$P_x(i)$ resides in a node $\in V$." Hence, routing can be viewed as changing the value of $P_x(i)$ from $x$, its origin, to $\pi(x)$, its destination, step by step for each piece $P_x(i)$.

A packet is **reconstructible** if at least $m_0$ of its pieces arrive at its destination at the end of the routing. A routing is **successful** if all the packets are reconstructible despite possibly loss of some pieces due to buffer overflow and link failures. A routing scheme **tolerates** $t$ **random link failures with probability** $p$ if its probability of successful routing is $p$ when links fail independently with probability $t/u$, where $u$ is the total number of links — the expected number of link failures is hence $t$. Note that, by the definition of successful routing, the above probability $p$ takes into account buffer overflow as well. We assume faulty links only make the pieces disappear or change their contents in a detectable way. Buffer size and length of a piece or packet are measured as the number of characters unless stated otherwise. By **constant size buffer** we mean buffer of size $O(L)$, space for routing information *not* counted. The terms **queue** and **buffer** will be used interchangeably. So will **link, edge**, and **wire**. We may refer to integral values such as the number of pieces, the number of links, etc. using numbers that may not be integral. Rounding those non-integral numbers does not affect our proofs and basic results.

We assume each packet of "reasonable" length requires unit time to traverse a link. A packet is of "reasonable" length if its length, routing information excluded, is $O(L)$. All packets will be of reasonable length in our schemes.

All our schemes run in epochs: in each epoch, pieces that are in the same node and demand transmission to the same neighbor in that epoch are **bundled (concatenated)** together to form a single packet and sent, much like the relation between railroad car and train. Since each buffer will have length $cL$ for some constant $c > 0$, a bundled packet has length at most $cL$. Now that each link is traversed by at most one (bundled) packet in each epoch, the number of epochs *is* the **run-time**.

The bundling of pieces into packets gives rise to two possible buffer strategies for handling overflow: (1) the whole packet is rejected and all its constituent pieces lost; or (2) the buffer takes in as many of the packet's constituent pieces as its capacity allows. The first one is more efficient, but the second one makes the probability of unsuccessful routing even smaller. In any case, the correctness of our results does not depend on the choice made since our analysis will depend only on the number of overflows in the routing, regardless of how the overflow is handled.

We say a buffer $x$ does not **overflow** in epoch $t$ if at most $b$ pieces make $x$ their destination in that epoch, where $b$ is $x$'s **capacity**. However, that there is no overflow in all the epochs in *this* sense when each buffer has capacity for $b$ pieces does not preclude overflow since there might be a time *during* epoch $t$ when the number of pieces in $x$ exceeds $b$, though that number eventually decreases to be at most $b$. To handle this anomaly, we only need to increase every buffer's capacity to $2b$. Now, if there is no overflow in the above sense, then, after the increase, since each node $x$ originally has at most $b$ pieces and at most $b$ pieces make $x$ their destination in any epoch, the number of pieces in $x$ will never exceed $2b$ during any epoch, and the anomaly disappears. To make our presentation more concise, we will still say an overflow occurs at $x$ in epoch $t$ if the number of pieces that make $x$ their destination in epoch $t$ — equivalently, the number of pieces *at the end* of epoch $t$, non-destructive model assumed — surpasses the buffer capacity.

We remark that our model is different from previous models for routing. In our model, packets are initially split into smaller pieces, and pieces are combined into packets during routing. Clearly, when $IDA(n_0, m_0)$ is used such that $n_0/m_0 = O(1)$, $\Theta(n_0)$ pieces can be combined into a packet whose length is in the same order as that of the original packet, and we assume such a packet takes unit time to traverse a link; in practice, however, each piece would carry $\Theta(\log N)$ bits of routing information. This issue is overcome for the hypercube in Section 5.6. We also do not count the time spent in splitting and reconstruction of packets in the analysis of run-time; the complexity of IDA has been discussed in Chapter 2.

Define $B(m, N, q)$ to be the probability that at least $m$ of the $N$ independent Bernoulli trials, each with success probability $q$, are successful. Clearly, we have

$$B(m, N, q) = \sum_{i=m}^{N} \binom{N}{i} q^i (1-q)^{N-i}. \tag{5.2}$$

Chernoff's bound will prove to be an extremely useful tool.

**Fact 5.6** ([87])

$$B(m, N, q) \le \left(\frac{Nq}{m}\right)^m \left(\frac{N - Nq}{N - m}\right)^{N-m}$$

*for* $m \ge Nq$.

Using the inequality $((N - Nq)/(N - m))^{N-m} \le e^{m-Nq}$, we can derive Fact 5.3 from Fact 5.6. The next lemma also follows easily from Chernoff's bound.

**Lemma 5.7** $B(m/2, m, q) < 2^m q^{m/2}$ *for* $q \le 1/2$.

**Proof:** Apply Fact 5.3 to get

$$B(m/2, m, q) \le (2q)^{m/2} [2(1-q)]^{m/2} < 2^m q^{m/2}.$$

Q.E.D.

The following lemma's corollary can often shorten lengthy arguments.

**Lemma 5.8** *Let* $0 < q < d < 1$. *Then* $f(q) = \left(\frac{q}{d}\right)^d \left(\frac{1-q}{1-d}\right)^{1-d} < 1$ *and* $B(dn, n, q) \le f(q)^n$.

**Proof:** It is easy to see that $f'(q) = \left(\frac{q(1-d)}{d(1-q)}\right)^{d-1} - \left(\frac{q(1-d)}{d(1-q)}\right)^d \ge 0$. As $f(0) = 0$ and $f(d) = 1$, we conclude that $f(0) = 0 < f(q) < 1 = f(d)$ for $0 < q < d < 1$. Using Chernoff's bound, we also have

$$
\begin{aligned}
B(dn, n, q) &\le \left(\frac{nq}{dn}\right)^{dn} \left(\frac{n - nq}{n - dn}\right)^{n - dn} \\
&= \left[ \left(\frac{q}{d}\right)^d \left(\frac{1-q}{1-d}\right)^{1-d} \right]^n \\
&= f(q)^n.
\end{aligned}
$$

Q.E.D.

**Corollary 5.9** *Let* $0 < d < 1$ *be a constant and* $q = N^{-c}$ *for some constant* $c > 0$. *Then* $B(dn, n, q) < N^{-cdn + o(1)} = N^{-\Theta(n)}$.

## 5.3 Routing on the Fault-Free Hypercube

### 5.3.1 Definitions

The **$n$-dimensional hypercube** $C_n$, also called **$n$-cube**, has $N = 2^n$ nodes. Each node $x$ is denoted by $x_0 \cdots x_{n-1}$, where $x_i \in \{0, 1\}$ is called $x$'s $i^{\text{th}}$ **bit** or **dimension**. The subsequence $x_i \cdots x_j$ of $x$ is denoted by $x[i : j]$. For $0 \le i < n$ and $x \in V(C_n)$, we define $x//i \stackrel{\text{def}}{=} x_0 \cdots \overline{x_i} \cdots x_{n-1}$. The set of $nN$ directed edges of $C_n$ is

$$E(C_n) = \{ (x, x//i) \mid x \in V(C_n),\ 0 \le i < n \},$$

where $(x, x//i)$ is called an **edge of dimension** $i$. To **travel** *via* **dimension** $i$ means to traverse an edge of dimension $i$. Given two binary numbers $x$ and $y$,

$x \circ y$ denotes the concatenation of $x$ and $y$, in that order. Assume $n = 2^k$ in this section to simplify the analysis and notations. We will leave comments on the simple modifications needed in the algorithm and in the analysis if $n$ is not of this form till the end of this section. Given a number $i$ such that $0 \leq i < 2^k = n$, let $bits_k(i)$ denote $i$'s $k$-bit binary representation.

The concept of subcube lies at the heart of our routing algorithm. Let $C_{n-k}(y)$ be the subgraph, or **subcube**, of $C_n$ induced by the following node set

$$\{ x \in V(C_n) \mid x[\, 0 : k - 1\,] = bits_k(y) \},$$

where $0 \leq y < n = 2^k$. In other words, $C_{n-k}(y)$ contains nodes whose first $k$ bits equal $bits_k(y)$. Clearly, there are $n$ subcubes, and each subcube has $N/n$ nodes. Since $C_{n-k}(y)$ is isomorphic to $C_{n-k}$, it is in fact an $(n-k)$-cube. Distinct subcubes are node-disjoint, that is,

$$C_{n-k}(i) \cap C_{n-k}(j) = \emptyset \quad \text{for} \quad i \neq j. \tag{5.3}$$

We remark that Rennels [298] in a different setting also suggests the use of subcubes in his proposed fault-tolerant hypercube parallel computer, in which each subcube is provided with one spare processor through the $n^{\text{th}}$ dimension.

### 5.3.2   SRA: description and preliminary analysis

Choose $n_0 = n$ and $m_0 = n/2$ for IDA. Assume each buffer has enough capacity to hold $5\,n$ pieces. The description of SRA appears in Figure 5.1.

We now sketch SRA. Each $P_x$ is split into $n$ pieces by IDA: $P_x(0), \ldots, P_x(n-1)$. The algorithm then proceeds in two phases. In Phase 1 piece $P_x(i)$ is routed **in order of dimension** first to the subcube $C_{n-k}(i)$, and then to a randomly chosen node in that subcube. $P_x(i)$ is next routed **in reverse order of dimension** to its destination in Phase 2. "In order of dimension" and "in reverse order of dimension" will be made precise in Comment 5.10 below. The key observation here is that $P_x(i)$ is routed within the subcube $C_{n-k}(i)$ during Subphases 1.2–2.1. SRA is clearly **testable**, which means it has the same probabilistic behavior for all permutation requests [371].

**Comment 5.10** By *in order of dimension* we mean that in epoch $i$ of Phase 1 only edges of dimension $i$ are traversed. Symmetrically, by *in reverse order of dimension* we mean only edges of dimension $n-i-1$ are traversed in epoch $i$ of Phase 2. Phase 1 is hence equivalent to "Route $P_x(i)$ to a node chosen randomly from $C_{n-k}(i)$" and Phase 2 to "Route $P_x(i)$ to $\pi(x)$." Note that a piece might be delayed at a node for

**Algorithm** SRA

**For** $x \in V(C_n)$:

**Cobegin**

  Split $P_x$ into $n$ pieces, $P_x(0), \ldots, P_x(n-1)$, using $IDA(n, n/2)$;

  Phase 1: ($n$ epochs, in order of dimension)

    Subphase 1.1: Route $P_x(i)$ to $bits_k(i) \circ (x[k : n-1]) \in C_{n-k}(i)$

      in $k$ epochs;

    Subphase 1.2: Route $P_x(i)$ to $R_x(i)$ in $n - k$ epochs, where

      $R_x(i)$ is chosen randomly from $C_{n-k}(i)$;

  Phase 2: ($n$ epochs, in reverse order of dimension)

    Subphase 2.1: Route $P_x(i)$ to $bits_k(i) \circ (\pi(x)[k : n-1]) \in C_{n-k}(i)$

      in $n - k$ epochs;

    Subphase 2.2: Route $P_x(i)$ to $\pi(x)$ in $k$ epochs;

**Coend.**

Figure 5.1: SRA ("SUBCUBE ROUTING ALGORITHM").

certain number of epochs before proceeding, but this is due not to queueing delay, where a piece loses the competition with other pieces for a link, but simply to the fact that each piece has to wait until the epoch assigned to it to proceed.

**Lemma 5.11** *At the end of each epoch $t$, where $0 \leq t < k$ (i.e., Subphase 1.1), there are $n$ pieces at each node. Furthermore, exactly $n/2$ pieces are sent to neighbors in epoch $t$, and all via the same dimension $t$.*

**Proof:** Since this subphase is completely symmetric for any node, we can prove this lemma by considering the node $x = \overbrace{00 \cdots 0}^{n}$ only. At the end of epoch $t$, node $x$ has only pieces originating from nodes

$$y = \underbrace{\overbrace{y_0 \cdots y_t}^{t+1} 0 \cdots 0}_{k} \overbrace{0 \cdots 0}^{n-k}$$

($x$ itself included). There are $2^{t+1}$ possible $y$'s. Distinct pieces originating from any given such $y$ are destined to

$$z = \underbrace{\overbrace{0 \cdots 0}^{t+1} z_{t+1} \cdots z_{k-1}}_{k} \overbrace{0 \cdots 0}^{n-k}$$

for *distinct* $z_{t+1} \cdots z_{k-1}$'s. Since there are $2^{k-t-1}$ distinct $z$'s, node $x$ must have received $2^{k-t-1}$ pieces from *each* $y$ at the end of epoch $t$. In total $x$ has $2^{t+1} 2^{k-t-1} = n$ pieces.

For the second claim, observe that exactly half of the $z$'s have $z_{t+1} = 1$ and only pieces destined to those $z$'s will be transmitted in epoch $t+1$ for $0 \le t+1 < k$, and *via* dimension $t+1$ by Comment 5.10.
Q.E.D.

The next lemma can be proved by letting the pieces run in the reverse direction in Lemma 5.11.

**Lemma 5.12** *At the end of any epoch $t$, where $2n - k \le t < 2n$ (i.e., Subphase 2.2), there are $n$ pieces at each node. Furthermore, exactly $n/2$ pieces are sent to neighbors in epoch $t$, and all via the same dimension $2n - t - 1$.*

**Comment 5.13** The $n$ pieces that each node has at the end of Subphases 1.1 and 2.1 are from *distinct* packets since any packet's pieces by then have reached *different* and hence disjoint subcubes. Also, each packet has exactly *one* piece in each subcube in Subphases 1.2–2.1. Note that each subcube in Subphases 1.2–2.1 of SRA performs $\log(N)$-relation routing (of pieces).

Observe that a packet's pieces do not take node-disjoint paths in Subphases 1.1 and 2.2. For example, a failed link of dimension 0 incident from node $x$ can wipe out $n/2$ of $P_x$'s $n$ pieces in epoch 0 since they all traverse this link by Lemma 5.11; see Figure 5.2 for illustration. The issue of fault tolerance will be addressed by FSRA in Section 5.4.

### 5.3.3   Analysis of SRA

The next theorem proves Rabin's conjecture in the affirmative.

**Theorem 5.14** SRA *runs in $2 \log N$ time with probability of successful routing at least $1 - N^{-2.419n+1.5}$ using buffers of size $10L$.*

**Proof:** SRA clearly runs in $2n$ time. Since each buffer can hold up to $5n$ pieces and each piece has length $2L/n$, the buffer size is $10L$.

By Lemmas 5.11 and 5.12, we only have to analyze Subphases 1.2–2.1 for overflow. Assume the non-destructive model for the analysis. We analyze the subcube $C_{n-k}(0)$ only; the other $n - 1$ subcubes can be identically treated.

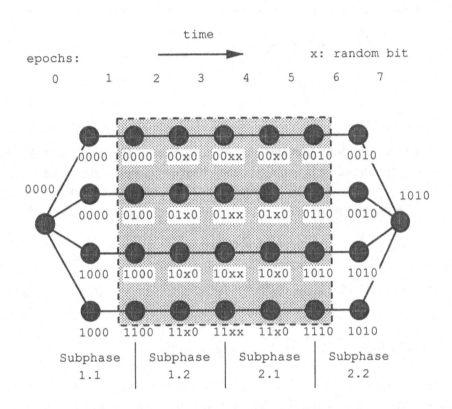

Figure 5.2: THE WORKING OF SRA ON $C_4$. Here we show how $P_x$'s four pieces travel from their origin $x = 0000$ to their destination $\pi(x) = 1010$ in epochs. Note that the four routes are not node-disjoint in either Subphase 1.1 or 2.2; for example, the last two pieces both travel to node 1000 in Subphase 1.1. However, they are in node-disjoint sub-cubes in Subphases 1.2–2.1 (within the dotted box).

Consider a node $y \in C_{n-k}(0)$ and an epoch $t$ where $k \leq t < n$ in Subphase 1.2. The condition for buffer $BF(y)$ to overflow in epoch $t$ is that more than $5n$ pieces make $y$ their destination in epoch $t$. Since each node has $n$ pieces at the beginning of Subphase 1.2 by Lemma 5.11 and since each piece is routed independently, traversing the assigned dimension in each epoch with probability $\frac{1}{2}$, Subphase 1.2 is an $n$-SPCS. Corollary 5.5 implies that the probability of overflow at $BF(y)$ in epoch $t$ is less than $(e^4/5^5)^n$. Since this holds for any $y \in C_{n-k}(0)$ and any epoch in Subphase 1.2, and since Subphase 2.1 is symmetric to Subphase 1.2, we have

$$
\begin{aligned}
p &\overset{\text{def}}{=} Pr(\text{overflow occurs in } C_{n-k}(0) \text{ in Subphases 1.2--2.1}) \\
&\leq 2\left(e^4/5^5\right)^n (N/n)(n-k) \\
&< 2N\left(e^4/5^5\right)^n \\
&\overset{\text{def}}{=} p_0.
\end{aligned}
\tag{5.4}
$$

This inequality clearly holds for any of the $n$ subcubes. By Comment 5.13, each packet has exactly one piece in each subcube. Hence the probability of unsuccessful routing due to overflow is at most the probability that overflow occurs in more than $n/2$ of the $n$ subcubes, which is

$$
\begin{aligned}
&\leq B(n/2, n, p_0) \\
&< Np_0^{n/2} \tag{5.5} \\
&= N^{3/2+n/2}\left(e^4/5^5\right)^{n^2/2} \\
&< N^{-2.419n+1.5}, \tag{5.6}
\end{aligned}
$$

where (5.5) is by Lemma 5.7 (note that $p < p_0 < 1/2$).
Q.E.D.

We can compare SRA with Valiant's scheme. His scheme runs in $2n + o(n)$ time with probability $1 - N^{-k}$ for some constant $k > 0$ [357]. In contrast, SRA runs in $2n$ time and with probability of successful routing at least $1 - N^{-2.419n+1.5}$. Furthermore, SRA runs in the said time bound, while Valiant's scheme may have long queueing delay, albeit with vanishing probability. Valiant's analysis uses all $\log N$ edges of each node in every step; in our scheme only *one* is traversed in each step (epoch). SRA can also be made fault-tolerant, as we shall show later. Of course, such comparison cannot establish superiority because the two schemes use different models and computation time for doing IDA is not counted.

We briefly comment on what if $n \neq 2^k$ for any $k$. Say, $n = 2^{k'} + l$, where $l < 2^{k'}$. Choose $n_0 = 2^{k'}$ for IDA and replace $k$ with $k'$ in SRA. Clearly, Lemmas 5.11 and

**For** $x \in V(C_n)$:

**Cobegin**

    Split $P_x$ into $n$ pieces, $P_x(0), \ldots, P_x(n-1)$, using IDA;

    Phase 1: ($n$ epochs, in order of dimension)

        Route $P_x(i)$ to $R_x(i)$, chosen randomly from $V(C_n)$;

    Phase 2: ($n$ epochs, in reverse order of dimension)

        Route $P_x(i)$ to $\pi(x)$;

**Coend.**

Figure 5.3: A ROUTING SCHEME WITHOUT THE SUBCUBE CONCEPT. See text.

5.12 still hold with $k'$ replacing $k$ and $2^{k'}$ replacing $n$. Hence, there is no overflow in Subphases 1.1 and 2.2. Now, we have $2^{k'}$ $(n-k')$-cubes, and a packet's pieces still travel within disjoint subcubes during Subphases 1.2–2.1. Theorem 5.14's proof is still valid with $k'$ replacing $k$ and $2^{k'}$ replacing $n$. So the probability of unsuccessful routing is at most $B(2^{k'}/2, 2^{k'}, p)$, where, following the above substitution and the steps leading to (5.4), we have $p < p_0 = N^{-\Theta(1)}$. Hence, if $k' = \Theta(\log n)$, then Corollary 5.9 implies that $B(2^{k'}/2, 2^{k'}, p) < N^{-c \log N + o(1)}$ for some $c > 0$.

### 5.3.4   Remarks on the tightness of bounds

We can demonstrate the power of the subcube concept by considering the routing scheme in Figure 5.3. Assume each buffer has capacity for $5n$ pieces as before and $n \geq 5$. We will calculate the probability that a given packet is not reconstructible due to overflow in epoch 5 of Phase 1. This value is surely a lower bound on the overall probability of unsuccessful routing.

    Clearly, a piece travels *via* dimension $i$ in epoch $i$ of Phase 1 with probability $1/2$. Consider a node $x \in V(C_n)$ and five of its $n$ neighbors, $y_0, \ldots, y_4$, where $y_l$ is linked to $x$ *via* an edge of dimension $l$. The probability that $P_x$'s $n$ pieces stay in $x$ during epochs 0 to 4 is $2^{-5n} = N^{-5}$. For any $i$ where $0 \leq i < 5$, the probability that $P_{y_i}$'s $n$ pieces stay in $y_i$ during epochs 0 to $i-1$, move to $x$ in epoch $i$, and then remain in $x$ during epochs $i+1$ to 4 is also $N^{-5}$. Hence, with probability $N^{-5} \left(N^{-5}\right)^5 = N^{-30}$, $P_{y_4}$'s $n$ pieces would find a full buffer at $x$, their common destination, in epoch 4 since each of $P_x$, $P_{y_0}$, $P_{y_1}$, $P_{y_2}$, and $P_{y_3}$ has contributed $n$ pieces to $x$, and all these pieces stay in $x$ in epoch 4. Hence, $P_{y_4}$'s pieces would all be lost, rendering $P_{y_4}$ not reconstructible. In summary, the probability of unsuccessful routing for the above scheme is at least $N^{-30}$.

We can use the same argument to show that any given packet can lose its piece in each subcube during SRA's Subphases 1.2–2.1, which use the above scheme,[1] with probability $q \geq N^{-30}$. Furthermore, since $q \leq p_0 = N^{-\Theta(1)}$ from (5.4), we have $q < 1/2$ for $n$ sufficiently large. From (5.2) and the easily verifiable fact that $q\,(1 - q) \geq q/2$ for $0 \leq q \leq 1/2$, it is easy to show that the probability of unsuccessful routing for SRA, $B(n/2, n, q)$, is at least

$$\binom{n}{n/2} q^{n/2} (1 - q)^{n/2} \geq \binom{n}{n/2} (q/2)^{n/2}$$

$$\geq \sqrt{\frac{2}{\pi}} \frac{2^n}{\sqrt{n}} \frac{N^{-15n}}{2^{n/2}}$$

$$= N^{-\Theta(n)}$$

for $n$ sufficiently large. Our bound of $N^{-2.419\,n+1.5}$ is hence asymptotically tight for SRA.

## 5.4   Routing on the Hypercube with Faults

### 5.4.1   Definitions

Assume $n = 2^k + k$ for some $k > 0$ to simplify the presentation. The modifications needed in the routing algorithm and its analysis if $n$ is not of this form should become obvious later. Note that $k < \log n$ but $k \approx \log n$.

Denote by $C_{n-k-1}(i : l)$ the subgraph induced by the set of nodes whose first $k$ bits equal $bits_k(i)$ and whose $(k + i)^{\text{th}}$ bit is $l$, i.e.,

$$\{ x \in V(C_n) \mid x[0 : k - 1] = bits_k(i) \quad \text{and} \quad x_{k+j} = l \},$$

where $0 \leq i < 2^k$, $0 \leq j < n - k$, and $l \in \{0, 1\}$. Clearly $C_{n-k-1}(i : l)$ is an $(n - k - 1)$-cube, and we have

$$C_{n-k-1}(i_0 : l_0) \cap C_{n-k-1}(i_1 : l_1) = \emptyset, \quad \text{if } i_0 \neq i_1 \text{ or } l_0 \neq l_1$$

$$\text{and} \tag{5.7}$$

$$C_{n-k-1}(i : l) \subset C_{n-k}(i).$$

---

[1]Of course, it is on a slightly smaller hypercube network: $C_{n-k}$ instead of $C_n$. However, our arguments leading to the $N^{-30}$ bound are independent of the size of the cube (note that the $N$ in $N^{-30}$ was derived from the number of pieces, $\log N$, in a node, *not* the size of the network) except that we require $n - k \geq 5$ so that $x$ has at least 5 neighbors in the subcube.

Algorithm FSRA

**For** $x \in V(C_n)$:

**Cobegin**

    Split $P_x$ into $n - k$ pieces, $P_x(0), \ldots, P_x(n - k - 1)$, using $IDA(n - k, (n/2) - k)$;

    Let $s_i = \overline{x_{k+i}}$ and $t_i = \overline{(\pi(x))_{k+i}}$ for $0 \le i < n - k$ ;

    Phase 1: ($n$ epochs, in order of dimension in each subphase)

        Subphase 1.1: Route $P_x(i)$ to $x^{(i)}$ in one epoch;

        Subphase 1.2: Route $P_x(i)$ to $bits_k(i) \circ \left( x^{(i)}[\,k : n - 1\,] \right)$ in $k$ epochs;

        Subphase 1.3: Route $P_x(i)$ to $R_x(i)$ in $n - k - 1$ epochs, where

                $R_x(i)$ is chosen randomly from $C_{n-k-1}(i : s_i)$;

    Bridging-Phase: ( 1 epoch)

            Send $P_x(i)$ to $R_x(i)(i : t_i)$;

    Phase 2: ($n$ epochs, in reverse order of dimension in each subphase)

        Subphase 2.1: Route $P_x(i)$ to $bits_k(i) \circ \left( \pi(x)^{(i)}[\,k : n - 1\,] \right)$

            in $n - k - 1$ epochs;

        Subphase 2.2: Route $P_x(i)$ to $\pi(x)^{(i)}$ in $k$ epochs;

        Subphase 2.3: Route $P_x(i)$ to $\pi(x)$ in one epoch;

**Coend.**

Figure 5.4: FSRA ("FAULT-TOLERANT SUBCUBE ROUTING ALGORITHM").

Note that $C_{n-k}(i)$ is a subcube of size $N/(n - k)$ and there are now $n - k = 2^k$ such subcubes. Given $l \in \{0, 1\}$, let $x^{(i)} \overset{\text{def}}{=} x//(k + i)$ and $x(i : l)$ be derived from $x$ by setting its $(k + i)^{\text{th}}$ bit to $l$.

## 5.4.2 Description of FSRA

Choose $n_0 = n - k$ and $m_0 = (n/2) - k$ for IDA, meaning each packet can afford to lose $n/2$ pieces. The buffer size is $5\,L\,(n - k)/((n/2) - k)$, enough for $5\,n$ pieces.

    The description of FSRA appears in Figure 5.4. Observe that $P_x(i)$ considers traversing, in sequence, dimensions $k + i, 0, 1, \ldots, k + i - 1, k + i + 1, \ldots, n - 1$ in Phase 1. For Phase 2, just reverse the above sequence.

    We now explain FSRA. In Subphase 1.1, $P_x(i)$ is routed *via* dimension $k + i$ to negate its $(k + i)^{\text{th}}$ bit to $s_i$. This bit is not changed for the rest of Phase 1. $P_x(i)$ is next sent to the subcube $C_{n-k-1}(i : s_i)$ in Subphase 1.2. In Subphase 1.3, $P_x(i)$ is routed to a randomly chosen node in $C_{n-k-1}(i : s_i)$. Phase 2 mirrors Phase 1: just reverse the above sequence with $x$ replaced by $\pi(x)$ and $s_i$ replaced by

$t_i = \overline{(\pi(x))_{k+i}}$, the complement of the $(k+i)^{\text{th}}$ bit of $\pi(x)$. But, executing Phases 1 and 2 alone would not constitute a complete routing scheme since $P_x(i)$'s $(k+i)^{\text{th}}$ bit at the end of Phase 1 (i.e., $s_i = \overline{x_{k+i}}$) might not be equal to $P_x(i)$'s $(k+i)^{\text{th}}$ bit at the beginning of Phase 2 (i.e., $t_i = \overline{(\pi(x))_{k+i}}$). The sandwiched *Bridging-Phase* remedies that by simply correcting that bit, if necessary. Note that $P_x(i)$ travels within $C_{n-k-1}(i : s_i) \subset C_{n-k}(i)$ in Subphase 1.3, within $C_{n-k}(i)$ in *Bridging-Phase*, and within $C_{n-k-1}(i : t_i) \subset C_{n-k}(i)$ in Subphase 2.1; see Figure 5.5 for illustration.

We can now see the reason for assuming $n = 2^k + k$. Consider $P_x$. In Subphase 1.1, $P_x(i)$ travels *via* dimension $i + k$: there are $n - k$ possible $i$'s. $P_x(i)$ then reaches $C_{n-k}(i)$ by correcting the first $k$ bits in Subphase 1.2: there are $2^k$ possible $i$'s. Since both $n - k$ and $2^k$ denote the number of pieces into which $P_x$ is split, they must be equal.

Note that if we pick $\pi$ to be the identity permutation, no pieces would move in *Bridging-Phase,* but if we pick $\pi$ to be, for example,

$$\pi(x_0 \cdots x_{n-1}) = \overline{x_0} \cdots \overline{x_{n-1}},$$

all $(n - k)\,N$ pieces move in *Bridging-Phase.* In other words, FSRA's behavior in *Bridging-Phase* depends on $\pi$. This is not a serious matter since Phases 1 and 2 are still testable and *Bridging-Phase* takes only one epoch.

### 5.4.3  Analysis of FSRA under the fault-free model

FSRA performs as well as SRA under the fault-free model, as shown by the next theorem.

**Theorem 5.15** *If no faults occur,* FSRA *runs in* $2 \log N + 1$ *time with probability of successful routing at least* $1 - N^{-2.419\,n+1.5}$ *using buffers of size at most* $20\,L$ *for* $n \geq 6$.

**Proof:** FSRA clearly runs in $2\,n + 1$ time. Each buffer has size

$$5\,L\,\frac{n - k}{(n/2) - k} \leq 20\,L$$

for $k \geq 2$. The rest of the proof follows closely that of Theorem 5.14.

Assume the non-destructive model. Arguments similar to those used in proving Lemma 5.11 can show that each node has $n - k$ pieces during Subphases 1.1–1.2 and 2.2–2.3. Now that there is no overflow in Subphases 1.1–1.2 and 2.2–2.3, since each node can hold $5\,n > n - k$ pieces, we only have to analyze Subphase 1.3, *Bridging-Phase,* and Subphase 2.1 for overflow. Without loss of generality, we consider only $C_{n-k}(0)$; the other subcubes can be identically analyzed.

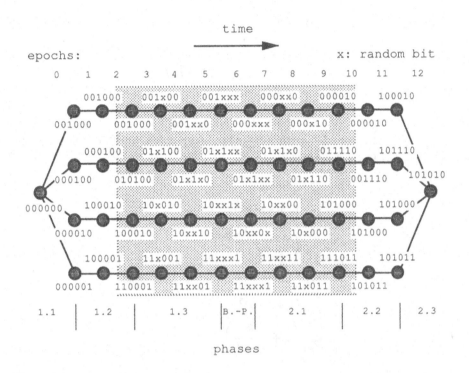

Figure 5.5: THE WORKING OF FSRA ON $C_6$. Here we show how $P_x$'s four pieces travel from their origin $x = 000000$ to their destination $\pi(x) = 101010$ in epochs. Note that the four routes are node-disjoint in each of the three phases. Furthermore, they are routed within node-disjoint subcubes in Subphases 1.3–2.1 (within the dotted box).

Consider an epoch $t$ in Subphase 1.3 and a buffer $BF(y)$, where $y \in C_{n-k}(0)$. It is easy to see that Subphase 1.3 is an $(n-k)$-SPCS. Hence the probability of overflow at $BF(y)$ in epoch $t$ of Subphase 1.3 is at most

$$\left( \frac{e^{\frac{5n}{n-k}-1}}{\left(\frac{5n}{n-k}\right)^{\frac{5n}{n-k}}} \right)^{n-k} \tag{5.8}$$

$$= \left(\frac{e^4}{5^5}\right)^n \left( \frac{e^{\frac{k}{n}}}{\left(1+\frac{k}{n-k}\right)^5} \right)^n$$

$$< \left(\frac{e^4}{5^5}\right)^n, \tag{5.9}$$

where (5.8) is by Theorem 5.4 with $(1+\delta)(n-k) = 5n$ and (5.9) is true because (below, ln denotes the natural logarithm)

$$e^{k/n} = n^{k/(n \ln n)}$$

$$< \left(n^{5/\log e}\right)^{k/(n \ln n)}$$

$$= \left(2^{5 \ln n}\right)^{k/(n \ln n)}$$

$$< \left(\left((1+k/n)^{n/k}\right)^{5 \ln n}\right)^{k/(n \ln n)}$$

$$= (1+k/n)^5$$

$$< \left(1+\frac{k}{n-k}\right)^5.$$

Now, the probability that overflow occurs in $C_{n-k}(0)$ in Subphase 1.3 is less than

$$\left(\frac{e^4}{5^5}\right)^n \left(\frac{N}{n-k}\right)(n-k-1) < \frac{p_0}{2},$$

where $p_0$ is defined in (5.4) on page 60. Since Subphase 2.1 is symmetric to Subphase 1.3, similarly, the probability that overflow occurs in $C_{n-k}(0)$ in Subphase 2.1 is less than $p_0/2$. Combining the above two observations, we have

$$q \stackrel{\text{def}}{=} Pr(\text{overflow occurs in } C_{n-k}(0) \text{ in Subphases 1.3--2.1})$$

$$= Pr(\text{overflow occurs in } C_{n-k}(0) \text{ in Subphase 1.3 or 2.1}) \tag{5.10}$$

$$\leq Pr(\text{overflow occurs in } C_{n-k}(0) \text{ in Subphase 1.3})$$

$$+ Pr(\text{overflow occurs in } C_{n-k}(0) \text{ in Subphase 2.1})$$

$$< 2\frac{p_0}{2}$$

$$= p_0. \tag{5.11}$$

Eq. (5.10) holds because the beginning of *Bridging-Phase* happens to be the end of Subphase 1.3 and the end of *Bridging-Phase* the beginning of Subphase 2.1. In other words, *Bridging-Phase* need not be analyzed separately for overflow as its analysis is already covered by that of the other two subphases.

Employing arguments given in Comment 5.13, one can easily show that each packet has one piece in each of the $n - k$ subcubes during Subphases 1.3–2.1. Hence the probability of unsuccessful routing is at most the probability that overflow occurs to more than $n/2$ subcubes in Subphases 1.3–2.1, which is at most $B(n/2, n-k, q) < B(n/2, n, q)$. Using Lemma 5.7 and the fact that $q < p_0 < 1/2$, we finally have

$$B(n/2, n, q) < Nq^{n/2} < Np_0^{n/2} < N^{-2.419 n+1.5},$$

where (5.6) of page 60 is used.

Q.E.D.

### 5.4.4  Analysis of FSRA under random fault models

We first show that $P_x$'s $n - k$ pieces take node-disjoint paths in Phase 1, Phase 2, and *Bridging-Phase*.

**Lemma 5.16** *A packet's pieces take node-disjoint paths in Phase 1.*

**Proof:** Consider two of $P_x$'s pieces, $P_x(i)$ and $P_x(j)$, where $i \neq j$. In Subphase 1.2, $P_x(i)$'s $(k+j)^{\text{th}}$ bit is $x_{k+j}$ but $P_x(j)$'s $(k+j)^{\text{th}}$ bit is $\overline{x_{k+j}}$; hence they take node-disjoint paths in Subphases 1.1–1.2. $P_x(i)$ and $P_x(j)$ also take node-disjoint paths in Subphase 1.3, since $P_x(i)$ travels in $C_{n-k}(i)$ but $P_x(j)$ in $C_{n-k}(j)$, a subcube node-disjoint from $C_{n-k}(i)$.

Now consider the case where $P_x(i)$ and $P_x(j)$ are in *different* subphases. Without loss of generality assume $P_x(i)$ is in Subphases 1.1–1.2 and $P_x(j)$ in Subphase 1.3. Since $P_x(i)$'s $(k+j)^{\text{th}}$ bit is $x_{k+j}$ but $P_x(j)$'s $(k+j)^{\text{th}}$ bit is $\overline{x_{k+j}}$, due to Subphase 1.1, they cannot pass through the same node.

Q.E.D.

Symmetrically, the same is true of Phase 2.

**Lemma 5.17** *A packet's pieces take node-disjoint paths in Phase 2.*

The same conclusion is true of *Bridging-Phase*.

**Lemma 5.18** *A packet's pieces take node-disjoint paths in* Bridging-Phase.

**Proof:** In *Bridging-Phase,* each packet's pieces travel within distinct subcubes, which are node-disjoint (see (5.7)).
Q.E.D.

The next result follows from the above three lemmas.

**Lemma 5.19** *For each packet $P_x$, FSRA produces $n - k$ node-disjoint paths for its $n - k$ pieces in each of the three phases.*

Node-disjointness implies edge-disjointness, and, in fact, only edge-disjointness is needed in the proofs of the next two theorems. The following observation leads to sharper constant terms in our analysis of fault tolerance.

**Lemma 5.20** *A packet's pieces take edge-disjoint paths from Phase 1 to Bridging-Phase.*

**Proof:** In the light of Lemmas 5.16 and 5.18, we only have to prove that any two distinct pieces, $P_x(i)$ in Phase 1 and $P_x(j)$ in *Bridging-Phase,* do not pass through the same edge. Suppose $P_x(j)$ traverses an edge of dimension $k + j$, say $(a, b)$, in *Bridging-Phase* (if it does not traverse any edge, this lemma certainly holds). Now $P_x(i)$ can traverse an edge of the *same* dimension, say $(a', b')$, only in Subphase 1.3. But $a \neq a'$ since the two pieces are in disjoint subcubes; hence these two edges must be distinct.
Q.E.D.

In our first fault model every link has a failure probability of

$$(8\,e\,n\,(n+1))^{-1} = O(n^{-2}),$$

and links fail independently. The expected number of link failures is then

$$(8\,e\,n\,(n+1))^{-1}\,n\,N = N/(8\,e\,(n+1)) = \Theta(N/\log N).$$

Since each packet produces $n - k$ pieces, the expected number of disconnected paths for each packet is at most $(n - k)\,(8\,e\,n)^{-1}$ throughout Phase 1 and *Bridging-Phase,* where each path is of length at most $n + 1$, and at most $(n - k)\,(8\,e\,(n + 1))^{-1} < (n - k)\,(8\,e\,n))^{-1}$ during Phase 2, where each path is of length at most $n$. If we let $Y_i$ denote the event that $P_x$'s $i^{\text{th}}$ path fails, then Fact 5.3 is applicable to the $Y_i$'s due to edge-disjointness. Hence the probability that at least $n/8$ of $P_x$'s $n - k$ paths fail in Phase 1 and *Bridging-Phase* is at most

$$\left( \frac{e^{(e\,n^2/(n-k))-1}}{(e\,n^2/(n - k))^{(e\,n^2/(n-k))}} \right)^{(n-k)/(8\,e\,n)} \tag{5.12}$$

$$\approx \quad \left(\frac{n-k}{n^2}\right)^{n/8}, \tag{5.13}$$

where (5.12) is by Fact 5.3 with $\delta = (e\,n^2/(n-k))-1$ and exponent $(n-k)\,(8\,e\,n)^{-1}$. The same inequality holds for Phase 2. Now, the probability that at least $n/4$ of $P_x$'s $n-k$ pieces are lost due to link failures is at most

$$Pr(\geq n/8 \text{ of } P_x\text{'s } n-k \text{ paths fail in Phase 1 and } \textit{Bridging-Phase})$$
$$+Pr(\geq n/8 \text{ of } P_x\text{'s } n-k \text{ paths fail in Phase 2})$$
$$< \quad 2\left(\frac{n-k}{n^2}\right)^{n/8}, \tag{5.14}$$

where (5.14) follows from (5.13). Finally, the effects of overflow and link failures on the reconstructibility of packets combined, the probability that $P_x$ is not reconstructible becomes, as $n$ goes to infinity,

$$Pr(\text{more than } n/2 \text{ of } P_x\text{'s } n-k \text{ pieces are lost})$$
$$\leq \quad Pr(\text{at least } n/4 \text{ of } P_x\text{'s } n-k \text{ pieces lost due to overflow})$$
$$+Pr(\text{at least } n/4 \text{ of } P_x\text{'s } n-k \text{ pieces lost due to link failures})$$
$$\leq \quad 2\left(\frac{n-k}{n^2}\right)^{n/8}, \tag{5.15}$$

where (5.15) is due to (5.14) and the fact that Corollary 5.9 can be used to show that the probability of more than $n/4$ pieces lost due to overflow is $N^{-\Theta(n)}$, negligible in comparison with $2\left(\frac{n-k}{n^2}\right)^{n/8}$. Since there are $N$ packets, we have proved the next theorem.

**Theorem 5.21** FSRA *tolerates* $N/(8\,e\,(n+1)) = \Theta(N/\log N)$ *random link failures with probability at least*

$$1 - 2N\left(\frac{n-k}{n^2}\right)^{n/8} = 1 - N^{-\Theta(\log\log N)}.$$

Consider another fault model: every link has a failure probability of $\frac{1}{c\,(n+1)}$ and links fail independently. The expected number of link failures is then $\frac{nN}{c\,(n+1)} = \Theta(N)$. The constant $c$ will be chosen to be $5\,(5/4)^4\,2^{10} \approx 12,500$.

Since each path uses at most $n+1$ links during Phase 1 and *Bridging-Phase*, it has probability at most $(n+1)\,(c\,(n+1))^{-1} = 1/c$ to fail. Hence the probability that at least $n/5$ of $P_x$'s $n-k$ paths fail in Phase 1 and *Bridging-Phase* is at most

$$B(n/5, n-k, 1/c)$$

$$
\begin{aligned}
&< \quad B(n/5, n, 1/c) \\
&\leq \quad \left(\frac{n/c}{n/5}\right)^{n/5} \left(\frac{n - n/c}{n - n/5}\right)^{n-(n/5)} \qquad\qquad \text{by Fact 5.6}\\
&< \quad \left(\frac{5}{c}\right)^{n/5} \left(\frac{5}{4}\right)^{4n/5} \\
&= \quad N^{-2}.
\end{aligned}
$$

The same inequality also holds for Phase 2. Now, the probability that at least $2\,n/5$ of $P_x$'s $n - k$ pieces are lost due to link failures is at most

$$
\begin{aligned}
&Pr(\geq n/5 \text{ of } P_x\text{'s } n - k \text{ paths fail in Phase 1 and } \textit{Bridging-Phase})\\
&+ Pr(\geq n/5 \text{ of } P_x\text{'s } n - k \text{ paths fail in Phase 2})\\
&< \ 2\,N^{-2}.
\end{aligned}
$$

Finally, we combine the effects of buffer overflow and link failures on the reconstructibility of packets. The probability that $P_x$ is not reconstructible is

$$
\begin{aligned}
&Pr(\text{more than } n/2 \text{ of } P_x\text{'s } n - k \text{ pieces are lost})\\
&\leq \ Pr(\text{at least } n/10 \text{ of } P_x\text{'s } n - k \text{ pieces lost due to overflow})\\
&\quad + Pr(\text{at least } 2\,n/5 \text{ of } P_x\text{'s } n - k \text{ pieces lost due to link failures})\\
&\leq \ N^{-\Theta(n)} + 2\,N^{-2},
\end{aligned}
$$

where Corollary 5.9 is used in the last inequality. Since there are $N$ packets, we have proved the next theorem.

**Theorem 5.22** FSRA *can tolerate* $\Theta(N)$ *random link failures with probability* $1 - O(N^{-1})$.

**Comment 5.23** The above result holds for *node* failures if each node can fail with the same probability as link and if by successful routing we mean packets that come from, and are going to, *non*-faulty nodes are delivered to their destinations [150, 216, 218]. The reason is that the paths chosen for each packet's pieces are *node*-disjoint in each phase by Lemma 5.19 and a path using $l$ links passes through $l + 1$ nodes, or, *probabilistically* equivalently, $2\,l + 1$ links in each phase under the *original* model. Hence, we can analyze FSRA *as if* only links fail and each piece passes at most $2\,n + 1$ in Phase 1, at most 1 in *Bridging-Phase*, and at most $2\,n + 1$ *links* in Phase 2. With $c$ appropriately adjusted, the same conclusion would hold.

## 5.5   Routing on the de Bruijn Network

### 5.5.1   Definitions

In this section, we consider the de Bruijn network $N_{d,n}$ with $N = d^n$ nodes and dimension $d > 1$. Each node $x$ is denoted by $x_0 \cdots x_{n-1}$, where $0 \leq x_i < d$ is called $x$'s $i^{\text{th}}$ **digit**. The $dN$ *directed* edges of $N_{d,n}$ are

$$E(N_{d,n}) = \{\, (x,y) \mid x_{k-1} = y_k \text{ for } 1 \leq k < n \,\}.$$

In other words, there is an edge from $x$ to $y$ if $y$'s last $n-1$ digits equal $x$'s first $n-1$ digits. This suggests the following definition.

**Definition 5.24** *Let* $x \in V(N_{d,n})$ *and* $0 \leq k < d$. *The operation* $SH$ *is defined as*

$$SH(k \rightarrow x) = k\, x_0 \cdots x_{n-2}.$$

*So,* $SH(k \rightarrow x)$ *shifts* $x$ *to the right by one digit and makes* $k$ *the most significant digit.*

Hence, $E(N_{d,n})$ can be equivalently defined as

$$\{\, (x,y) \mid y = SH(k \rightarrow x) \quad \text{for some } 0 \leq k < d \,\}.$$

**Definition 5.25** *Let* $x \in V(N_{d,n})$. *Define* $ROT$ *as*

$$ROT(x) \stackrel{\text{def}}{=} SH(x_{n-1} \rightarrow x) = x_{n-1}x_0 \cdots x_{n-2}.$$

*That is,* $ROT$ *rotates* $x$*'s digits to the right by one digit.*

A path from node $\alpha$ to node $\zeta$ is denoted by $\alpha \rightarrow \cdots \rightarrow \zeta$. A special kind of path between two nodes, called the **canonical path**, is at the heart of our scheme.

**Definition 5.26** *Let* $x, y \in V(N_{d,n})$. *The* **canonical path** *from* $x$ *to* $y$ *is*

$$x \;\rightarrow\; y_{n-1} x_0 \cdots x_{n-2} \;\rightarrow\; y_{n-2}\, y_{n-1}\, x_0 \cdots x_{n-3} \;\rightarrow\; \cdots \;\rightarrow\; y_0 \cdots y_{n-1}.$$

*In other words,* $y = y_0 \cdots y_{n-1}$ *is reached from* $x = x_0 \cdots x_{n-1}$ *by "shifting in"* $y$*'s digits one by one from the left.*

Note that the canonical path might not be the shortest path between two nodes. Since the canonical path is of length $n$ if we include self-loops, any node can be reached from any other *via* $n$ links. Hence, the diameter of $N_{d,n}$ is $n = \log_d N$, proving the asymptotic optimality[2] of $N_{d,n}$. In contrast, the hypercube network is far from optimal, as a graph with degree $\log N$ is expected to have a diameter of roughly $\log_{\log N} N = \log N / \log \log N$, not $\log N$.

Our routing scheme RABN is SRA-like but has a *Bridging-Phase* as FSRA. RABN is also fault-tolerant. Bounds at least as good as FSRA's on the run-time, buffer size, tolerance for random link failures, and probability of successful routing will be obtained for a class of de Bruijn networks.

A counterpart to the subcube concept in the hypercube network is needed to achieve the sharp probabilistic bound.

**Definition 5.27** *Let $0 \leq i < n$ and $0 \leq l < d$. The graph $N_{d,n}(i:l)$ is an induced subgraph of $N_{d,n}$ by the node set:* $\{ x \in V(N_{d,n}) \mid x_i = l \}$.

Unlike the hypercube case, $N_{d,n}(i:l)$ is *not* itself a de Bruijn network. We call each $N_{d,n}(i:l)$ a **subnetwork**. Each subnetwork has $d^{n-1}$ nodes. Clearly we have

$$N_{d,n}(i:l_0) \cap N_{d,n}(i:l_1) = \emptyset \qquad \text{if } l_0 \neq l_1. \tag{5.16}$$

## 5.5.2   RABN: description and preliminary analysis

Choose $n_0 = d$ and $m_0 = d/2$ for IDA. At every node $y$, let $|BF(y)| = 10\,L$, enough to hold $5\,d$ pieces. The description of RABN appears in Figure 5.6. Recall that $P_x(i)$ also denotes the node the piece $P_x(i)$ resides in. RABN clearly runs in $2\,n + 1$ epochs/time.

We now explain RABN. Piece $P_x(i)$ is first sent to $SH(i \to x)$ in Subphase 1.1. At the end of this step, distinct pieces from a packet are already on disjoint subnetworks: $P_x(i) \in N_{d,n}(0:i)$. In the next $n - 1$ epochs, $P_x(i)$ is routed randomly: in every epoch, $P_x(i)$ is sent from its current node, say $y$, to $SH(\beta \to y)$ with $\beta$ chosen randomly from $\{0, \ldots, d-1\}$. Phase 1 for $P_x(i)$ can be seen schematically as follows:

$$x \to i x_0 \cdots x_{n-2} \to \alpha_{n-1} i x_0 \cdots x_{n-3} \to \cdots \to \alpha_1 \cdots \alpha_{n-1} i, \tag{5.17}$$

where the $\alpha_i$'s are picked randomly from $\{0, \ldots, d-1\}$. Phase 1 is hence equivalent to:

> Pick $y \in N_{d,n}(n-1:i)$ randomly and route $P_x(i)$ to $y$ *via* the canonical path.

The concept of piece-set will play the same role as that of subcube.

---

[2]We call a network **asymptotically optimal** if its diameter is $\Theta(\log_d N)$, asymptotically the best possible, where $N$ is the number of nodes and $d$ the maximum degree of the network [139, 371].

Algorithm RABN
**For** $x \in V(N_{d,n})$:
**Cobegin**

Split $P_x$ into $d$ pieces, $P_x(0), \ldots, P_x(d-1)$, using $IDA(d, d/2)$;

Phase 1: ($n$ epochs)

Subphase 1.1: Send $P_x(i)$ to $SH(i \to x) \in N_{d,n}$ $(0 : i)$ in one epoch;

Subphase 1.2: Route $P_x(i)$ randomly for $n - 1$ epochs;

Bridging-Phase: (1 epoch)

Send $P_x(i)$ to $ROT(P_x(i)) \in N_{d,n}$ $(0 : i)$;

Phase 2: ($n$ epochs)

Route $P_x(i)$ to $\pi(x)$ *via* the canonical path;

**Coend.**

Figure 5.6: RABN ("ROUTING ALGORITHM FOR THE DE BRUIJN NETWORK").

**Definition 5.28** *For* $0 \le i < d$, *let* $P(i) = \{ P_x(i) \mid x \in V(N_{d,n}) \}$. *That is,* $P(i)$ *contains all the packets'* $i^{\text{th}}$ *pieces. Each* $P(i)$ *is called a* **piece-set**.

In SRA, $P_x(i)$ travels within the subcube $C_{n-k}(i)$ during Subphases 1.2–2.1. The following lemma is its counterpart for the de Bruijn network.

**Lemma 5.29** *At the end of epoch* $t$ *for* $0 \le t < n$ *(i.e., Phase 1),* $P_x(i)$ *is in* $N_{d,n}$ $(t : i)$; *in other words,* $N_{d,n}(t : i)$ *contains all and only pieces in the piece-set* $P(i)$.

**Proof:** The digit $i$ moves to the right by one position in each epoch starting from epoch 0, as shown in (5.17).
Q.E.D.

**Comment 5.30** The above lemma says that if there is overflow at any node, say $x = x_0 \cdots x_{n-1}$, in any epoch, say $t$, only pieces in $P(x_t)$ can be affected; that is, from a packet's viewpoint, that overflow can potentially affect only its $x_t^{\text{th}}$ piece. Furthermore, pieces from the same piece-set not only are routed within the same subnetwork but also never meet pieces from a different piece-set. This shows a packet's pieces can be lost to overflow *independently*.

*Bridging-Phase* can be seen schematically as

$$\alpha_1 \cdots \alpha_{n-1} \beta \to \beta \alpha_1 \cdots \alpha_{n-1}.$$

**Comment 5.31** *Bridging-Phase* does not create *new* overflow since *ROT* is a bijection on $V(N_{d,n})$.

Let $\pi(x) = z_0 \cdots z_{n-1}$. Phase 2 can be viewed schematically as

$$i\,\alpha_1 \cdots \alpha_{n-1} \rightarrow z_{n-1}\,i\,\alpha_1 \cdots \alpha_{n-2} \rightarrow \cdots \rightarrow z_1 z_2 \cdots z_{n-1}\,i \rightarrow z_0 z_1 \cdots z_{n-1}.$$

In fact, Phase 2 mirrors Phase 1, which can be seen in the following way. Reverse the direction of the path in the above schema to get

$$z_0 z_1 \cdots z_{n-1} \rightarrow z_1 z_2 \cdots z_{n-1}\,i \rightarrow z_2 z_3 \cdots z_{n-1}\,i\,\alpha_1 \rightarrow \cdots$$

$$\cdots \rightarrow z_{n-1}\,i\,\alpha_1 \cdots \alpha_{n-2} \rightarrow i\,\alpha_1 \cdots \alpha_{n-1}.$$

Next, reverse the direction of digit-shifting to *left-to-right* to get

$$z_0 z_1 \cdots z_{n-1} \rightarrow i\,z_0 z_1 \cdots z_{n-2} \rightarrow \alpha_{n-1}\,i\,z_0 \cdots z_{n-3} \rightarrow \cdots$$

$$\cdots \rightarrow \alpha_3 \cdots \alpha_{n-1}\,i\,z_0 z_1 \rightarrow \alpha_2 \cdots \alpha_{n-1}\,i\,z_0 \rightarrow \alpha_1 \cdots \alpha_{n-1}\,i.$$

But this is Phase 1; see (5.17). Recall that the $\alpha_i$'s are chosen randomly. Figure 5.7 illustrates the working of RABN.

We need the following lemma for Subphase 1.1.

**Lemma 5.32** *At the end of Subphase* 1.1, *each node has $d$ pieces, all from distinct packets.*

**Proof:** Consider $x = x_0 x_1 \ldots x_{n-1} \in V(N_{d,n})$. At the end of Subphase 1.1, node $x$ receives $P_y$'s $x_0^{\text{th}}$ piece for $y = x_1 x_2 \ldots x_{n-1} z$ where $0 \leq z < d$. There are exactly $d$ such $y$'s since there are $d$ possible $z$'s.
Q.E.D.


## 5.5.3   Analysis of RABN under the fault-free model

The analysis of RABN follows that of SRA and FSRA closely.

**Theorem 5.33** *If $n\,d^{n-1}\,(e^4/5^5)^d < 1/4$, RABN runs in $2n+1$ time with probability of successful routing at least*

$$1 - \left(8\,n\,d^{n-1}\,(e^4/5^5)^d\right)^{d/2}$$

*using buffers of size $10\,L$.*

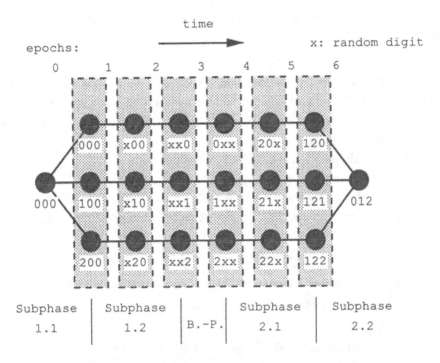

Figure 5.7: THE WORKING OF RABN ON $N_{3,3}$. Here we show how $P_x$'s three pieces travel from their origin $x = 000$ to their destination $\pi(x) = 012$ in epochs. Note that the three routes may not be node-disjoint in each phase. However, pieces are in node-disjoint subnetwork (enclosed by dotted boxes) at the end of each epoch.

**Proof:** Since the bounds on time and buffer size are already established, we proceed to analyze the probability part.

We will analyze Phase 1 only for overflow because Phase 2 is symmetrical to Phase 1 and *Bridging-Phase*, as Comment 5.31 demonstrates, does not cause new overflow. Lemma 5.29 shows overflow in $N_{d,n}(t:i)$ in epoch $t$ affects pieces only in $P(i)$. In other words, pieces in distinct piece-sets can be lost due to overflow in the *same* epoch *independently*. Hence, we can consider only pieces in the piece-set $P(0)$ and, consequently, only the following subnetworks in which pieces in $P(0)$ are routed through:

$$N_{d,n}(0:0), N_{d,n}(1:0), \ldots, N_{d,n}(n-1:0).$$

The other $d-1$ piece-sets can be identically analyzed. Since each node has $d$ pieces at the end of epoch 0 by Lemma 5.32, there is no overflow in Subphase 1.1. We now analyze Subphase 1.2 for overflow. Consider epoch $t$ for $0 < t < n$. Again, assume the non-destructive model.

We show that Subphase 1.2 is a $d$-SPCS. Consider node $x = x_0 \cdots x_{n-1}$ and epoch $t$. Every node of the form $z = x_{t+1} \cdots x_{n-1} a_0 \cdots a_t$, where $a_i \in \{0, \ldots, d-1\}$, has probability $1/d^t$ of sending its $x_t^{\text{th}}$ piece to $x$. Furthermore, no other nodes could have sent any piece to $x$ in epoch $t$. So the expected number of pieces at $x$ in epoch $t$ is

$$\frac{1}{d^t} | \text{number of } z\text{'s} | = \frac{1}{d^t} d^{d+1} = d.$$

Besides, each piece is routed independently by the routing algorithm.

Corollary 5.5 then implies

$$Pr(\text{overflow at } BF(y) \text{ in epoch } t) \leq \left(\frac{e^4}{5^5}\right)^d.$$

As this holds for any $y \in N_{d,n}(t:0)$ and $0 < t < n$, we have

$$\begin{aligned}
q &\overset{\text{def}}{=} Pr(\text{some pieces in } P(0) \text{ encounter overflow in Subphase 1.2}) \\
&\leq (n-1) d^{n-1} \left(\frac{e^4}{5^5}\right)^d \\
&< n\, d^{n-1} \left(\frac{e^4}{5^5}\right)^d \\
&\overset{\text{def}}{=} q_0.
\end{aligned} \tag{5.18}$$

Note that (i) the above inequality holds for any piece-set $P(i)$, where $0 \leq i < d$, (ii) each piece-set encounters overflow independently of the other piece-sets by Lemma 5.29 and Remark 5.30, (iii) each packet has exactly one piece in each piece-set, and

(iv) Phase 2 is symmetric to Phase 1. Now, the probability of unsuccessful routing due to overflow is at most the probability that overflow occurs to more than $d/2$ of the $d$ piece-sets, which is less than

$$
\begin{aligned}
& B(d/2, d, 2\,q) \\
\leq\ & 2^d\,(2\,q)^{d/2} \\
\leq\ & 2^d\,(2\,q_0)^{d/2} \\
=\ & \left(8\,n\,d^{n-1}\left(\frac{e^4}{5^5}\right)^d\right)^{d/2},
\end{aligned}
$$
(5.19)
(5.20)

where (5.19) follows from Lemma 5.7 (note that $q < q_0 < 1/4$ by the assumption) and (5.20) from (5.18).
Q.E.D.

**Corollary 5.34** RABN *on* $N_{\lceil n \ln n \rceil, n}$ *(i.e., $d = \lceil n \ln n \rceil$) runs in $\approx 2 \ln N / \ln \ln N$ time with probability of successful routing greater than $1 - N^{-\ln N/2}$ using only constant size buffers.*

**Proof:** Note that $n\,(\ln n + \ln \ln n) \approx \ln N$ since $N = (\lceil n \ln n \rceil)^n$; hence, $n \ln n \approx \ln N - n \ln \ln n$. Theorem 5.33 implies that the probability of unsuccessful routing is at most

$$
\begin{aligned}
& \left(8\,n\,d^{n-1}\left(\frac{e^4}{5^5}\right)^d\right)^{d/2} \\
<\ & \left(8\,n\,d^{n-1}\,e^{-4d}\right)^{d/2} \\
\approx\ & \left(8\,n\,(n \ln n)^{n-1}\,e^{-4n \ln n}\right)^{n \ln n/2} \\
=\ & \left(\frac{8\,(\ln n)^{2n-1}}{n^{2n}}\right)^{n \ln n/2}\,\left((n \ln n)^n\right)^{-n \ln n/2} \\
\approx\ & \left(\frac{8\,(\ln n)^{2n-1}}{n^{2n}}\right)^{n \ln n/2}\,N^{n \ln \ln n/2}\,N^{-\ln N/2} \\
<\ & N^{-\ln N/2},
\end{aligned}
$$
(5.21)

where (5.21) is true because $e^4/5^5 < e^{-4}$. The last inequality can be verified by checking that the natural logarithm of

$$
\left(\frac{8\,(\ln n)^{2n-1}}{n^{2n}}\right)^{n \ln n/2}\,N^{n \ln \ln n/2}
$$

is indeed less than zero.

With $N = (\lceil n \ln n \rceil)^n$, we clearly have $n \approx \ln N / \ln \ln N$. So, RABN runs in $\approx 2 \ln N / \ln \ln N$ time on $N_{\lceil n \ln n \rceil, n}$.

Q.E.D.

**Example 5.35** Theorem 5.33 says for a network of size $N = \lceil 4 \ln 4 \rceil^4 = 1\,296$, the probability of unsuccessful routing is at most $9.49 \cdot 10^{-22}$.

Valiant and Brebner's scheme on $N_{\lceil n \ln n \rceil, n}$ [371, Theorem 2] implies a scheme that runs in $2\,(n + en)$ time with probability at least $1 - (\ln n)^{-en} \approx 1 - N^{-\ln \ln n / \ln n}$ (this probabilistic bound may be improvable). In contrast, RABN runs in $2\,n + 1$ time with probability of success $1 - N^{-\Theta(\ln N)}$. RABN is also fault-tolerant, to be shown in the coming subsection. Of course, such comparison is only superficial as we do not take into account factors such as the time spent in doing IDA.

### 5.5.4    Analysis of RABN under a random fault model

Consider $N_{\lceil n \ln n \rceil, n}$ for $n > 2$. Assume every link fails with probability $(12\,n \ln n)^{-1}$ and link failures are independent. The expected number of link failures is then

$$(12\,n \ln n)^{-1} \lceil n \ln n\,N \rceil \approx N/12.$$

Although a packet's pieces may not take node-disjoint paths in Phases 1 and 2, at least $d - n$ of them do, as the next lemma shows.

**Lemma 5.36** *For* RABN *running on* $N_{d,n}$, *each packet has at least* $d - n$ *pieces that take node-disjoint paths in each of Phases 1 and 2.*

**Proof:** Fix a node $x = x_0 \cdots x_{n-1}$ and let $U = \{\,x_0, \ldots, x_{n-1}\,\}$. Now, consider only those pieces $P_x(i)$ that satisfy $i \notin U$. There are at least $d - n$ such pieces. Suppose any two of them, $P_x(i)$ and $P_x(j)$, passed through the same node $y = y_0 \cdots y_{n-1}$ at the end of different epochs, $t_i$ and $t_j$ where $t_i < t_j$ (they cannot pass through the same node in the same epoch according to Lemma 5.29). Then, we would have

$$y_0 \cdots y_{n-1} \quad = \quad \alpha_0 \cdots \alpha_{t_i - 1}\, i\, x_0 \cdots x_{n-2-t_i}$$

$$\text{and}$$

$$y_0 \cdots y_{n-1} \quad = \quad \beta_0 \cdots \beta_{t_j - 1}\, j\, x_0 \cdots x_{n-2-t_j}$$

and, hence, $j = x_{t_j - t_i - 1}$, contradicting the assumption that $j \notin U$.

Q.E.D.

Lemma 5.36 says that each packet has a set of at least $d - n$ pieces such that a link failure can in each of Phases 1 and 2 destroy at most one in the set.

The next lemma shows any two of a packet's pieces take node-disjoint links in *Bridging-Phase*.

**Lemma 5.37** $P_x(i)$ *and* $P_x(j)$ *take node-disjoint links in* Bridging-Phase *for* $i \neq j$.

**Proof:** Assume $P_x(i)$ travels from node $\alpha$ to node $\beta$ and $P_x(j)$ travels from node $\gamma$ to node $\delta$. Since $\alpha_{n-1} = \beta_0 = i$, $\gamma_{n-1} = \delta_0 = j$, and $i \neq j$, we must have $\alpha \neq \gamma$ and $\beta \neq \delta$.
Q.E.D.

**Theorem 5.38** RABN *tolerates* $\lfloor N/12 \rfloor = \Theta(N)$ *random link failures on* $N_{\lceil n \ln n \rceil, n}$ *with probability at least* $1 - 2 N^{-(\ln \ln n/6)+(7/6)}$.

**Proof:** Consider Phase 1 (Phase 2 can be treated identically) and a packet $P_x$. Let $x = x_0 \cdots x_{n-1}$ and $U = \{ x_0, \ldots, x_{n-1} \}$. From now on we consider only pieces $P_x(i)$ such that $i \notin U$ (there are at least $n \ln n - n$ of them, which Lemma 5.36 ensures all take node-disjoint paths) and treat other pieces as if they were all lost. Clearly, the result thus obtained is an upper bound on the probability of unsuccessful routing. Since $n \ln n - n \approx n \ln n$, the result would still be asymptotically correct if we simply assume that *all* of $P_x$'s $n \ln n$ pieces take node-disjoint paths. This allows us not to have to keep track of small order terms which do not contribute anything to the final bound at all.

Any link failure affects at most one of $P_x$'s pieces. Now, the probability that at least $n \ln n/6$ of $P_x$'s $n \ln n$ pieces are lost due to link failures is the probability that at least $n \ln n/6$ of $P_x$'s $n \ln n$ paths fail. Since $P_x$'s $n \ln n$ paths totally use at most $n^2 \ln n$ links, as each path has length at most $n$, the above probability is in turn at most the probability that at least $n \ln n/6$ out of the at most $n^2 \ln n$ links used by $P_x$ fail, which is finally bounded by

$$B(n \ln n/6, \ n^2 \ln n, \ 1/(12\, n \ln n))$$

$$\leq \left( \frac{n/12}{n \ln n/6} \right)^{n \ln n/6} \left( \frac{n^2 \ln n - n/12}{n^2 \ln n - (n \ln n/6)} \right)^{n^2 \ln n - (n \ln n/6)}$$

$$< (2 \ln n)^{-n \ln n/6} \left( \frac{n}{n - \frac{1}{6}} \right)^{n^2 \ln n}$$

$$< (n \ln n)^{\frac{-n \ln n \ln(2 \ln n)}{6 \ln(n \ln n)}} e^{\frac{n^2 \ln n}{6n-1}}$$

$$\approx (n \ln n)^{\frac{-n \ln \ln n}{6}} n^{\frac{n}{6}}$$

$$= \left( \frac{n}{(n \ln n)^{\ln \ln n}} \right)^{n/6}$$

$$< \left( (n \ln n)^{1 - \ln \ln n} \right)^{n/6}$$

$$= N^{-\frac{\ln \ln n - 1}{6}}$$

as $n$ goes to infinity. Since Lemma 5.37 implies $d = n \ln n$ links are used in *Bridging-Phase* for each packet's $d$ pieces, the probability that $n \ln n/15$ of them fail in *Bridging-Phase* is at most

$$B(n \ln n/15, \, n \ln n, \, 1/(12 n \ln n))$$

$$\leq \left( \frac{1/12}{n \ln n/15} \right)^{n \ln n/15} \left( \frac{n \ln n - \frac{1}{12}}{n \ln n - \frac{n \ln n}{15}} \right)^{n \ln n - (n \, lnn/15)}$$

$$< \left( \frac{5}{4 n \ln n} \right)^{n \ln n/15} \left( \frac{15}{14} \right)^{14 n \ln n/15}$$

$$= \left( \frac{5 \cdot 15^{14}}{4 \cdot 14^{14} n \ln n} \right)^{\frac{n \ln n}{15}} .$$

Now, the probability that $P_x$ cannot be reconstructed is at most the probability that at least $n \ln n/2$ of $P_x$'s $n \ln n$ pieces are lost, which is at most

$$Pr(\geq 2 n \ln n/5 \text{ of } P_x\text{'s } n \ln n \text{ pieces lost due to link failures})$$
$$+ Pr(\geq n \ln n/10 \text{ of } P_x\text{'s } n \ln n \text{ pieces lost due to overflow})$$
$$\approx \quad Pr(\geq 2 n \ln n/5 \text{ of } P_x\text{'s } n \ln n \text{ pieces lost due to link failures})$$
$$\leq \quad Pr(\geq n \ln n/6 \text{ of } P_x\text{'s } n \ln n \text{ pieces lost in Phase 1})$$
$$+ Pr(\geq n \ln n/15 \text{ of } P_x\text{'s } n \ln n \text{ pieces lost in } \textit{Bridging-Phase})$$
$$+ Pr(\geq n \ln n/6 \text{ of } P_x\text{'s } n \ln n \text{ pieces lost in Phase 2})$$
$$< \quad 2 N^{-\frac{\ln \ln n - 1}{6}} + \left( \frac{5 \cdot 15^{14}}{4 \cdot 14^{14} n \ln n} \right)^{\frac{n \ln n}{15}}$$
$$\approx \quad 2 N^{-\frac{\ln \ln n - 1}{6}} .$$

As before, the probability of unsuccessful routing due to buffer overflow can be shown to be negligible in comparison with that due to link failures. This theorem is proved since there are totally $N$ packets.
Q.E.D.


**Comment 5.39** Since $n \approx \ln N / \ln \ln N$, the probabilistic bound in Theorem 5.38 is $\approx 1 - N^{-\frac{\ln \ln \ln N}{6}}$.

## 5.6 On Time Bounds and Models

In this section, we briefly discuss how SRA and FSRA can be made to run in $O(\log N)$ time under the more traditional model. In this model, every piece is routed as a separate entity without being bundled with other pieces, and we count as taking one time step a piece crossing a link. We note that, since a piece can be much smaller than the original packet due to the use of IDA, the actual running time can potentially be much smaller than other $O(\log N)$-time schemes where we count as taking one time step a packet crossing a link. For the rest of this section, we will assume the new model for analyzing the running time.

Clearly, Subphases 1.1 and 2.3 of FSRA can be completed in one step. We need a result of Valiant to analyze the middle parts of FSRA and SRA.

**Fact 5.40** ([370, p. 952]) $\Theta(\log N)$-*relation on an* $N$-*node hypercube can be routed in time* $O(\log N)$ *with probability at least* $1 - N^{-\Theta(1)}$.

Note that each subcube during SRA's Subphases 1.2–2.1 routes a $\log N$-relation (see Comment 5.13), and each subcube during FSRA's Subphases 1.3–2.1 routes an $(n-k)$-relation, where $n = \log N$ and $k < \log \log N$ as $n = 2^k + k$. Consequently, in both cases, the routing can be completed in time $O(\log N)$ with probability $1 - N^{-\Theta(1)}$ by Fact 5.40. As there are $\Theta(\log N)$ subcubes, we can apply Corollary 5.9 to conclude that, in both cases, the routing can be completed in time $O(\log N)$ with probability $1 - N^{-\Theta(\log N)}$.

We now only have SRA's Subphases 1.1 and 2.2 and FSRA's Subphases 1.2 and 2.2 to analyze. For this purpose, we have to solve the following problem on the hypercube [55, 166, 306, 307]: how can every node send a distinct packet to every other node efficiently? This important problem has appeared under such names as **total exchange problem** [55, 124] and **all-to-all personalized communication** [166].

We can easily show that the total exchange problem requires at least $2^{n-1}$ steps on the $n$-cube. Each node has $\binom{n}{i}$ packets that require $i$ hops, and at most $n\,2^n$ links can be working at any one time; hence the total running time is at least

$$\frac{2^n \sum_{i=1}^n i \binom{n}{i}}{n\,2^n} = 2^{n-1}.$$

We can solve the total exchange problem in $2^n - 1$ steps. This can be achieved by (1) solving it on each of the subcubes $C_{n-1}(0)$ and $C_{n-1}(1)$ for packets destined to nodes within the same subcube, (2) each node $x$ sending its $2^{n-1}$ packets destined to nodes in the other subcube to node $x//0$, then finally (3) solving the problem on each subcube for the packets destined to nodes within the same subcube again [55, 56]. With (1) and (2) simultaneously executed, one can show that the above algorithm runs in time at most $2^n - 1 = \Theta(N)$ [56, p. 62]. We remark that, cleverly overlapping (2) with (1) and (3), Bertsekas, Özveren, Stamoulis, Tseng, and Tsitsiklis [55] are able to reduce the running time to the lower bound $2^{n-1}$.

Now, observe that SRA's Subphase 1.1 is nothing but a total exchange problem for a $k$-cube, as each node $x = x_0 \cdots x_{n-1}$ sends a distinct piece to each node $i_0 \cdots i_{k-1} x_k \cdots x_{n-1}$, where $i_j \in \{0, 1\}$ for $0 \le j < k$. Recall that $k = \log \log N$. The same holds for SRA's Subphase 2.2 and FSRA's Subphases 1.2 and 2.2 (except that, now, $k < \log \log N$). Hence, in each case, the running time is $O(\log N)$.

We therefore conclude that, indeed, both SRA and FSRA can be made to run in $O(\log N)$ with probability at least $1 - N^{-\Theta(\log N)}$ under the traditional model where pieces are not concatenated.

## 5.7   A General Framework for IDA-Based Schemes

We generalize Rabin's hypercube routing scheme in Figure 5.8 and call it **Rabin's paradigm**. We use $IDA(n_0, n_0/2)$ there for convenience. We have the following theorem.

**Theorem 5.41** *Assume $G$ is node-symmetric with connectivity $k \ge n_0 = \Omega(\log N)$. If each path in each of the two phases is of length at most $l$, then Rabin's paradigm tolerates $|E|/l$ random link failures with high probability using constant size buffers.*

We sketch its proof in the next paragraphs. Since the intermediate nodes are chosen randomly and the network is node-symmetric, we immediately have an $n_0$-SPCS. Hence, with each buffer able to hold, say, $5n_0$ pieces and $n_0 = \Theta(\log N)$, Corollary 5.5 says the probability of having even one[3] buffer overflow is $N^{-\Omega(1)}$. We remark that, although node-disjoint paths are needed for fault tolerance, they are not relevant for analyzing buffer overflow.

Suppose each link fails independently with probability $(dl)^{-1}$ for some constant $d > 1$. The probability that a path in Phase 1 fails is hence at most $1/d$. The probability that a packet loses $n_0/4$ of its pieces to link failures in Phase 1 is

$$B(n_0/4, n_0, 1/d) = N^{-\Omega(1)}$$

---

[3]It seems difficult to analyze the probability that $n_0/2$ buffers encounter overflow without the subcube idea used by SRA and FSRA, which guarantees independence of overflow for each of a packet's pieces.

**Rabin's Paradigm for** $G(V, E)$
**For** $x \in V$:
**Cobegin**
    Split $P_x$ into $n_0$ pieces, $P_x(0), \ldots, P_x(n_0 - 1)$, using $IDA(n_0, n_0/2)$;
    Each buffer can hold $\Theta(n_0)$ pieces;
    Phase 1: ( $m$ epochs):
        Route pieces to randomly chosen intermediate nodes
        *via* node-disjoint paths;
    Phase 2: ( $m$ epochs):
        Route pieces to their destination *via* node-disjoint paths;
**Coend.**

Figure 5.8: RABIN'S PARADIGM.

by Fact 5.6 for a suitable $d$. The same conclusion holds for Phase 2. The probability that more than $n_0/2$ pieces are lost to link failures is therefore $N^{-\Omega(1)}$. The theorem is now proved by combining the two cases — link failure and buffer overflow.

We make several remarks before leaving this section. It is easy to show that there exist node-disjoint paths from any node to any other $k$ nodes for a graph with connectivity $k$ [71, Theorem 2.6]. So paths used in the paradigm exist; however, it is *NP*-hard to find short paths [108, 160]. Paths of optimal lengths have been known for the hypercube [285], the generalized hypercube [160], the loop network [160], the de Bruijn network [108], and the Kautz network [108], among which the first three are node-symmetric. Similar results have also been obtained for the star network [101], which is node-symmetric, except that it is not clear if the paths thus obtained are of optimal length. For graphs that are not node-symmetric, the choice of the paths becomes crucial, as we can no longer rely upon symmetry to obtain SPCSs. Routing on the de Bruijn network provides a good example. The de Bruijn network is not node-symmetric because, for example, some of the nodes have self-loops but some not (see Figure 3.3). Indeed, using Rabin's paradigm to do routing for the de Bruijn network may not produce an SPCS.

## 5.8  FSRA **under a More Realistic Fault Model**

Assume each link may fail independently with constant probability $p > 0$. This constant $p$ may be maintained by periodic replacement of wires (see Chapter 8). Assume FSRA uses IDA with $n_0 = n - k$ and $m_0 = n_0/8$ and each buffer has capacity for $5\,n$ pieces. Observe that a path of length $l$ has probability $1 - (1-p)^l$ to fail. The probability that $P_x$ cannot be reconstructed is

$$Pr(\text{more than } 7\,n_0/8 \text{ of } P_x\text{'s } n_0 \text{ pieces are lost})$$
$$\leq \quad Pr(\geq 3\,n_0/8 \text{ of } P_x\text{'s } n_0 \text{ paths fail in Phase 1 \& } \textit{Bridging-Phase})$$
$$+Pr(\geq 3\,n_0/8 \text{ of } P_x\text{'s } n_0 \text{ paths fail in Phase 2})$$
$$+Pr(\geq n_0/8 \text{ of } P_x\text{'s } n_0 \text{ pieces lost due to overflow})$$
$$\leq \quad \frac{\left(8\,e\left(1-(1-p)^{n+1}\right)/3\right)^{3\,(n-k)/8}}{e^{(n-k)\,(1-(1-p)^{n+1})}} + \frac{\left(8\,e\left(1-(1-p)^{n}\right)/3\right)^{3\,(n-k)/8}}{e^{(n-k)\,(1-(1-p)^{n})}}$$
$$\approx \quad \frac{2\,\left(8\,e\left(1-(1-p)^{n+1}\right)/3\right)^{3\,(n-k)/8}}{e^{(n-k)\,(1-(1-p)^{n+1})}},$$

where Fact 5.3 is used to bound the first two terms. We ignore the third term since it is in the order of a negligible $N^{-\Theta(\log N)}$. Thus we have the following theorem.

**Theorem 5.42** FSRA *tolerates* $p\,|E(C_n)|$ *random link failures with probability at least*

$$1 - 2\,N\,\frac{\left(8\,e\left(1-(1-p)^{n+1}\right)/3\right)^{3\,(n-k)/8}}{e^{(n-k)\,(1-(1-p)^{n+1})}}. \tag{5.22}$$

Theorem 5.42 can partially answer the question: given $p$, does the network have acceptable routing performance?

**Example 5.43** Take $p = 10^{-7}$. If $k = 3$, the cube has $2^{11}$ nodes and the probability of unsuccessful routing is at most $2.6958 \cdot 10^{-12}$, a small number indeed.

We observe that the formula in the above theorem eventually goes to $-\infty$ as $n \to \infty$. In Figure 5.9, we take a log-plot of the formula

$$2\,N\,\frac{\left(8\,e\left(1-(1-p)^{n+1}\right)/3\right)^{3\,(n-k)/8}}{e^{(n-k)\,(1-(1-p)^{n+1})}}$$

and the tendency is, as predicted, towards infinity. To make the probability of failure tend to zero, we need replication of computation, as is done in Chapter 9, and the reconstruction of packets as pieces move towards their destinations, as is done by Aumann and Ben-Or in [24].

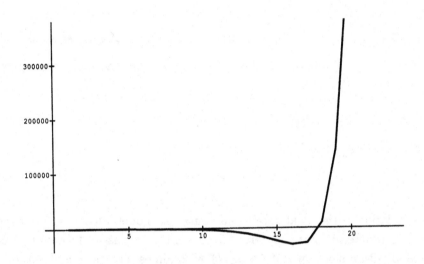

Figure 5.9: UNSUCCESSFUL ROUTING UNDER $O(1)$ LINK FAILURE PROBABILITY. Here we plot (5.22), which is an upper bound on the probability of unsuccessful routing, against $k$, with $p = 10^{-7}$. This is a log-plot.

# Chapter 6

# Simulation of the PRAM

> But it is the theory of another world [. . .].
>
> —Joseph Alois Schumpeter

The simulation of the ideal parallel computation model, PRAM, on the hypercube network is considered in this chapter. It is shown that a class of PRAM programs can be simulated with a slowdown of $O(\log N)$ with almost certainty and without using hashing, where $N$ denotes the number of processors. Also shown is that general PRAM programs can be simulated with a slowdown of $O(\log N)$ with the help of hashing. Both schemes are IDA-based and fault-tolerant.

# 6.1 Introduction

Parallel algorithms are notoriously hard to write and debug. Hence, it is only natural to turn to ideal models that provide good abstraction. As these models do not assume any particular hardware configuration, they should have the additional benefit that programs written for them can be executed on any hardware that supports the model, similar to the situation in the sequential case where the existence of a, say, C compiler on a particular platform implies standard C programs can be compiled and executed there [370]. The PRAM (**"Parallel Random Access Machine"**) is one such model. It completely abstracts out the cost issue in communication and allows us to focus on the computational aspect. However, such convenience and generality is not without its price: the PRAM model, unlike the von Neumann machine model, is not physically feasible to build [369]. The simulation of PRAMs by feasible computers is therefore important and forms the major theme of this chapter.

Although some network-specific algorithms and primitives like sort, scans [67, 68], and broadcasting [166] will and should continue to be used — perhaps made available to the programmer as a library — to achieve maximum efficiency, other computational problems may benefit from more general and network-independent treatments due to the difficulty of designing efficient network-specific algorithms and the need for generality and portability; many authors, notably Valiant, champion this view [242, 243, 370]. It is at this juncture that general-purpose computation models like the PRAM are attractive and their efficient simulation becomes valuable.

The PRAM model and its simulation problem are discussed in Section 6.2. Then in Section 6.3 we focus on the simulation of a class of PRAM programs which do not require hashing and rehashing of all the PRAM variables, as seem to be needed for the simulation of general PRAM programs. The main result there says this class of programs can be simulated with a slowdown of at most $8 \log N$ with almost certainty using constant size buffers plus wait buffers with capacity for $O(\log^2 N)$ pieces (Theorem 6.1). Each wait buffer, in fact, accumulates only $O(\log N)$ pieces *on the average*. Our scheme is moreover fault-tolerant. Our identifying such a class of programs is an attempt to find a potentially rich class of PRAM programs whose simulation can be practical, since expensive hashing of all the variables is not needed and the slowdown is only $O(\log N)$ with almost certainty. In the Appendix, we sketch a general PRAM simulation scheme based on Ranade's algorithm with ideas from FSRA to achieve fault tolerance. Both of our simulation schemes use IDA.

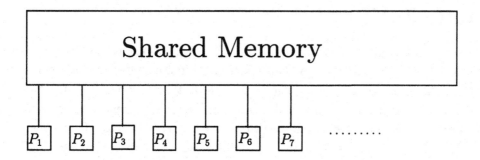

Figure 6.1: THE PRAM MODEL OF COMPUTATION. The $P_i$ are processors that can access any memory cell in unit time.

## 6.2   The PRAM Model

The most popular theoretical model for parallel computation is the PRAM model, for which most parallel algorithms in the literature are designed [9, 130, 172, 174, 249, 282, 313]. The PRAM model is introduced by Fortune and Wyllie [122].

A PRAM consists of some finite number of sequential processors, all of which operate synchronously on a shared memory consisting of memory **cells/variables**; see Figure 6.1. In every step, each processor carries out some local computation and then reads from a variable or writes to a variable. We assume, without loss of generality, that PRAM processors all read or all write in each step. The PRAM idealizes communication by postulating that every access to the memory is completed in $O(1)$ time. Hence it is convenient for expressing parallel algorithms as well as their design and analysis, as one need concentrate only on the computational aspect of a problem. The PRAM model has several variations [75, 181, 303, 330]:

EREW (Exclusive-Read Exclusive-Write) PRAM. No simultaneous reads and writes are allowed. This model is originally called **Parallel Random Access Computer (PRAC)** [225].

CREW (Concurrent-Read Exclusive-Write) PRAM. No simultaneous writes are allowed. This model is originally called PRAM [122].

CRCW (Concurrent-Read Concurrent-Write) PRAM. Various choices for defining the effects of simultaneous writes to the same cell exist.

- Only simultaneous writes of the *same* value are permitted [319].

- An arbitrarily chosen processor succeeds in storing its value.

- The processors are given a **priority** ordering, and the highest priority processor's write always succeeds in storing its value; in [134], for example, the lowest numbered processor does.

- Reads, writes, and replace-adds/fetch-and-adds[1] are all allowed to simultaneously access the same cell. The results correspond to those that would be obtained if these operations occurred in some *serial* order [313]. This is called **paracomputer serialization principle** [139].

Besides PRAMs, there exist many other parallel computation models ("there are probably more models of parallel machines than there are real parallel machines." [214]). **Circuits** and **alternating Turing machines** (ATMs) are two other theoretical models for parallel computation. See [74, 111, 170] for the definition of circuits, [304] for uniform circuit complexity as a model of parallel complexity, [275] for the "Nick's class" (or $\mathcal{NC}$: roughly, problems solvable by parallel machines in $O(\log^{O(1)} N)$ time using $N^{O(1)}$ processors with $N$ being the size of the input), [338] for simulation of PRAMs by circuits, [83] for the definition of ATM and an ATM characterization of $\mathcal{NC}$, [90, 261, 337] for surveys of parallel computation complexity, and [69, 83, 134, 135, 172] for discussions of the **Parallel Computation Thesis**, which states that, within composition with a polynomial, parallel *time* is equivalent to Turing machine *space*. Issues surrounding various parallel computation models are discussed by several authors in [309].

## 6.2.1 Simulation of the PRAM

The PRAM is not a realistic parallel computer, since even future technology does not seem to make it realizable. The PRAM model also does not accurately reflect costs [332], because it is doubtful that access to the shared memory can be accomplished in constant time, although, in this respect, optical devices may alleviate some of the restrictions placed by electronics [113, Chapter 10 and Appendix I].

To justify writing programs in the PRAM model one must demonstrate that PRAMs can be efficiently simulated by *feasible* machines, implemented by processors linked *via* a sparse network [367]. In this chapter, we assume the direct interconnection schemes, where each node is attached to by a PE, consisting of a processor and a memory module; see Figure 3.2. We call such a parallel computer **Ultracomputer** [313], with $N$-Ultracomputer meaning one with $N$ PEs. By $(N, M)$-PRAM we mean

---

[1]Fetch-and-Add $(X, e)$ would in one indivisible step returns the value of $X$ and adds $e$ to it [11]. Replace-Add $(X, e)$ is similar except that it returns $X + e$ [138]. See [137, 138, 229] for the use and implementation of such operations for real parallel machines.

a PRAM consisting of $N$ processors using $M$ variables. Throughout this chapter, $N$ and $M$ denote the number of PRAM processors and that of PRAM variables, respectively, unless noted otherwise. The shared variables of the PRAM are to be allocated among the memory modules of the simulating Ultracomputer before, and maybe even during, the simulation.

The simulating Ultracomputer behaves like the simulated PRAM. In each step, processors can access the memory, the main difference being that access to the memory has to be conducted by routing through the interconnection network in the Ultracomputer. The **simulation problem** is concerned with finding (i) a **storage allocation** scheme for the PRAM shared variables and (ii) a routing scheme for communication such that the *same* $(N, M)$-PRAM program runs on an $N$-Ultracomputer efficiently [368].[2] The existence of efficient and explicit simulation schemes also implies a general-purpose translation process whereby PRAM programs can be executed on Ultracomputers.

A simulation is said to have a **slowdown** of $s$ if it takes $sT$ time to simulate $T$ PRAM steps. For the sake of brevity, the term "network $G$" will also denote an Ultracomputer with $G$ as its interconnection network.

## 6.2.2   **Previous work on simulation of** PRAMs

If a network can sort in $r(N)$ time, then it can simulate an $(N, N)$-CRCW PRAM step in $O(r(N))$ time [75, the conference version]. For the more general and common case where $M \gg N$, in a sequence of papers [34, 374, 246, 364, 12] the time bound for *deterministic* simulation of each PRAM step has been reduced to $O(\log M)$ on a completely connected network and $O(\log N \log M)$ on a bounded-degree network (hence $O(\log N)$ and $O(\log^2 N)$, respectively, if $M$ is polynomial in $N$). The simulation algorithms in [12], however, are non-uniform, that is, not given explicitly. Aumann and Schuster [26, 27] show that IDA can be employed to reduce the memory blowup to a constant and avoid the use of time stamps.

Another approach is to use *probabilistic* methods. In a sequence of papers [246, 362, 171, 291] the slowdown of a bounded-degree network to simulate $T$ $(N, M)$-PRAM steps, where $M$ is polynomial in $N$, is reduced to: $O(\log N)$ with probability tending to one as $N$ and/or $T$ go to infinity (the buffer size is also reduced to $O(1)$, measured as the number of packets). In the last two papers, due to Karlin and Upfal [171] and

---

[2]Allowing the simulating machine to have less processors than the simulated machine, a concept called **parallel slackness** by Valiant, can attain optimality in terms of the product of parallel runtime and number of processors, or **work** [181, 368]. Such a simulation is said to be **work-preserving** or have constant **inefficiency**.

Ranade [291], universal hash functions [82] are used to distribute the PRAM variables among the memory modules, an idea first proposed by Mehlhorn and Vishkin [246], and rehashings may have to be carried out several times throughout the simulation. Sorting is used in [171]; combining of packets is used in [291]. Valiant [368] has a scheme that uses neither combining nor full-scale sorting. The beautiful algorithm of Ranade's is currently being investigated as a basis for a general-purpose parallel computer in Germany [1]. Aumann [23] shows, using IDA, that each PRAM step can be simulated by a faulty hypercube where $O(N)$ links are randomly disconnected in $O(\log N)$ steps with probability $1 - N^{-O(1)}$. Allowing a slackness of $\Omega(\log N)$, Aumann and Ben-Or [24] show that the use of IDA and slackness of $\Omega(\log N)$ can lead to work-preserving simulation of PRAM on a hypercube that allows dynamic faults where each node fails with a constant probability.

### 6.2.3 Combining in the priority model

Memory contention can be reduced if requests to the *same* cell are **combined** into one. So, besides the regular buffers that hold packets temporarily during routing, we need a **wait buffer** at each node to record each act of such combining. When read requests are combined, those not forwarded are deposited in the wait buffer to be later substantiated by the return value from the memory and then routed back to their issuing nodes. No such records are needed when write requests are combined, and those not advanced are simply discarded, since only one value can be written into a cell.

The combining of write requests does create a special problem for IDA-based routing schemes. Suppose both $P$ and $Q$ issue a write request to variable $x$, and each request is split by IDA into two pieces: $P_1$ and $P_2$ for $P$'s request; $Q_1$ and $Q_2$ for $Q$'s request. If during the routing, $P_1$ over-writes $Q_1$ and $Q_2$ over-writes $P_2$ in combining, then the final request, reconstructed from $P_1$ and $Q_2$, may be neither $P$'s request nor $Q$'s! As a result, CRCW PRAMs with **priority** are assumed. Whether $P$'s pieces should over-write $Q$'s or *vice versa*, in the above example, can now be determined by $P$'s and $Q$'s relative priority. Priority will be set to be the number of the issuing processor.

We now return to combining. Two requests are **combinable** if their destination addresses are identical. There are two cases to consider:

- **Combining of two read requests.** When a read request arrives at a node, it is matched to all the read requests in the (regular) buffer and those in the wait buffer. If a match occurs in the buffer, one of the matched pair — it does not matter which — is deposited to the wait buffer. If no match occurs in the buffer

but one occurs in the wait buffer, the incoming read request is deposited to the
wait buffer. Finally, if no match occurs, the incoming read request is queued in
the buffer.

- **Combining of two write requests.**    When a write request arrives at a node, it is
  matched to all the write requests in the (regular) buffer. If a match occurs, the
  one with a lower priority, that is, the one issued by a processor with a lower
  priority, is discarded, and the one with a higher priority is kept in the buffer.

## 6.2.4    A digression on "hot spot" contention

The issue of "**hot spot**" contention — concurrent requests to same memory locations
— has been extensively studied for MINs [164, 186, 190, 200, 206, 207, 208, 209, 256,
274, 300, 351, 359, 384]. Synchronizing through locks in order to have exclusive access
to some shared data provides a good example of hot spot access pattern: when a lock is
released, waiting processors rush to grab it [224]. Here is the "hot spot" traffic *model*:
concurrent requests to a *single* shared variable form a fixed fraction $h$ of the total
memory traffic with the rest accessing each memory module with *equal* probability,
constituting the **background traffic**. It is proposed by Pfister and Norton to model
non-uniform traffic patterns that lead to serious degradation in performance even
for small $h$ [274], and the **tree saturation** phenomenon is invoked to explain why
"hot spot" traffic degrades performance; see Figure 6.2.    It has been well-known
that memory contention can significantly degrade performance when many processes
are accessing the same memory module and that it limits the scalability of parallel
computers [382].

Combining can be found in designs and implementations such as the Columbia
CHoPP computer [343], where it is first proposed,[3] the NYU Ultracomputer [137],
the IBM RP3 [273], the Cedar machine of the University of Illinois [187], and the
BBN Monarch [299]. Some, like the Cedar machine, limit the extent of combining:
requests are combined only at the memory modules but not in the network [206, 385].
Since **pairwise combining**, where only two requests can be combined into one, is
not effective [208], the more general $k$-**way combining** for $k > 2$ is also proposed
[207].

Hardware combining has been studied and implemented. Two separate copies of
MINs are employed for the IBM RP3, one for regular requests and the other for "hot
spot" requests [273]. Recently, Tzeng [359] proposes a structure called **combining
tree** with only $1/\log N$ the cost of a combining network. Another possibility to save

---

[3]The idea already appears in the first supercomputer, the IBM 7030, STRETCH [312].

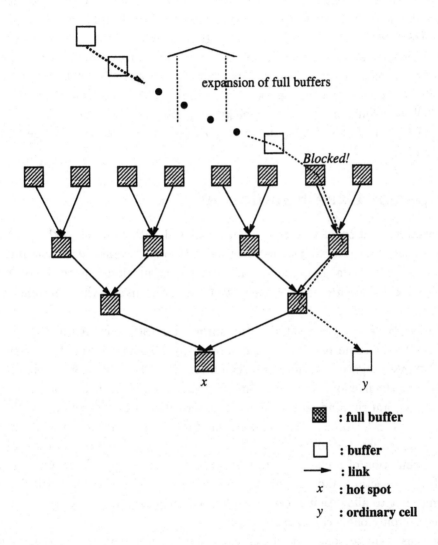

Figure 6.2: TREE SATURATION. Since $x$ is a "hot spot" variable, nodes neighboring $x$ first see their buffers filled up with requests to $x$. Then nodes neighboring these nodes in turn do likewise, etc. Worse, even requests to memory modules that do not host the "hot spot" variable can be severely delayed by buffers filled up with requests to $x$.

cost is to restrict combining to, say, only read requests; in contrast, the IBM RP3 and the NYU Ultracomputer support the (pairwise) combining of the more complicated but powerful fetch-and-OP operations.

Hardware combining being in general expensive to implement [274] (but see [100]), software combining or software-hardware combination, if applicable, may be a good alternative [384, 164]. Another software support to alleviate "hot spot" contention is to scatter the data evenly among the memory modules using randomization, interleaving, and/or careful algorithmic and data structure designs [256, 299, 300]. Other proposals include diversion of the packets in routing [200], redundant paths in the network [300], and different network topology; for example, the hypercube network is claimed to support single "hot spots" with "barely perceptible effect on the background traffic" [2].

## 6.3    Special Case Simulation

Fast, universal simulation of PRAMs has been achieved with hashing as the storage allocation scheme. Since rehashings may be needed throughout the simulation during which time — and it is a long time — no useful computation can be done, it is legitimate to ask if there are useful classes of PRAM programs for which hashing can be avoided.

An Ultracomputer program satisfies the **same cell (SC) condition** if, in each step, accesses to the same memory module are all to the same cell in that module. An $(N, M)$-PRAM program satisfies the SC condition if its shared memory cells can be allocated among the memory modules of an $N$-Ultracomputer in such a way that the same PRAM program running on the Ultracomputer satisfies the SC condition. With SC programs, we can focus on routing and assume that the SC condition is enforced by some storage allocation method; see [184] for a survey of the related **data alignment problem**. Simulation of a class of CRCW PRAM SC programs by Ultracomputers is considered in this section, and our general conclusion still holds if the SC condition is relaxed somewhat to allow that accesses to the same memory module be directed to $O(1)$, instead of only one, cells in that module.

SC programs seem to constitute a rich class. For example, access of an array of size at most $N$ can satisfy the SC condition by simply allocating each element of the array to *distinct* memory modules. If each element $a_{i,j}$ of an $N \times N$ array $A$ is allocated to node $i + j \bmod N$, access of each row and each column satisfies the SC condition; moreover, each memory module receives either zero or two requests for each diagonal element access.

## 6.3.1 The simulation algorithm and results

The simulation algorithm will be FSRA running on the hypercube network with the combining mechanism described in Subsection 6.2.3. We denote this simulation scheme by **sim-FSRA**. The following subsections will establish, *if* the memory **access patterns** satisfy Assumption 6.8 on page 99, that with almost certainty, the time slowdown is $O(\log N)$.

**Theorem 6.1** *A $T$-step CRCW PRAM $(N, M)$-PRAM SC program can be simulated by an $N$-Ultracomputer in $2\,(2 \log N + 1)\,(2\,T - 1) \approx 8\,T \log N$ time with probability $1 - N^{-\Theta(T \log N)}$. Furthermore, each regular and wait buffer has capacity for $O(\log N)$ and $O(\log^2 N)$ pieces, respectively. Each wait buffer actually accumulates $O(\log N)$ pieces on the average, even without assuming Assumption 6.8. We also do not assume $M$, the number of PRAM variables, is polynomial in $N$.*

Our simulation is fault-tolerant in the sense that each packet's pieces take node-disjoint paths in each of FSRA's three phases. Conventions that simplify the proof but have otherwise no essential effects on our general results follow.

- Assume SRA instead of FSRA is employed as the routing algorithm.

- Assume $N = 2^n$ and $n = 2^k$ for some $k > 0$.

- Each read request in the **return phase**, after the reading is completed, takes the *same* route, but in the reverse direction, as it did when being routed to its destination. Hence, *new* overflow is created in neither the regular nor the wait buffers. We therefore need to analyze only the **forward phase**.

- During an epoch, each node first sends out pieces and then performs combining on the received pieces. We analyze each epoch *after* the combining is done, that is, the end of each epoch; since only one incoming link is used for packet delivery in each epoch of SRA, doubling the buffer size afterwards is enough to accommodate *pre*-combining pieces at each node in each epoch.

- The non-destructive model (Comment 5.2 in Section 5.1) is assumed.

We assume the combining mechanism is switched on only during Subphase 2.1, possibly plus the last epoch of Phase 1. If the combining mechanism is on throughout the routing, clearly that benefits only the *regular* buffers by removing pieces from them, and it remains an open question if the whole Theorem 6.1 can then be extended to *all* SC programs. On the other hand, we will show at the end of Subsection 6.3.3 that the bounds for the average size of wait buffers still hold if combining is on throughout the routing.

Some useful definitions follow.

**Definition 6.2** *The number of packets directed to node $x$ is denoted by $n_x$, and $\{n_x\}_{x \in V}$ defines the* **access pattern**.

By the SC condition, the $n_x$ packets go to the same cell in node $x$ and, clearly, $\sum_{x \in V(C_n)} n_x = N$. Analysis can be much simplified if we assume, for notational reasons only, that each node at the end of Subphase 2.1 has exactly $n$ pieces but some may be **ghost pieces** and non-existent. We stress that pieces are ghosts not because they are lost during the routing — note that the non-destructive model is assumed — but because they simply do not exist in the first place. We use **"piece"** to denote a piece, ghost or otherwise, and reserve the unquoted word for non-ghost (real) pieces.

**Definition 6.3** *"Pieces" at node $x$ at the end of Subphase 2.1 are labeled as $\beta_x(0)$, ..., $\beta_x(n-1)$, where $\beta_x(l)$ is destined to node $v_x(i) \stackrel{\text{def}}{=} bits_k(i) \circ x_k \dots x_{n-1}$.*

So, $\beta_y(l)$ is a ghost piece if and only if node $v_x(l)$ is not a target of *any* packet, or, what amounts to the same thing, $n_{v_x(l)} = 0$. Again, note that we assume the non-destructive model.

**Definition 6.4** *$\beta_x(l)$ may be a result of several acts of combining, and all these pieces involved are called its* **ancestors**.

A (bundled) packet contains no combinable pieces since it is assembled and sent *after* combining. When a packet arrives at a node, each of its constituent pieces is matched to existing pieces at that node (each piece is a request). Since each packet and each buffer contain no combinable pieces, in a sense 2-way (pairwise) combining is used because no more than two pieces can be combined into a single piece.

### 6.3.2   Analysis of size of regular buffers

We will show that, for some $D > 0$, capacity for $Dn$ pieces at each regular buffer is enough for sim-FSRA to simulate each PRAM step with a slowdown of $\approx 4 \log N$ with extremely high probability.

There is no overflow in Subphase 2.2 because, at the end of Subphase 2.1, each buffer has $n$ "pieces," and Lemma 5.12 implies that each buffer has at most $n$ pieces in each epoch of Subphase 2.2. There is also no overflow in Phase 1.1 by Lemma 5.11. So, we need analyze only Subphases 1.2–2.1 for overflow.

The analysis of Theorem 5.14 can be applied to Subphase 1.2 since combining is switched on only in Subphase 2.1. Therefore, each subcube has overflow in Subphase

1.2 with probability at most $p_0/2$ for some $D$, say $D_1$. The definition for $p_0$ can be found on page 60.

We now turn to Phase 2. Consider epoch $t$ and node $y$. Without loss of generality, let $y$ be in the subcube $C_{n-k}(0)$. The cases for the other $n-1$ subcubes can be identically treated. To simplify notations, we assume Phase 2 starts with epoch 0 instead of $n$. Since Subphase 2.2 has no overflow, we can further assume $0 \leq t < n-k$, that is, any epoch in Subphase 2.1. Recall that the $(n-t-1)^{\text{th}}$ dimension is used for sending out pieces in epoch $t$.

**Definition 6.5** $A_t(y) \stackrel{\text{def}}{=} \{ z \in V(C_{n-k}(0)) \mid z_{n-t-1} = y_{n-t-1}, \ldots, z_{n-1} = y_{n-1} \}$. *Clearly*, $|A_t(y)| = 2^{n-k-t-1}$.

**Definition 6.6** *Let* $a_t \stackrel{\text{def}}{=} 1 - 2^{-(n-k-t-1)}$ *for* $0 \leq t < n-k$. *Note that* $a_{n-k-1} = 0$, $a_{n-k-2} = 1/2$, *and* $a_0 = 1 - (2 \, n/N)$.

Let $Y_{x,l}$ be the random variable that is 1 if one of $\beta_x(l)$'s ancestors is at $y$'s buffer in epoch $t$ and 0 otherwise. We next derive the expectation of $\sum_{x,l} Y_{x,l}$, the number of pieces at $y$'s buffer in epoch $t$, *after* combining. Since the routing is in reverse order of dimension, each of $\beta_x(l)$'s ancestors is in some node $w \in V(C_{n-k}(0))$ with $w_i = x_i$ for $n-t-1 \leq i < n$ at the end of epoch $t$. So, $Y_{x,l} = 0$ for $x \notin A_t(y)$. By a standard theorem in probability theory, we have

$$E\left[\sum_{x,l} Y_{x,l}\right] = \sum_{x,l} E[Y_{x,l}] = \sum_{x \in A_t(y)} \sum_{l=0}^{n-1} E[Y_{x,l}]. \tag{6.1}$$

**Definition 6.7** $B_t(y) \stackrel{\text{def}}{=} \{ z \in V(C_{n-k}(0)) \mid z_k = y_k, \ldots, z_{n-t-2} = y_{n-t-2} \}$. *Clearly*, $|B_t(y)| = 2^{t+1}$.

For $x \in A_t(y)$ and $0 \leq l < n$, consider piece $\beta_x(l)$, a result of combining $n_{v_x(l)}$ pieces. First, consider $t < n-k-1$. An ancestor of $\beta_x(l)$ can be at $y$'s buffer in epoch $t$ only if it is in $B_t(y)$ when Phase 2 starts; see Figure 6.3. This happens with probability $|B_t(y)|/2^{n-k} = 2^{-(n-k-t-1)}$. The probability that one of $\beta_x(l)$'s ancestors is at $y$'s buffer in epoch $t$ is hence $1 - \left(1 - 2^{-(n-k-t-1)}\right)^{n_{v_x(l)}} = 1 - a_t^{n_{v_x(l)}}$, which is zero when $n_{v_x(l)} = 0$, as it should be. Eq. (6.1) now becomes

$$\sum_{x \in A_t(y)} \sum_{l=0}^{n-1} \left(1 - a_t^{n_{v_x(l)}}\right) = \sum_{x \in A_t(y)} \left(n - a_t^{n_{v_x(0)}} - \cdots - a_t^{n_{v_x(n-1)}}\right). \tag{6.2}$$

On the other hand, if $t = n-k-1$ (i.e., the end of Subphase 2.1), the number of pieces at $y$'s buffer at the end of epoch $t$ is exactly the total number of packets

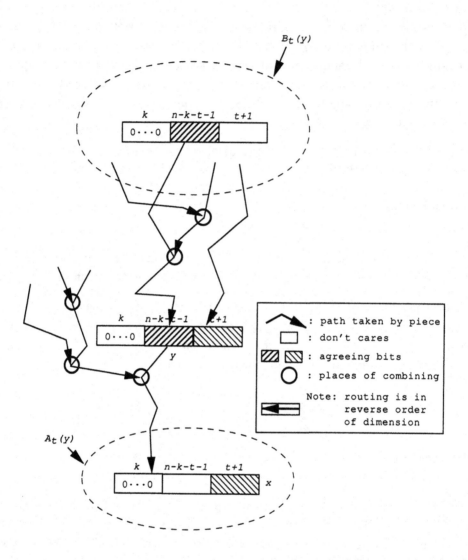

Figure 6.3: HOW PIECES GOT COMBINED IN SUBPHASE 2.1. Consider node $y$, epoch $t$, and ancestors of $\beta_x(l)$. Only pieces falling within the upper ellipse — nodes whose middle $n - k - t - 1$ bits agree with $y$'s at the beginning of Phase 2 — may reach $y$ in epoch $t$. Those outside may themselves be combined somewhere, but they will not pass *through* $y$ on their way to $x$.

destined to nodes $v_y(0), \ldots, v_y(n-1)$, which is at most $n$ by the SC condition. Before proceeding, we assume the following proposition, which basically says the number of pieces at any node is on the average $O(\log N)$ in each epoch.

**Assumption 6.8** *The access pattern satisfies: there exists a constant $c > 0$ such that (6.2) is at most $cn = O(n)$ for any $y$ and $0 \le t < n - k$.*

With this assumption on the access pattern, the expected number of pieces at $y$'s buffer in epoch $0 \le t < n - k$ is $O(n)$. Since the $Y_{x,l}$'s are clearly independent Bernoulli trials and the expectation of their sum is $O(n)$, Fact 5.3 applied to the $Y_{x,l}$'s shows that $y$'s buffer has overflow in epoch $t$ with probability at most $N^{-d}$ for some $d > 0$. Since there are $N/n$ nodes in each subcube and $n - k$ epochs in Subphase 2.1, the probability that a subcube has overflow is at most $(N/n)(n-k)N^{-d}$, which can be made at most $p_0/2$ for some $D$, say $D_2$. Each subcube hence has overflow in Subphases 1.2–2.1 with probability at most $p_0$ if we pick $D = \max(D_1, D_2)$. We conclude that the routing is unsuccessful with probability at most $B(n/2, n, p_0) \le N p_0^{n/2} \le N^{-2.419 \log N + 1.5}$ by using the argument in the proof of Theorem 5.14. We summarize our findings below.

**Lemma 6.9** *Given Assumption 6.8, sim-FSRA takes $2(2 \log N + 1)$ time to simulate each CRCW PRAM step with probability of success at least $1 - N^{-2.419 \log N + 1.5}$ using buffers with capacity for $O(\log N)$ pieces.*

Many familiar access patterns satisfy Assumption 6.8:

- **Permutation.** In this case, $n_{v_x(l)} = 1$ for any node $x$ and $0 \le l < n$. Eq. (6.2) produces $n$ with these numbers, as expected.

- **All-to-one communications.** Here, all the packets are destined to a single node, $\beta$. Hence $n_{v_x(l)} = 0$ except for pairs of $x$ and $l$ with $v_x(l) = \beta$, in which case $n_{v_x(l)} = N$. Calculation shows (6.2) is at most $1 - a_t^N < 1$. Hence, the expected number of *pre*-combining pieces at each buffer is less than 2. Indeed, if all the packets are destined to $\beta$, there is at most one piece left at each buffer in each epoch after combining since *all* the pieces are combinable, and each incoming packet contains at most one piece.

- **Relatively uniform communications.** Assume $n_{v_x(l)} \le C/2$ in (6.2) for each $x$ and $0 \le l < n$, that is, each memory module is the target of at most $C/2$ packets. Then, (6.2) becomes

$$2^{n-k-t-1}\left(n - n\, a_t^{C/2}\right) = 2^{n-t-1}\left(1 - \left(1 - 2^{-(n-k-t-1)}\right)^{C/2}\right) < C\, n/2.$$

The expected number of pre-combining pieces at each buffer is hence less than $Cn = O(n)$.

Without Assumption 6.8 buffers with capacity for $\Omega(\sqrt{N})$ pieces would be needed for sim-FSRA. This can be seen as follows. Pick any node $y$. Let $n_{v_x(l)} = 2^{t+1}$ for $x \in A_t(y)$ and $t + 1 = n/2$. Then, (6.2) becomes

$$2^{n-k-t-1}\left(n - n\,a_t^{2^{t+1}}\right)$$
$$= 2^{n-t-1}\left(1 - \left(1 - 2^{-(n-k-t-1)}\right)^{2^{t+1}}\right)$$
$$= \sqrt{N}\left(1 - (1 - \tfrac{n}{\sqrt{N}})^{\sqrt{N}}\right)$$
$$= \Omega(\sqrt{N}).$$

In the above situation, all the $N$ packets are destined to the nodes within a radius of $n/2$ from node $y$. Restructuring of programs, such as trying a different allocation scheme or using software combining, should be carried out for these bad cases. It is not unknown if the simpler method of switching on the combining mechanism throughout the routing, instead of just in Subphase 2.1, can solve the problem.

### 6.3.3 Analysis of size of wait buffers

We show that each wait buffer accumulates on the average $W = O(n)$ pieces at the end of Phase 2; henceforth, this conclusion can carry over to the whole Phase 2 since no pieces are deleted from wait buffers in the forward phase. This conclusion, we note, holds *without the need of Assumption 6.8*. Then we show in Comment 6.16 that if each wait buffer has capacity for $O(n^2)$ pieces, the simulation of each PRAM step by sim-FSRA is successful with probability $1 - N^{-\Theta(n)}$.

We assume the combining mechanism is switched on from the end of Phase 1, that is, epoch $n - 1$. Since the expected number of pieces at each regular buffer at the end of Phase 1 is $n$, the expected number of pieces deposited to each wait buffer *then* is $n - 1 < n$. We will analyze wait buffers for Subphase 2.1 and later add $n$ to the derived expected number of pieces to obtain an upper bound on $W$. We again assume Phase 2 starts with epoch 0 instead of $n$ to simplify the presentation.

Consider epoch $0 \le t < n - k$ and node $y$. Without loss of generality, assume $y \in V(C_{n-k}(0))$. Recall that the $(n - t - 1)^{\text{th}}$ dimension is used for sending out pieces in epoch $t$.

**Definition 6.10** *Define* $B_t^i(y) \stackrel{\text{def}}{=} B_t(y) \cap \{z \mid z_{n-t-1} = i\}$, *where* $i \in \{0, 1\}$. *Clearly,* $|B_t^0(y)| = |B_t^1(y)| = 2^t$ *and* $B_t^0(y) \cap B_t^1(y) = \emptyset$.

Let $Z_{t,x,l}$ be the random variable that is 1 if two of $\beta_x(l)$'s ancestors are combined at $y$ in epoch $t$ and 0 otherwise, where $x \in A_t(y)$ and $0 \le l < n$ (it is easy to see that $Z_{t,x,l} = 0$ for $x \notin A_t(y)$; consult Figure 6.4. We now derive the expectation of $\sum_{t=0}^{n-k-1} \sum_{x,l} Z_{t,x,l}$, the total number of pieces deposited to $y$'s wait buffer in Phase 2.1. Note that

$$E\left[\sum_{t=0}^{n-k-1} \sum_{x,l} Z_{t,x,l}\right] = \sum_{t=0}^{n-k-1} \sum_{x \in A_t(y)} \sum_{l=0}^{n-1} E[Z_{t,x,l}]. \tag{6.3}$$

For $x \in A_t(y)$ and $0 \le l < n$, consider $\beta_x(l)$, a result of combining $n_{v_x(l)}$ pieces. Two conditions must hold for two of $\beta_x(l)$'s ancestors to be combined at $y$ in epoch $t$: (i) $n_{v_x(l)} \ge 2$, and (ii) at least one ancestor is in $B_t^0(y)$ and at least one ancestor is in $B_t^1(y)$ at the beginning of Phase 2. Condition (i) is obvious: it takes two pieces to combine. As for Condition (ii), observe that if two pieces are combined at $y$ in epoch $t$, then they must meet for the *first* time there and then. Thus, although they must be in $B_t(y)$ at the beginning of Phase 2, their residing nodes' $(n-t-1)^{\text{th}}$ bits must differ at that time, which is precisely Condition (ii); see Figure 6.4.

The probability that a piece is in $B_t^i(y)$, where $i \in \{0,1\}$, at the beginning of Phase 2 is $|B_t^i(y)|/2^{n-k} = 2^{-(n-k-t)}$. Now, assume first that $0 \le t < n - k - 1$. The probability that (ii) is satisfied is, by the inclusion-exclusion principle,

$$1 - 2\left(1 - 2^{-(n-k-t)}\right)^{n_{v_x(l)}} + \left(1 - 2^{-(n-k-t-1)}\right)^{n_{v_x(l)}} = 1 - 2\,a_{t-1}^{n_{v_x(l)}} + a_t^{n_{v_x(l)}},$$

where $n_{v_x(l)} \ge 2$ is assumed. This formula happens to be zero when $n_{v_x(l)} \in \{0, 1\}$, as desired. If $t = n - k - 1$, on the other hand, this formula gives $1 \ominus 2\,a_{n-k-2}^{-n_{v_x(l)}} = 1 \ominus 2^{-(n_{v_x(l)}-1)}$, where $a \ominus b \overset{\text{def}}{=} \max(0, a - b)$.

The expectation (6.3) is now at most

$$\sum_{x \in A_{n-k-1}(y)} \sum_{l=0}^{n-1} \left(1 \ominus 2^{-(n_{v_x(l)}-1)}\right) + \sum_{t=0}^{n-k-2} \sum_{x \in A_t(y)} \sum_{l=0}^{n-1} \left(1 - 2\,a_{t-1}^{n_{v_x(l)}} + a_t^{n_{v_x(l)}}\right)$$

$$\le \sum_{x \in A_{n-k-1}(y)} \sum_{l=0}^{n-1} \left(1 \ominus 2^{-(n_{v_x(l)}-1)}\right) + \sum_{t=0}^{n-k-2} \sum_{x \in A_t(y)} \sum_{l=0}^{n-1} \left(1 - a_t^{n_{v_x(l)}}\right), \tag{6.4}$$

since $2\,a_{t-1}^{n_{v_x(l)}} - a_t^{n_{v_x(l)}} \ge a_t^{n_{v_x(l)}}$. We want an upper bound on (6.4) subject to the constraint that

$$\sum_{\substack{x \in V(C_{n-k}(0)) \\ 0 \le l < n}} n_{v_x(l)} = N,$$

since there are $N$ packets. The maximum of the following formula is clearly as large

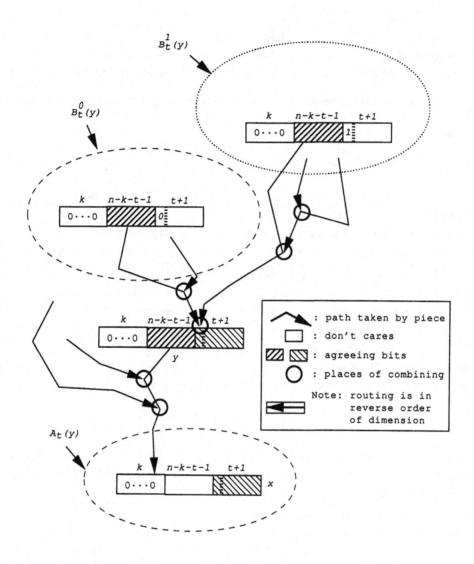

Figure 6.4: COMBINING AND WAIT BUFFERS IN SUBPHASE 2.1. Consider node $y$, epoch $t$, and ancestors of $\beta_x(l)$. Only if there are pieces falling within the upper left ellipse *and* there are pieces falling within the upper right ellipse at the beginning of Phase 2 will there be combining of $\beta_x(l)$'s ancestors at $y$ in epoch $t$.

as (6.4)

$$\sum_{x \in A_{n-k-1}(y)} \sum_{l=0}^{n-1} \left( 1 \ominus 2^{-(X(n-k-1,x,l)-1)} \right) + \sum_{t=0}^{n-k-2} \sum_{x \in A_t(y)} \sum_{l=0}^{n-1} \left( 1 - a_t^{X(t,x,l)} \right), \qquad (6.5)$$

where the $X(t, x, l)$'s are *non*-negative *real* numbers for $0 \le t < n - k$, $x \in V(C_{n-k}(0))$, and $0 \le l < n$, and they satisfy

$$\sum_{t=0}^{n-k-1} \sum_{x \in V(C_{n-k}(0))} \sum_{l=0}^{n-1} X(t, x, l) = N. \qquad (6.6)$$

Since $A_{n-k-1}(y) = \{ y \}$, the first term in (6.5) is at most $n$; hence (6.5) is at most

$$n + \sum_{t=0}^{n-k-2} \sum_{x \in A_t(y)} \sum_{l=0}^{n-1} \left( 1 - a_t^{X(t,x,l)} \right), \qquad (6.7)$$

subject to the constraint (6.6).

Let $X^*(t, x, l)$ be the value of $X(t, x, l)$ at the maximum of (6.7). Clearly, $X^*(n - k - 1, x, l) = 0$ and $X^*(t, x, l) = 0$ for $x \notin A_t(y)$ since they do not appear in Eq. (6.7). The use of Lagrange's multipliers and the second derivatives [17] can show that

$$a_t^{X^*(t,x,l)} \ln a_t = a_{t'}^{X^*(t',x',l')} \ln a_{t'} \qquad (6.8)$$

for $0 \le t, t' < n - k - 1$, $x, x' \in A_t(y)$, and $0 \le l, l' < n$. Note that $a_t \ne 0$ for $0 \le t < n - k - 1$. Eq. (6.8) moreover implies $X^*(t, x, l) = X^*(t, x', l')$ for $0 \le t, t' < n - k - 1$, $x, x' \in A_t(y)$, and $0 \le l, l' < n$.

With the definition that $X^*(t) \stackrel{\text{def}}{=} X^*(t, x, l)$, where $0 \le t, t' < n - k - 1$, $x, x' \in A_t(y)$, and $0 \le l, l' < n$, the constraint (6.6) becomes

$$\sum_{t=0}^{n-k-2} |A_t(y)| \, n \, X^*(t) = \sum_{t=0}^{n-k-2} 2^{n-t-1} X^*(t) = N, \qquad (6.9)$$

and (6.7) at its maximum becomes $n + \sum_{t=0}^{n-k-2} \gamma_t$, where $\gamma_t \stackrel{\text{def}}{=} 2^{n-t-1} \left( 1 - a_t^{X^*(t)} \right)$ for $0 \le t < n - k - 1$.

We prove a series of claims below.

**Claim 6.11** $\gamma_t \le 2 \, n \, X^*(t)$.

**Proof:** Case 1: $X^*(t) \ge 1$. Since $(1 - a)^b \ge 1 - a \, b$ for $b \ge 1$, we have

$$\gamma_t = 2^{n-t-1} \left( 1 - \left( 1 - 2^{-(n-k-t-1)} \right)^{X^*(t)} \right) \le 2^k \, X^*(t) = n \, X^*(t).$$

Case 2: $0 \le X^*(t) < 1$. Let $c_a = \left( X^*(t) \ln \left( 1 - 2^{-(n-k-t-1)} \right) \right)^a / a!$. Then, by $\left( 1 - 2^{-(n-k-t-1)} \right)^{X^*(t)} = e^{X^*(t) \ln \left( 1 - 2^{-(n-k-t-1)} \right)}$ and the power series expansion $e^x = 1 + x + x^2/2! + \cdots$, we have

$$\gamma_t = 2^{n-t-1} \left( 1 - \sum_{a=0}^{\infty} c_a \right) = -2^{n-t-1} \left( \sum_{a=1}^{\infty} c_a \right).$$

Since $\sum_a c_a$ is an alternating series where $\{|c_a|\}$ is a monotonic decreasing sequence with limit 0, Leibniz's rule [16, Theorem 10.14] says that $0 \ge \sum_a c_a \ge c_1$. Hence, $\gamma_t \le -2^{n-t-1} c_1$. But,

$$\begin{aligned}
c_1 &= X^*(t) \ln \left( 1 - 2^{-(n-k-t-1)} \right) \\
&= -X^*(t) \left( 2^{-(n-k-t-1)} + \left( 2^{-(n-k-t-1)} \right)^2 / 2 + \cdots \right) \\
&> -X^*(t) \, 2^{1-(n-k-t-1)}.
\end{aligned}$$

Hence, $\gamma_t \le 2^{n-t-1} X^*(t) \, 2^{1-(n-k-t-1)} = 2 \, n \, X^*(t)$.
Q.E.D.

The next claim follows from $X^*(t) \le 2^{t+1}$ (due to (6.9)) and Claim 6.11.

**Claim 6.12** $\gamma_t \le n \, 2^{t+2}$ and $\sum_{t=0}^{m-1} \gamma_t \le n \, 2^{m+2}$ for $m > 0$.

**Claim 6.13** $0 \le \ln a_0 / \ln a_t \le 2^{-t}$.

**Proof:** Applying the power series of $\ln(1 + x)$, we have

$$\begin{aligned}
\ln a_0 / \ln a_t &= \frac{(2 \, n/N) + (2 \, n/N)^2/2 + \cdots}{(2 \, n \, 2^t/N) + (2 \, n \, 2^t/N)^2/2 + \cdots} \\
&\le \frac{(2 \, n/N) + (2 \, n/N)^2/2 + \cdots}{2^t \, (2 \, n/N) + 2^t \, (2 \, n/N)^2/2 + \cdots} \\
&= 2^{-t}.
\end{aligned}$$

Q.E.D.

**Claim 6.14** *For any* $0 \le x, y < 1$,

$$\frac{1 - (y \ln a_0 / \ln a_t)}{1 - (y \ln a_0 / \ln a_{t+1})} \ge x$$

*for* $t \ge -\log(1 - x)$.

**Proof:** By Claim 6.13, if we choose $t \geq m = -\log(1-x)$, then $0 \leq \frac{\ln a_0}{\ln a_t} \leq 1 - x \leq \frac{1-x}{y}$ and $0 \leq \frac{\ln a_0}{\ln a_{t+1}} x \leq \frac{1-x}{2} x \leq \frac{1-x}{y}$. Thus,

$$1 - x \geq y \left( \frac{\ln a_0}{\ln a_t} - \frac{\ln a_0}{\ln a_{t+1}} x \right).$$

From here, it is easy to see that

$$1 - \frac{\ln a_0}{\ln a_t} y \geq x - \frac{\ln a_0}{\ln a_{t+1}} x y.$$

The claim can now be proved by rearranging the terms.
Q.E.D.

Now, for any $\epsilon > 0$, let $t \geq m = -\log(\epsilon/2)$. Then

$$
\begin{aligned}
\gamma_t / \gamma_{t+1} &= 2 \frac{1 - a_t^{X^*(t)}}{1 - a_{t+1}^{X^*(t+1)}} \\
&= 2 \frac{1 - a_0^{X^*(0) \ln a_0 / \ln a_t}}{1 - a_0^{X^*(0) \ln a_0 / \ln a_{t+1}}} \\
&\geq 2 - \epsilon
\end{aligned}
$$

by Claim 6.14. Hence, $n + \sum_{t=0}^{n-k-2} \gamma_t$ is at most

$$n + \sum_{t=0}^{m-1} \gamma_t + \sum_{t=m}^{\infty} \gamma_t < n + n \, 2^{m+2} + \sum_{t=0}^{\infty} (2 - \epsilon)^{-t} \gamma_m = \left( 1 + \frac{8}{\epsilon} + \frac{\frac{8}{\epsilon}}{1 - \frac{1}{2-\epsilon}} \right) n = \Theta(n)$$

by Claim 6.12 and $2^{m+2} = 8/\epsilon$. Finally, we add $n$ to the above value to account for combining in Phase 1 and get the next lemma.

**Lemma 6.15** *The expected number of pieces accumulated in the wait buffer is $O(n)$ under sim-*FSRA.

Note that this conclusion holds *without* the help of Assumption 6.8. Moreover, the expected number of pieces accumulated in a wait buffer is *independent* of the size of the regular buffers. Below, we combine the analysis of regular and wait buffers.

**Comment 6.16** Assume Assumption 6.8 and that each wait buffer has capacity for $C \log^2 N$ pieces. Consider node $y \in V(C_{n-k}(0))$ and epoch $0 \leq t < n - k$ as before.

The number of pieces deposited to $y$'s wait buffer in epoch $t$ is the random variable $Z(t) \overset{\text{def}}{=} \sum_{x,l} = Z_{t,x,l}$. Employing the same arguments leading to (6.4), we have

$$
E[Z(t)] \leq
\begin{cases}
\displaystyle\sum_{l=0}^{n-1}\left(1 \ominus 2^{-\left(n_{v_y(l)}-1\right)}\right) \leq n & \text{if } t = n - k - 1 \\[2em]
\displaystyle\sum_{x \in A_t(y)}\sum_{l=0}^{n-1}\left(1 - a_t^{n_{v_x(l)}}\right) & \text{if } 0 \leq t < n - k - 1
\end{cases}
$$

The second case is $O(n)$ since it is at most (6.4), which is $O(n)$ by Lemma 6.15. For $Z(-1)$, the number of pieces deposited to $y$'s wait buffer at the end of Phase 1, $E[Z(-1)] < n$. In summary, $E[Z(t)] = O(n)$ for $-1 \leq t < n - k$. Since each $Z(t)$ is a sum of independent Bernoulli trials, the probability that $y$'s wait buffer accumulates more than $Cn$ pieces in epoch $t$ is $N^{-\Theta(1)}$ by Fact 5.3. As a result, each subcube contains a buffer — regular or wait — that overflows under sim-FSRA with probability at most $p_0 = N^{-\Theta(1)}$, given suitable choices of $C$ and $D$. Finally, the simulation is unsuccessful only if more than $n/2$ of the subcubes have buffers that overflow, which occurs with probability at most $N p_0^{n/2} < N^{-2.419\,n+1.5}$ by (5.6).

It is easy to show that switching on the combining mechanism in Phase 1 contributes only $O(n)$ extra pieces to each wait buffer on the average. Consider epoch $0 \leq t < n$ of Phase 1 and, without loss of generality, node $y \in V(C_{n-k}(0))$. It is easy to see that Subphase 1.1 does not contribute more than $O(n)$ pieces. Hence, we can consider $t \geq k$. For two pieces to be combined at $y$ in epoch $t$, it must be that they are combinable and one is at $B_t^0(y)$ and the other at $B_t^1(y)$ at the beginning of Subphase 1.2. In the worst scenario, *every* piece at a node in $B_t^0(y)$ is combinable with a piece at a node in $B_t^1(y)$. Since a piece from $B_t^0(y) \cup B_t^1(y)$ reaches $y$ in epoch $t$ with probability $2^{-t-1}$ and since each node starts with at most $n$ pieces at the beginning of Subphase 1.2, the expected number of pieces combined at $y$ in epoch $t$ is at most $|B_t^0(y)|\, n\, 2^{-2\,(t+1)} = n\, 2^{-t-2}$. Finally, the expected number of pieces in $y$'s wait buffer at the end of Subphase 1.2 is at most

$$
\sum_{t=0}^{n-k-1} n\, 2^{-t-2} = O(n),
$$

as desired.

## 6.3.4   Analysis of slowdown

Let $p$ be the probability that the simulation of a PRAM step is successful. By Lemma 6.9 and Comment 6.16, $p > 1 - N^{-2.419\,n+1.5}$, if Assumption 6.8 holds. Let $q = 1 - p$.

Now assume we are simulating $T+1$ CRCW PRAM steps. The probability that sim-FSRA takes at least $2T+1$ rounds of routing to finish the simulation successfully is

$$
\begin{aligned}
\gamma &= \sum_{i \geq 2T} \binom{i}{T} p^{T+1} q^{i-T} \\
&= p^{T+1} \binom{2T}{T} \left( q^T + \tfrac{2T+1}{T+1} q^{T+1} + \tfrac{(2T+2)(2T+1)}{(T+2)(T+1)} q^{T+2} + \cdots \right) \\
&< p^{T+1} q^T \binom{2T}{T} \left( 1 + 2q + (2q)^2 + \cdots \right) \\
&= p^{T+1} q^T \binom{2T}{T} (1 - 2q)^{-1}.
\end{aligned}
$$

Since $\binom{2T}{T} = 2\binom{2T-1}{T-1} < 2 \cdot 2^{2T-1}/2 = 4^T/2$, we have

$$
\begin{aligned}
\gamma &< p^{T+1} q^T 4^T (1-2q)^{-1}/2 \\
&< (4q)^T \\
&< (4N^{-2.419n+1.5})^T
\end{aligned}
$$

for $n \geq 2^2$.

We remark that the slowdown can be pushed to $O(1)$ if the return value of each read request is ahead of its use (computation, conditional **if**-statements, etc.) by $2(2\log N + 1)$ PRAM instructions, because we can then pipeline the routing: in step 0 the first routing is started; then in step 2 the second routing is started while the first one enters epoch 1; etc. Here we assume the number of PRAM instructions to be simulated is $\Omega(\log N)$, since FSRA runs in $\Theta(\log N)$ time. FSRA running in certain order of dimension, routings in progress do not congest any particular dimension. Finally, the buffer size has to be increased by a factor of $\log N$ because, at any one time, $O(\log N)$ routings are being carried out.

# Appendix: A Universal Simulation Scheme

We sketch how the simulation of $(N, M)$-CRCW PRAMs with $M$ polynomial in $N$ can be achieved with a slowdown of $O(\log N)$ with probability tending to one as $N$ and/or $T$ go to infinity. By a standard technique [171], we only have to show that each PRAM step can be simulated in $O(\log N)$ steps with probability $1 - N^{-\Theta(1)}$, henceforth, "with high probability (w.h.p.)."

We first adapt Ranade's algorithm to handle cases where each node originally has $A(N) = O(\log N)$, instead of one, packets. First, embed $A(N)$ butterfly networks onto the hypercube network such that each edge of the hypercube network is used by $O(1)$ butterfly networks and each mapping to the nodes of the hypercube network from the nodes of the butterfly network is *onto* [142]. Assign the $A(N)$ packets at each node of the hypercube network to the corresponding nodes in the $A(N)$ butterfly networks such that each gets at most one packet. Now, let the hypercube network run Ranade's algorithm for the $A(N)$ embedded butterfly networks *concurrently* (this is called **multiplexing** [51]). Various parameters suitably adjusted in the universal hash functions, Ranade's result still holds for the hypercube network when each node starts with $O(\log N)$ packets instead of only one. Call this scheme $R'$.

Before we give the three-phase simulation scheme, the reader may want to review the terms in Subsections 5.3.1 and 5.4.1. We do not specify constant terms as they can be chosen to keep our conclusion correct.

Fix a hypercube network $C_n$ where $n = 2^k + k$ for some $k > 0$ and $N = 2^n$. $C_n$ is to simulate the $(N, M)$-CRCW PRAM. Assume $\mathcal{H}$ is picked as the hash function so that each variable $a$ is located in node $\mathcal{H}(a)$. Consider $P_x$, a request to variable $y$ located in node $\mathcal{H}(y)$. First, $P_x$ is split by IDA into $2^k = \Theta(\log N)$ pieces, as in FSRA. In Phase 1, $P_x(i)$ is routed to $x^{(i)}$ and then to $bits_k(i) \circ (x^{(i)}[k : n-1]) \in V(C_{n-k}(i))$ as in Subphases 1.1–1.2 of FSRA. Thus, $P_x$'s pieces take node-disjoint paths. In Phase 2, $P_x(i)$ first traverses the $(k+i)^{\text{th}}$ dimension (call this step $\alpha$) if the $(k+i)^{\text{th}}$ bit of its destination $\mathcal{H}(y)$ is the same as that of its current node, as FSRA's *Bridging-Phase* does. Each node still has $O(\log N)$ pieces after $\alpha$.[4] Let $w(i) \stackrel{\text{def}}{=} (\mathcal{H}(y)[k : n-1])^{(i)}$. For the rest of Phase 2, apply $R'$ to route $P_x(i)$ to $bits_k(i) \circ w(i) \in V(C_{n-k}(i))$. $P_x$'s pieces take node-disjoint paths here since they are on disjoint subcubes. Phase 2 runs in $O(\log N)$ time w.h.p.

Now, each node $x \in V(C_{n-k}(i))$ has $2^k$ **buckets** with the $l^{\text{th}}$ bucket holding pieces destined to node $v_x(l)^{(l)}$. Since each node is a target of $O(\log N/\log\log N)$ packets w.h.p. due to universal hashing, $x$ at the end of Phase 2 contains $O(\log N/\log\log N)$ pieces to $v_x(l)^{(l)}$ for each $0 \le l < 2^k$ w.h.p; hence, each bucket has $O(\log N/\log\log N)$ pieces w.h.p. [213, p. 567]. Now, bundle the first piece from each bucket to form "packet" $P_x^1$, the second piece from each bucket to form $P_x^2$, etc. Each $x$ ends up with $O(\log N/\log\log N)$ "packets" w.h.p. Now, apply FSRA's Subphases 2.2–2.3 to deliver each "packet" in $k+1$ time (epochs), giving a run-time of $O((k+1)\log N/\log\log N) = O(\log N)$. This bound can be improved to $O(\log N/\log\log N)$ if pipelining is used. Again, any packet's pieces take node-disjoint paths in this phase.

The simulation is fault-tolerant. In each of the three phases, any packet's pieces take node-disjoint paths. Consequently, if we use IDA with more redundancy, then, various constants suitably adjusted, the same analysis as in Subsection 5.4.4 can show

---

[4]Take any node $x$ and assume $x$ is in the subcube $C_{n-k}(j)$. *Only* the neighbor across the $(k+j)^{\text{th}}$ dimension could have sent pieces to $x$ at $\alpha$ (note that pieces in the subcube $C_{n-k}(j)$ are sent *via* the $(k+j)^{\text{th}}$ dimension at $\alpha$). As each node totally has $O(\log N)$ pieces before $\alpha$, node $x$ still has $O(\log N)$ pieces after it.

that FSRA, hence our simulation scheme as well, tolerates $O(N)$ random link failures w.h.p. (instead of just with probability $1 - O(1/N)$).

Finally, we show that each queue is of constant size. As each queue in Ranade's algorithm needs to store only a constant number of packets *during* the simulation process, we need to worry only about the end of Phase 2 and Phase 3. Fortunately, we can show that each node has only $O(\log N)$ pieces at the end of Phase 2. Ranade's algorithm uses $O(\log N)$-wise independent hash functions [213]. Now, $x$ at the end of Phase 2 contains pieces to $\Theta(\log N)$ nodes: $v_x(l)^{(l)}$ for each $0 \le l < 2^k$. So $x$ has as many pieces as there are PRAM variables that are hashed to the above-mentioned set of $\Theta(\log N)$ nodes. That answer is $O(\log N)$ w.h.p. by using a result of Kruskal, Rudolph, and Snir [181, Corollary 4.20].

Hence, we have proved the following theorem.

**Theorem 6.17** *An $N$-node hypercube with combining can simulate an $(N, M)$-CRCW PRAM with a slowdown of $O(\log N)$ with probability tending to one as $N$ or the number of PRAM instructions approaches infinity. This simulation can tolerate $O(N)$ random link failures and uses only constant queue size.*

# Chapter 7

# Asynchronism and Sensitivity

The Lacedæmonians [advanced] slowly and to the music of
many flute-players [...], meant to make them advance evenly,
stepping in time, without breaking their order, as large
armies are apt to do in the moment of engaging.

—Thucydides

The routing algorithms in Chapter 5 can be converted into efficient asynchronous algorithms by replacing the global clock with a synchronization scheme based on message passing. We also demonstrate that asynchronous FSRA has low sensitivity to variations in link and processor speeds.

## 7.1 Introduction

The assumption of synchronism often greatly simplifies the design of algorithms, be they sequential or parallel. Many computation models — for example, RAM ("Random Access Machine") [5] in the sequential setting and PRAM in the parallel setting — assume the existence of a global clock. But, this assumption will become less desirable as the number of processors increases. For one thing, a global clock introduces a single point of failure.[1] A global clock also restrains each processor's degree of autonomy and renders the machine unable to exploit differences in running speed [42, 192], limiting the overall speed to, so to speak, that of the "slowest" component instead of the "average" one, thus wasting cycles. Tight synchronization also limits the size of the parallel computer, since it takes time to distribute the clock-signal to the whole system [316].

Proceeding in epochs, our routing schemes in Chapter 5 assume synchronism. In fact, the very definition of ECS assumes a global clock to synchronize epochs. We show in this chapter that with synchronization done *via* message passing, ECSs can be made asynchronous without loss of efficiency and without global control. Much work has been done in this area; see, for example, [31, 32, 33].

Bertsekas and Tsitsiklis identify three approaches to synchronization: **global synchronization**, **local synchronization**, and **rollback** [56]. In the first approach, the next phase is started only after it is detected that *all* the packets of the previous phase have been sent and received. In the second approach, a processor can start the next phase once it knows all the expected packets have been received. The second approach is generally superior to the first in that less time is wasted. Moreover, if each processor knows when it has received all the packets it is supposed to receive, the second approach can drastically cut down the number of synchronization messages. We adopt the second approach in this chapter. The third approach is used mainly in concurrency control of distributed databases.

With asynchronism, the dependence of run-time on link and processor speeds becomes subtle. Whereas the run-time should be measured by the *slowest* link or processor in the synchronous case, since each epoch has to wait until the slowest component completes its job, the effect of component speed on the run-time of asynchronous algorithms is not so straightforward. For example, both the algorithm and

---

[1]There are two practical approaches to this problem: making the global clock fault-tolerant and abolishing the global clock. In the FTMP ("Fault-Tolerant Multiprocessor") computer [158], common fault-tolerant clocking is achieved by hardware redundancy. In the SIFT ("Software Implemented Fault Tolerance") computer [377], in contrast, there is no common clock; instead, consensus about time is reached *via* periodical resynchronization.

the network topology can influence how sensitive the run-time is to variations in link and processor speeds. As the second focus of this chapter, we show that FSRA has low sensitivity in Section 7.4, after building up the framework for sensitivity analysis in Theorem 7.3.

## 7.2   Terminology and Definitions

Most of the terms in this section are adapted from [31, 33]. An asynchronous network is a store-and-forward direct network represented as a digraph $G(V, E)$. The local computations done in each node are assumed to take zero time without loss of generality. The packets sent over any link are received after finite but variable and unpredictable delay; in contrast, they are received within a fixed time in synchronous networks.

The **time complexity** of an asynchronous algorithm is the maximum number of time units from start to the completion of the algorithm, assuming that the inter-message delay and the propagation delay of a link are at most *one* time unit. The algorithm must work correctly without this assumption, introduced only for the purpose of performance evaluation. A **start node** will initiate the algorithm.

## 7.3   Asynchronous Routing Using Local Synchronization

Consider the following straightforward synchronization scheme, SA, to be inserted between epochs at each node; see Figure 7.1 for illustration.

> After all its packets that demand transmission in epoch $j$ have been sent, node $i$ sends "epoch $j$ finished"[2] to those neighbors *that may send packets to it in epoch $j + 1$* and wait. Node $i$ enters epoch $j + 1$ after it has received the same messages from all its neighbors *that are possible destinations of its packets in the next epoch, $j + 1$*.

Note that SA without the italicized parts is the well-known **acknowledgment synchronizer** [31, 126]. A **synchronizer** is a communication protocol that enables synchronous algorithms to run on asynchronous networks without modifications [32]. Such systems are called **self-timed** in VLSI [119]. In SA *local* pulses are generated at each processor such that pulse $p$ is generated by a processor only after it received

---

[2]A 1-bit message "the current epoch finished" suffices if each node keeps a counter and adds one to it each time the next epoch is started.

all the messages of the algorithm sent to it by its neighbors during their pulse $p - 1$ [270]. Clearly, SA is a synchronizer. We also note that, from each individual node's standpoint, the SA-synchronized system behaves like the original synchronous one, which can be seen by treating synchronization messages as if they were pulses from the original global clock.

Observe that no node $i$ waits forever for an "epoch $j$ finished" message from another node $k$. This is because, by the italicized sentences in SA, we know that if node $i$ *may* send a packet to node $k$, then node $k$ will send such a message to node $j$.

Messages sent by SA will be called **synchronization messages**. The italicized parts in SA are intended to minimize the number of synchronization messages. The scheme would still work correctly without them, but each node would then have to generate $d$ synchronization messages between epochs, where $d$ is the out-degree of the node. That number may be reduced if each node sends synchronization messages only to those nodes that are *senders* to it in the next epoch, telling them it is ready to receive, as is done in SA. Take SRA as an example. Since only one dimension is used in each epoch, only one (instead of $\log N$) synchronization message is sent between epochs by each node.

We assume one of the nodes also acts as the start node $s$ and broadcasts a wake-up message through **flooding** to all the other nodes. During the process, any node which is woken up by such messages sends the wake-up messages to all its neighbors which it does not receive the wake-up message from. A woken node starts epoch 0. Broadcasting by flooding is more fault-tolerant than that by using spanning trees, which, however, requires less packets. Such broadcasting will be completed in $d$ time, where $d$ is the diameter of the network. The main result of this section follows.

**Theorem 7.1** *An ECS can run asynchronously in at most $d + 3t$ time with buffer size $2c$ if it originally uses buffers of size $c$ and finishes in $t$ epochs, where $d$ is the diameter of the network and the buffer size is measured as the number of packets.*

**Proof:** We will prove this theorem using SA. In SA, when a node $x$ sends "epoch $j$ finished" messages to (some of) its neighbors, it might make some of them, say $y$, enter epoch $j + 1$ if $x$ is $y$'s last neighbor to finish epoch $j$. Furthermore, by the specification of SA, it is clear that prior to $x$'s doing so, none of $x$'s neighbors that will send packets to it in epoch $j + 1$ could enter epoch $j + 1$. Node $x$ may now be receiving packets of epoch $j + 1$ from $y$ and packets of epoch $j$ from other neighbors that have not finished epoch $j$. In summary, each node in epoch $j$ can receive packets of, and only of, epochs $j$ and $j + 1$. Hence, doubling the buffer size is enough for SA to prevent overflow not present in the execution of the original synchronous ECS.

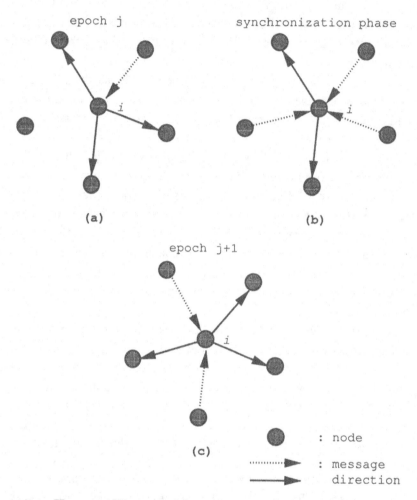

Figure 7.1: HOW SA WORKS. (a) In epoch $j$ node $i$ sends packets to its neighbors. (b) After finishing this, it sends synchronization messages to those neighbors that may send packets to it in the next epoch, and its neighbors do likewise. (c) After receiving synchronization messages from those neighbors that it will send packets *to* in the next epoch, it enters epoch $j + 1$ and starts sending packets (the dotted lines indicate same actions taken by $i$'s neighbors).

As for the run-time, consider epoch $i$ and the last node $x$ to enter epoch $i$. After at most unit time, node $x$ will complete sending its packets to its neighbors. After another unit time, node $x$ will send out the "epoch $i$ finished" messages. After still another unit time, it will have received all the needed synchronization messages since it is the *last* node to enter epoch $i$. As the last node enters epoch 0 at time $d$, the run-time is at most $d + 3t$ by induction on the last node to enter each epoch. Q.E.D.

The above theorem shows that both FSRA and RABN can run asynchronously with time complexity $n + 3(2n+1) = 7n+3$ on $C_n$ and $N_{d,n}$, respectively. Hence, neither the run-time nor the buffer size, only doubled, is much compromised.

Note that the above theorem still holds under fault models as long as there is a diagnostic mechanism for each node to know which of its incident links have failed. Some modifications of SA are needed then: nodes now wait only for neighboring nodes linked by a non-faulty link to reply. The wake-up process, however, can potentially take a long time to complete; in fact, in the worst case, it can take $N - 1$ steps to complete when all the links not on a Hamiltonian path are lost. A **Hamiltonian path** is a path that visits each node exactly once. But as the run-time of the wake-up process is equal to the diameter $d'$ of the hypercube network with faulty edges removed, the number of faulty links necessary to make $d'$ larger than $\log N$ is obviously at least $\log N - 1$, which happens with negligible probability if each link fails with a small probability.

We remark that there does exist a set of exactly $\log N - 1$ edges whose removal increases the diameter of the hypercube network by one. Consider the set $\mathcal{D} \overset{\text{def}}{=} \{(0,0//1), (0,0//2), \ldots, (0,0//(\log N - 1))\}$. If $\mathcal{D}$ is removed from the hypercube network, the distance from node $\overbrace{00 \cdots 0}^{\log N}$ to $\overbrace{01 \cdots 1}^{\log N}$ becomes $\log N + 1$ because any path between them must contain the link $(00 \cdots 0, 10 \cdots 0)$ *and* a path of length $\log N$ from $10 \cdots 0$ to $01 \cdots 1$. On the other hand, the distance between any two nodes $x$ and $y$ where $x \neq 00 \cdots 0$ or $y \neq 01 \cdots 1$ is still at most $\log N$ since the shortest path can be chosen in such a way as to either (i) avoid going through node $00 \cdots 0$ when $x \neq 00 \cdots 0$, thus making the removal of $\mathcal{D}$ irrelevant, or (ii) traverse at most $\log N$ links when $x = 00 \cdots 0$ but $y \neq 01 \cdots 1$. Case (ii) holds because, if $y = 1y_1 \cdots y_{n-1}$, then there is a path of length $1 + \sum_{i=1}^{n-1} y_i \leq \log N$ from $00 \cdots 0$ to $y$, while if $y = 0y_1 \cdots y_{n-1}$, then we can go from $00 \cdots 0$ first to $10 \cdots 0$, then to $1y_1 \cdots y_{n-1}$, and finally to $0y_1 \cdots y_{n-1}$ with a total length at most $1 + \sum_{i=1}^{n-1} y_i + 1$. Now, $\sum_{i=1}^{n-1} y_i \leq \log N - 2$ because $y = 0y_1 \cdots y_{n-1} \neq 01 \cdots 1$ by assumption. The general issue on the minimum number of nodes or edges to be deleted to increase the diameter of a graph is investigated in [70].

# 7.4   Run-Time Sensitivity to Component Speeds

A processor can run more slowly due to a variety of reasons: it may be inherently slower or it may be slowed due to transient causes such as doing backup for failures. A link can be slower because, say, it is longer. Hence, clearly, links or processors should not be expected to run at the same speed all the time.

Fix $\Delta t > 0$ throughout this section. Define **link delay** to be the time needed to transmit a packet across a link. In the previous sections, for example, the link delay is assumed to be one for all the links. In general, however, all links may not have the same delay. Suppose an algorithm $\mathcal{R}$ sees its run-time increased by $\Delta T(l, \Delta t)$ after link $l$ has its link delay increased by $\Delta t$. Define the **link sensitivity** of $\mathcal{R}$ to be $S = \max_{l \in E} \Delta T(l, \Delta t)/\Delta t$. An algorithm is said to have low link sensitivity if $S$ is a constant (i.e., $S = O(1)$), independent of the size of the network.

Processor sensitivity is defined analogously. A processor is said to be slowed by an amount of $\Delta t$ if it needs $\Delta t$ extra time for each unit work. The **processor sensitivity** of an algorithm is $\mathcal{S}_p = \max_{p \in V} \Delta T(p, \Delta t)/\Delta t$, where $\Delta T(p, \Delta t)$ is the increase in run-time if processor $p$ is slowed by $\Delta t$. An algorithm has low processor sensitivity if $\mathcal{S}_p = O(1)$.

To see why low sensitivity is a desirable property for asynchronous algorithms, consider an algorithm with link sensitivity equal to $\log N$, where $N$ is the size of the network. Then there exists a link which can increase the run-time by an additive amount of $\Delta t \log N$ if its link delay is increased by $\Delta t$. This slowdown is undesirable not only because of its magnitude but also because of its dependence on the size of the network, making the computer less scalable; for example, the link sensitivity is increased by one each time the machine size is doubled.

Various scenarios can lead to high sensitivity. Suppose the link delay of link $L$ from processor $A$ to processor $B$ is increased by $\Delta t$. Now, if $B$ receives $r$ packets from $A$, the completion time of the whole communication scheme must be increased by $\Omega(r \, \Delta t)$. More generally, assume the total number of packets — synchronization messages or otherwise — sent during the computation is $M$ and the total number of links in the network is $K$. As there must be a link which is traversed by at least $M/K$ packets, low sensitivity is possible only if $M/K = O(1)$, that is, the number of packets is proportional to the number of links. One final scenario is when $A$ sends a packet to $B$ but that packet is delayed by $r$ other packets all of which cross the slowed link $L$, leading to a sensitivity value of at least $r \, \Delta t$.

## 7.4.1  A general theorem

Let $G(V, E)$ be the graph on which an ECS $\mathcal{R}$ is run for $r$ epochs, $0, \ldots, r - 1$. Assume that SA is used for local synchronization, that each node $i \in V$ starts sending messages at time $t_i$, and that each edge $(i, j) \in E$ has link delay $L(i, j)$. Define $T(i)$ to be the completion time at node $i$. Hence, $\mathcal{R}$'s run-time is $\max_{i \in V} T(i)$. We categorize messages into two types: ECS **messages** in the original ECS and **synchronization messages** issued by SA. Furthermore, assume, for simplicity in the initial analysis, that only synchronization messages exist. For the rest of this section, by the sensitivity of an ECS we mean that of an SA-synchronized ECS.

A graph representation in the style of [56, pp. 91–94] captures the essence of the problem. Fix $l \in V$. Construct a graph from scratch recursively as follows. Start with node $N(l, r)$. Add node $N(k, j)$ and an incident link of weight $L(k, i)$ to node $N(i, j + 1)$ if node $k$ sends a synchronization message to node $i$ in epoch $j$ (so, $(k, i) \in E$). This process is repeated until $j = 0$. Now add a link of weight zero *from* $N(i, j)$ *to* $N(i, j+1)$ for each $i \in V$ and $0 \le j < r$, signifying the time dependence that epoch $j + 1$ can start only *after* epoch $j$ at each node $i$; see Figure 7.2a. In the end, we have a directed acyclic graph in which there is a path from every node $N(\cdot, \cdot)$ in the graph to $N(l, r)$. Call such a graph $l$-**graph** and $N(i, j)$ a node of **level** $j$. Clearly, the $l$-graph is a graph with $N(l, r)$ as its root and looks like Figure 7.2b.

An $l$-**path from** $i_0 \in V$ is a weighted path from level 0 to level $r$ in the $l$-graph

$$(N(i_0, 0), N(i_1, 1), \ldots, N(i_r, r)), \text{ where } i_r = l,$$

such that *each* edge $(N(i_j, j), N(i_{j+1}, j + 1))$ on the $l$-graph appears in the $l$-path with the same weight. Thus if there are $b$ parallel lines from $N(i_j, j)$ to $N(i_{j+1}, j+1)$ on the $l$-graph, there would be $b$ parallel lines in the $l$-path as well, in which case we say $(i_j, i_{j+1}) \in E$ is **used by the $l$-path $b$ times**. An $l$-path, in short, is the induced graph of a path from a node of level 0 to a node of level $r$ on the $l$-graph; see Figure 7.2c for illustration. The **weight** of an $l$-path from $i_0$ is defined to be $t_{i_0}$ plus all the weights of its links.[3]

It is easy to understand the $l$-graph. There is a link $(N(u, i), N(v, i + 1))$ on it for $u \ne v$ if $u$ sends a synchronization message to $v$, meaning that $u$ has completed epoch $i$ and $v$ may send packets to $u$ in epoch $i+1$. Node $v$ enters epoch $i+1$ only after all such $u$ (and itself) have finished epoch $i$, as confirmed by the synchronization

---

[3]As we consider synchronization messages only for the time being, there are no parallel lines in either $l$-graphs or $l$-paths; that is, $l$-paths are *simple* paths. But, as we add ECS packets to the picture, as will be done soon, parallel lines may be created.

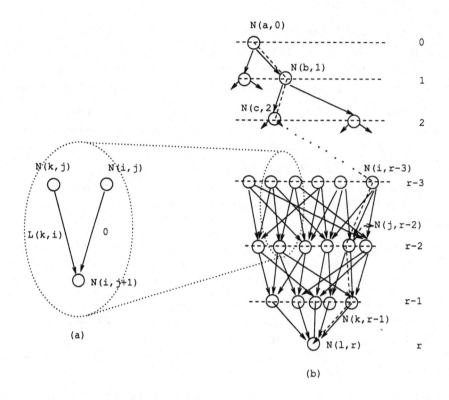

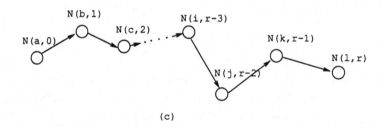

Figure 7.2: PROPERTIES OF THE *l*-GRAPH. (a) how the graph is constructed ($j = r-3$ here); (b) a completed *l*-graph; (c) an *l*-path from node *a* (note the correspondence with the dotted path in (b)). Weights are not shown in (b) and (c).

messages. An $l$-path is just a trace of the time dependence on the $l$-graph leading to node $l$'s completion. The following lemma can be easily proved by induction on the level of the $l$-graph.

**Lemma 7.2** ([56]) $T(l)$ *is equal to the weight of the heaviest $l$-path.*

Now, suppose $(u, v) \in E$ sees its link delay increased from $L(u, v)$ to $L(u, v) + \Delta t$. Consider $T'(l)$, the new completion time of node $l$. Suppose no $l$-paths use the slowed link $(u, v)$ more than $K$ times. Then $T'(i) \leq T(i) + K \Delta t$ since each $l$-path has its weight increased by at most $K \Delta t$. So, each node sees its completion time increased by no more than $K \Delta t$. The above inequality clearly holds in the more general case where more than one link is slowed by $\Delta t$ and no $l$-paths use the slowed links more than $K$ times in total. Hence the following observation is true:

(*) The link sensitivity of an ECS is at most $K$ if no $l$-graphs for $l \in V$ have an $l$-path that uses the slowed links more than $K$ times in total.

Figure 7.3 uses the above observation to analyze SRA's sensitivity.

Adding ECS packets does not complicate our general argument except that, now, between synchronization points at each node must be added the time to transmit ECS packets. Hence, in the construction of $l$-graphs, we now add a link of weight $L(k, i)$ from $N(k, j)$ to $N(i, j + 1)$ if node $k$ sends an ECS packet to node $i$ in epoch $j$. We can prove the following theorem by the same analysis leading to (*).

**Theorem 7.3** *The link sensitivity of an ECS is at most $K_1 + K_2$ if no $l$-graphs have an $l$-path that uses the slowed links more than $K_1$ and $K_2$ times in total, respectively for synchronization messages and ECSs.*

**Comment 7.4** Theorem 7.3 is general enough to cover the case where *processors* are slowed. Suppose processor $P$ is slowed by $\Delta t > 0$. Then, as far as the run-time of ECS is concerned, this situation is the same as the one where all the links incident *from* $P$ see their link delay increased by $\Delta t$, a situation obviously covered by the above theorem. Hence, the problem of processor sensitivity can be reduced to that of link sensitivity.

## 7.4.2 Sensitivity analysis of FSRA

Theorem 7.3 can be employed to show that FSRA has low sensitivity. Consider a link in the hypercube network. It may be used once in Phase 1, at most once in *Bridging-Phase*, and once in Phase 2. Hence, this link is used at most three times for ECSs. Similarly, it is used three times for SA's synchronization messages.

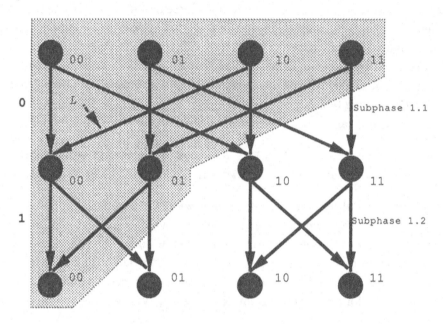

Figure 7.3: SENSITIVITY OF SRA ON $C_2$. Here we show all the time dependency in SRA's Phase 1 with all the $l$-graphs embedded in it (weights are not included). For example, those nodes enclosed by the dotted area induce the 00-graph. To see this, just label each node $x$ on level $i$ as $N(x, i)$. To see why SRA has low sensitivity, assume link $L$ is slowed by $\Delta t$. Then the completion time of node 00 is only slowed by $\Delta t$ since $L$ is used only once — each $L$ appears exactly once in the $l$-graph above. The above argument can be easily extended to include Phase 2 and holds for the completion time of any node given that any link or node is slowed. The same argument holds for both ECS packets and synchronization messages. Hence, SRA's link sensitivity is four.

**Corollary 7.5** *The link sensitivity of* FSRA *is at most* 6.

To derive FSRA's processor sensitivity, assume processor $x$ is slowed by $\Delta t$. Equivalently, by Comment 7.4, assume all the $n = \log N$ links incident from $x$ are slowed by $\Delta t$. Let

$$\mathcal{D} = \{\, (x, x/\!/0), (x, x/\!/1), \ldots, (x, x/\!/(n-1)) \,\}$$

and consider any $l$-path with $l \in V$. For ECS packets, this $l$-path uses at most one link in $\mathcal{D}$ in each of Phases 1 and 2, since each dimension is traversed at most once in each phase. This $l$-path also uses at most one link in $\mathcal{D}$ in *Bridging-Phase*, since only one link is traversed there. Similarly, each link is used once in each of FSRA's three phases for synchronization messages. We summarize our findings in the next corollary.

**Corollary 7.6** *The processor sensitivity of* FSRA *is at most* 6.

Theorem 7.3 can also be used to analyze the sensitivity value when more than one link or node is slowed. For example, the argument in Figure 7.3 can show that SRA's run-time would be increased by $4\,\Delta t$ — the sensitivity value hence is 4 — if all the links of dimension, say, 0 are slowed by $\Delta t$. This shows that the sensitivity value may remain constant as long as the slowed links are suitably distributed.

# 7.5   Communication Complexity and Sensitivity

We have shown that FSRA can run efficiently on asynchronous hypercube networks with low sensitivity. In fact, FSRA also has low **communication complexity**, defined as the number of synchronization messages used by SA: in total, $2^k < \log N$ synchronization messages are sent by each node in each of Subphase 1.1, *Bridging-Phase*, and Subphase 2.3, and one synchronization message is sent in each epoch of Subphases 1.2–1.3 and 2.1–2.2. The communication complexity is hence less than $5 N \log N$. Small communication complexity is necessary to achieve small sensitivity.

Suppose, instead of SA, we use a local synchronization scheme where each processor sends synchronization messages to *all* its neighbors, as the standard acknowledgment synchronizer does. Then, the node from which the slowed link is incident from would need $\Omega(\Delta t)$ extra time to transmit a message; hence the total increase in run-time would be $\Omega(\Delta t \log N)$ because FSRA runs in $2 \log N + 1$ epochs, suggesting a sensitivity of $\Omega(\log N)$. Of course, SA becomes the acknowledgment synchronizer, and thus has the same complexity, when every node is a potential packet receiver of every one of its neighbors; SA would have the same high sensitivity value as the acknowledgment synchronizer when applied to some communication schemes other than FSRA.

There exists a more efficient synchronizer due to Peleg and Ullman [270] that runs in $O(1)$ time and uses $\Theta(N)$ synchronization messages, as SA does when applied to SRA and FSRA (note that we are referring to each epoch of SA here, not SA-synchronized FSRA and SRA). However, its constant term is larger. Worse, it has high sensitivity when used with FSRA and SRA: since only $\Theta(N)$ edges are used for synchronization purposes and FSRA and SRA each runs in $\Theta(\log N)$ epochs, the sensitivity is $\Omega(\log N)$.

We remark that Peleg and Ullman's synchronizer has sensitivity value $\Omega(\log^{1/3} N)$ when used with FSRA and SRA even if we use randomness. A subgraph $G(V, E')$ is a **$t$-spanner** of a network $G(V, E)$ if the distance between $u$ and $v$ in $G(V, E')$ is at most $t$ for every $(u, v) \in E$ [270]. The following lemma is proved using results from coding theory (recall that $n = \log N$).

**Fact 7.7** ([270, Corollary 5.4]) *The $n$-cube $C_n$ has a 3-spanner with fewer than $7 \cdot 2^n$ edges for every $n \geq 0$.*

In Peleg and Ullman's synchronizer, synchronization messages are sent on the 3-spanner constructed in the above fact. Since a node has at most $d^t$ nodes that are at distance at most $t$ from it, where $d$ is the degree of the graph, Fact 7.7 implies each node in the 3-spanner has degree $\Omega(n^{1/3})$. Hence, as long as we do not have any prior knowledge about which link is slowed, the slowed link would be used on the spanner with probability $\Omega(n^{1/3}/n)$. Hence, the average link sensitivity of both SRA and FSRA would be $\Omega(n \, n^{-2/3}) = \Omega(n^{1/3})$. Of course, if we know which link is slowed, we can transform the $t$-spanner in such a way as to avoid it completely. In conclusion, as far as FSRA is concerned, SA seems to be the most efficient synchronizer.

# Chapter 8

# On-Line Maintenance

> The living clockwork of the State must be repaired
>
> while it is in motion, and here it is a case of
>
> changing the wheels as they revolve.
>
> —Friedrich Schiller

We demonstrate in this chapter that, if FSRA is used, a constant fraction of the wires in the hypercube network can be disabled simultaneously without disrupting the ongoing computation or degrading the routing performance. This general result can lead to efficient on-line maintenance procedures. This seems to be the first time that the important issue of on-line maintenance is addressed analytically.

## 8.1   Introduction

The fact that hardware deteriorates and the demand that machine be more available to the user make the property of on-line maintenance without performance penalty a desirable design goal. For example, in the Tandem/16 computer system [173], modular design allows some components to be replaced on-line. Periodic maintenance of the hardware is also key to ensuring consistent system performance; without it, one cannot safely say a particular component retains roughly the same failure rate at different times.

In this chapter we address the issue of on-line wire maintenance on the hypercube network with FSRA as the routing algorithm. It is shown that the set of edges can be partitioned into a constant number, 352, of disjoint edge sets of roughly equal sizes such that the probability of unsuccessful routing is exponentially small if any edge set in the proposed partition is disabled (Theorem 8.3). That implies little performance penalty as re-routing is extremely unlikely. The partition is also easily and locally computable.

The above result suggests several on-line maintenance procedures, two of which are given below. All nodes can disable and test their incident links in the *same* edge set, say once per minute, each edge set at a time, and report, disconnect, or replace unsatisfactory ones. The whole procedure can be completed in 352 minutes, *independent* of the size of the hypercube network. This procedure can then be either immediately repeated or done at longer intervals, depending on the reliability requirement. As a second example, maintenance engineers can replace all wires with new ones periodically by doing so to each edge set at a time. After a constant 352 steps the process is completed. All these can be done without disrupting the ongoing computation, stopping the machine, or degrading the routing performance, according to our result.

The second maintenance procedure also has implications for packaging. Wires in the same edge set should, if possible, be physically bundled together or put on the same board to facilitate the replacement process. The whole edge set can then be disconnected in one act. The simple alternative of replacing one wire at a time may become cumbersome as the number of wires grows larger.

## 8.2   On-Line Wire Maintenance on Hypercubes with FSRA

We are interested in the problem of partitioning the edges of the hypercube network into *large* and *disjoint* sets so that the disabling of all edges in any such set still keeps small the probability of unsuccessful routing. Specifically, we show in Theorem 8.3 that, under FSRA, the set of edges can be partitioned into 352 disjoint edge sets of roughly equal sizes such that the probability of successful routing is at least $1 - N^{-0.6 \log N}$ if any edge set in the proposed partition is disabled. Throughout this chapter $N$ denotes the size of the network.

The practical implication of the existence of such a partition is that a hypercube-based parallel computer can have its wires disabled in a systematic manner, one edge set at a time, without ever stopping the machine and with little routing performance penalty, hence bringing minimum inconvenience to the user. We insist that the partition consist of large sets so that the number of maintenance cycles, which is equal to the number of edges sets in the partition, is small. That the number of edge sets is a constant number, 352, independent of the size of the hypercube network, means the maintenance procedure can be completed in a constant number of cycles. Since no wires should be replaced twice in one maintenance cycle, node-disjointness is required.

Although FSRA tolerates random link failures, and the disabled wires can be considered faulty, they are not random faults. Instead, it is through a careful partition of the edges, with the routing algorithm in mind, that the sharp probabilistic bound is achieved.

## 8.2.1 Definitions and outline of approach

Let $S$ be a set of edges. A routing scheme **tolerates the disabling of $S$ with probability** $p$ if the probability of successful routing is $p$ when edges in $S$ are disabled and no other links fail. A set of subsets of $E(C_n)$, $\{S_i\}_i$, is a **partition** if any two of the sets are disjoint and $\bigcup_i S_i = E(C_n)$. Finally, a partition $\{S_i\}_i$ is a $p$-**complete disablement set** for a routing scheme $\mathcal{R}$ if $\mathcal{R}$ tolerates the disabling of each $S_i$ with probability at least $p$.

Our goal is to find a partition which is a $p$-complete disablement set for FSRA, where $p = 1 - N^{-cn}$ for some $c > 0$, such that each edge set in the partition is of size $\Theta(n N)$.

Here is an outline of our approach. Call a piece $P$ **safe** for an edge set $S$ under routing scheme $\mathcal{R}$ if $\mathcal{R}$ never chooses a path that contains edges in $S$ for $P$. We will define a partition $\mathcal{P}$ such that each packet has at least $(3/8)(n-k)$ safe pieces for any edge set in that partition under FSRA. Hence, if we use $IDA(n-k, (n-k)/4)$, then, for the routing to be unsuccessful, there must exist a packet which loses at least $(\frac{3}{8} - \frac{1}{4})(n-k) = (n-k)/8 = \Theta(n)$ of its pieces due to overflow. Corollary 5.9 easily puts its probability, which is at most $B((n-k)/8, n-k, q)$, where $q = N^{-\Theta(1)}$ is the probability that a subcube encounters overflow, to be $N^{-cn}$ for some constant

$c > 0$.

## 8.2.2  Partition $\mathcal{P}$

Assume $N = 2^n$, where $n = k + 2^k$ and $k > 2$. Our results need only nominal modifications if $n$ is not of this form.

We need two more definitions. Let $dim(i)$ denote the set of edges of dimension $i$, that is

$$dim(i) = \{ (x, x/\!/i) \mid x \in V(C_n) \}.$$

Let $bits_3(i)$ be the 3-bit representation of the integer $i$ for $0 \le i < 8$, that is

$$bits_3(i) = i_0 \, i_1 \, i_2, \qquad \text{where } i = \sum_{j=0}^{2} i_j \, 2^j.$$

We next divide the nodes of the hypercube network into 11 subsets. Let $0 \le l < 11$. Define

$$nodes(l) = \left\{ x \in V(C_n) \mid \sum_{i=k}^{n-1} x_i \, 2^{i-k} \equiv l \bmod 11 \right\}.$$

In other words, $x = x_0 \cdots x_{n-1} \in nodes(l)$ if the value of $x[k : n-1]$ is $l$ modulo 11. Now, for $0 \le i < 8$ and $0 \le l < 11$, let

$$L_{i,l} = \{ (x, y) \in E(C_n) \mid x \in nodes(l) \text{ and } x_0 x_1 x_2 = bits_3(i) \}.$$

So, an edge $(x, y)$ is in $L_{i,l}$ if the value of $x$'s last $n - k$ bits is $l$ modulo 11 and $x$'s first three bits are the binary representation of $i$. Note that an edge's membership in $L_{i,l}$ is independent of the node it is incident *to*.

Clearly, $L_{i,l} \cap L_{i',l'} = \emptyset$ if $i \ne i'$ or $l \ne l'$ because edges from $L_{i,l}$ and $L_{i',l'}$ are then incident *from* nodes distinct in the first three or the last $n - k$ bits, respectively. Furthermore, $\bigcup_{i,l} L_{i,l} = E(C_n)$ since any edge $(x, y)$ is in $L_{i,l}$ where $bits_3(i) = x_0 \, x_1 \, x_2$ and $\sum_{i=k}^{n-1} x_i \, 2^{i-k} \equiv l \bmod 11$. Hence, $\{ L_{i,l} \}_{i,l}$ is a partition.

One more refinement of $L_{i,l}$ is needed to obtain $\mathcal{P}$. For $0 \le i < 8$, $0 \le l < 11$, and $0 \le t < 4$, we define

$$E(i, l, t) \overset{\text{def}}{=} L_{i,l} \cap \left( \bigcup_{\substack{\lfloor k\,t/4 \rfloor \le r < \lfloor k\,(t+1)/4 \rfloor \\ k+2^{k-2} \, t \le r < k + 2^{k-2} \, (t+1)}} dim(r) \right).$$

The above lengthy formula simply says $E(i, l, t)$ contains those edges in $L_{i,l}$ that are of the following at least $\lfloor n/4 \rfloor$ dimensions:

$$\lfloor k\,t/4 \rfloor, \ldots, \lfloor k\,(t+1)/4 \rfloor - 1, k + 2^{k-2}\,t, \ldots, k + 2^{k-2}\,(t+1) - 1,$$

that is, the $(t+1)^{\text{th}}$ quarter of the first $k$ dimensions and the $(t+1)^{\text{th}}$ quarter of the remaining $n-k$ dimensions. Note that each node can easily and locally compute which of its incident links are in a given $E(i, l, t)$.

Observe that each $E(i, l, t)$ contains a constant fraction (about $1/4$) of the incident links of a constant fraction (about $1/(11 \cdot 8)$) of the nodes. More precisely, since $|L_{i,l}| \geq 2^{k-3} \lfloor 2^{n-k}/11 \rfloor$, we have

$$|E(i, l, t)| \geq \lfloor n/4 \rfloor \, 2^{k-3} \lfloor 2^{n-k}/11 \rfloor \approx n\,N/352.$$

It is easy to see that $E(i, l, t) \cap E(i', l', t') = \emptyset$ if $i \neq i'$, $j \neq j'$, or $t \neq t'$ and that $\bigcup_{i,l,t} E(i, l, t) = \bigcup_{i,l} L_{i,l} = E(C_n)$. Hence, $\mathcal{P} \stackrel{\text{def}}{=} \{\, E(i, l, t) \,\}_{i,l,t}$ is a partition.

## 8.2.3  Analysis of partition $\mathcal{P}$

Without loss of generality, assume edges in $E(7, 0, 0)$ are disabled and no other links fail. Hence, the dimensions of the disabled edges form the set

$$\mathcal{D} = \{\, 0, 1, \ldots, \lfloor k/4 \rfloor - 1, \, k, \, k+1, \ldots, k + 2^{k-2} - 1 \,\}.$$

We will eliminate unsafe pieces for each subphase until only safe ones remain. Since some unsafe pieces may not actually be lost, we are very conservative in calculating the final probability of successful routing. It will also become clear in the proof that, with $E(7, 0, 0)$, we are eliminating as many unsafe pieces as possible.

Consider $P_x$'s $2^k$ pieces: $P_x(0), \ldots, P_x(2^k - 1)$. In Subphases 1.1 and 2.3, only $P_x(0), \ldots, P_x(2^{k-2} - 1)$ are lost, hence unsafe, since only they travel *via* dimensions in $\mathcal{D}$ (the dimensions are $k, k+1, \ldots, k + 2^{k-2} - 1$). There are $2^{k-2}$ of them.

Now consider Subphases 1.3–2.1. Observe that only edges that are incident from nodes with $bits_3(7) = 111$ as their first three bits may be disabled. Consequently, any $P_x(i)$ with $i_0 i_1 i_2 \neq 111$ is safe here, since it travels within the subcube $C_{n-k}(i)$ where edges are incident from nodes with $i_0\,i_1\,i_2 \neq 111$ as their first three bits. So, at most $2^{k-3}$ pieces are unsafe here; they are $P_x(2^k - 2^{k-3}), \ldots, P_x(2^k - 1)$.

After the above two eliminations, we are left with the following $\beta = 2^k - 2^{k-2} - 2^{k-3} = 5 \cdot 2^{k-3}$ pieces:

$$P_x(2^{k-2}), \, P_x(2^{k-2} + 1), \ldots, P_x(2^k - 2^{k-3} - 1).$$

At this moment, we note that the particular choice of $E(7,0,0)$ affects only *which* pieces are safe, and this particular $E(7,0,0)$ gives a lower bound of their number. Finally, let us consider Subphases 1.2 and 2.2. First, a definition.

**Definition 8.1** *Let* $x \in nodes(a)$ *for* $0 \le a < 11$. *Define*

$$\Delta(x, i) = \begin{cases} a - 2^i \bmod 11 & \text{if } x_{k+i} = 1 \\ a + 2^i \bmod 11 & \text{if } x_{k+i} = 0 \end{cases}$$

The key point here is that $P_x(i) \in nodes(\Delta(x, i))$ at the end of Subphase 1.1 since dimension $k + i$ is traversed in Subphase 1.1. Define a vector of $\beta$ elements for $x \in nodes(a)$ as

$$\begin{aligned} \vec{\alpha}(x) &= (\Delta(x, 2^{k-2}), \Delta(x, 2^{k-2} + 1), \ldots, \Delta(x, 2^k - 2^{k-3} - 1)) \\ &= \left( a \pm 2^{2^{k-2}} \bmod 11, \, a \pm 2^{2^{k-2}+1} \bmod 11, \ldots, a \pm 2^{2^k - 2^{k-3} - 1} \bmod 11 \right). \end{aligned}$$

Observe that since $P_x(2^{k-2} + i) \in nodes(\Delta(x, 2^{k-2} + i))$ at the end of Subphase 1.1, $P_x(2^{k-2} + i) \in nodes(0)$ at the beginning of Subphase 1.2 only if $\vec{\alpha}(x)$'s $i^{\text{th}}$ component, $\vec{\alpha}_i(x)$, is zero.

We now consider the positions in $\vec{\alpha}(x)$ where 0 might occur. Let $j$ be the first position in $\vec{\alpha}(x)$ such that $\vec{\alpha}_j(x) = 0$ and $m > 0$. Note that $2^m \equiv 1 \bmod 11$ if and only if $10 \mid m$, and $-2^m \equiv 1 \bmod 11$ if and only if $10 \mid (m-5)$. Hence, 0 can appear only in positions $j + 5, j + 10, j + 15, \ldots$ in $\vec{\alpha}(x)$. Since $P_x(2^{k-2} + i) \in nodes(0)$ at the beginning of Subphase 1.2 only if $\vec{\alpha}_i(x) = 0$, at most $1/5$ of the $\beta$ $P_x(i)$'s are in $nodes(0)$ at the beginning of Subphase 1.2. Similarly, at most $1/5$ of the $\beta$ $P_x(i)$'s are in $nodes(0)$ at the end of Subphase 2.2. The rest of the $P_x(i)$'s are safe in Subphases 1.2 and 2.2 since all disabled edges are incident from nodes in $nodes(0)$ and these two subphases affect only the first $k$ bits, leaving every $P_x(i)$'s membership in the *nodes* set unchanged. We conclude that at least $(1 - \frac{2}{5})\beta = 3 \cdot 2^{k-3}$ pieces are safe.

**Lemma 8.2** *For any edge set in* $\mathcal{P}$, *each packet has at least* $3(n - k)/8$ *safe pieces under* FSRA.

Let the routing scheme be FSRA employing $IDA(n - k, n - k/4)$ with each buffer capable of holding $5n$ pieces. Since the disabling of any edge set in $\mathcal{P}$ leaves at least $3(n - k)/8$ of any packet's pieces safe, a packet is not reconstructible only if more than $(\frac{3}{8} - \frac{1}{4})(n-k) = (n-k)/8$ of its pieces are lost due to buffer overflow. The same arguments as in Theorem 5.15 show that the probability of unsuccessful routing is then at most the probability that overflow occurs to more than $(n - k)/8$ subcubes, which in turn is at most $B((n - k)/8, n - k, q)$, where $q < 2N(e^4/5^5)^n = N^{-\Theta(1)}$

is the probability that a subcube has overflow (see page 66). Chernoff's bound puts this latter bound to be at most $N^{(-4.839+(5.349/n))(n-k)/8} \approx N^{-0.6n}$. Hence we have proved the following theorem.

**Theorem 8.3** $\mathcal{P}$ *is a* $(1 - N^{-0.6n})$-*complete disablement set for* FSRA.

**Example 8.4** For $k = 3$, the hypercube network has $2^{11}$ nodes and each edge set in $\mathcal{P}$ has at least 46 edges. The probability of unsuccessful routing if any edge set in $\mathcal{P}$ is disabled is at most $7.91 \cdot 10^{-12}$, a small number indeed.

We make one final observation. Lemma 8.2 holds for any IDA-based routing scheme that uses the subcube concept. To be precise, that lemma is satisfied by any three-phase IDA-based routing scheme that has its Phases 1 and 2 the same as FSRA's Subphases 1.1–1.2 and Subphases 2.2–2.3, respectively, and has each piece $P_x(i)$ in the subcube $C_{n-k}(i)$ during its Phase 2, as in FSRA's Subphases 1.3–2.1. The general conclusion of Theorem 8.3 can be easily seen to hold for this class of algorithms. One example is our universal simulationalgorithm in the Appendix of Chapter 6.

# Chapter 9

# A Fault-Tolerant Parallel Computer

Man has more than twice the power

that he needs to support himself

—Leonardo da Vinci

In this final chapter, we briefly review techniques and concepts in fault-tolerant computing. Then we sketch the design of a fault-tolerant parallel computer, HPC ("hypercube parallel computer"), based on the results and ideas from previous chapters.

130

# 9.1   Introduction

A fault-free computer, or any human artifact, has never been built, and will never be. No matter how reliable each component is, there is always possibility, however small, that it will go wrong. Statistical principles dictate that, other things being equal, this possibility increases as the number of components increases. Such an event, if not anticipated and safe-guarded against, will eventually make the computer malfunction and lead to anything from small annoyance and inconvenience to disaster.

Recently, the same enormous decrease in hardware cost which makes parallel computers economically feasible also makes fault tolerance more affordable [297]. In other words, the low cost of hardware makes possible both high degree of fault tolerance using redundancy and high performance. Indeed, most fault-tolerant computers today employ multiple processors; see [241, 254, 317] for good surveys.

It is in the light of these backgrounds that we take this extra step toward designing a hypercube parallel computer (HPC for short). In the HPC processors are grouped into logical **clusters** consisting of physically *close* processors, and each program execution is replicated at all members of a cluster. Clusters overlap, however. The concept of cluster — logical or physical — introduces a two-level, instead of flat, organization and can be found in, for example, the Cm$^*$ [344], Cedar [187], and FTPP ("Fault Tolerant Parallel Processor") [148] computers. The structure of the clusters is chosen so that essentially no changes are needed for FSRA to serve as HPC's communication scheme. In addition, the IDA-based FILTERING turns each cluster into a **region of fault containment**, without which any single fault will spread throughout the whole system sooner or later.

In Section 9.2 the rich field of fault-tolerant computing is concisely surveyed. Then, in Section 9.3, the HPC is sketched. We conclude this book by mentioning possible directions for further investigations in the last section.

# 9.2   Introductory Fault-Tolerant Computing

## 9.2.1   Techniques

As semiconductor technology advances, components get rather complicated and their fault behaviors equally so. Faults also take countless forms. For the C.mmp/Hydra, it was reported that about "two-thirds of the failures were directly attributable to hardware problems" [382]. With the AT&T 1ESS processor, in contrast, "software faults account for 50 percent of the downtime" [354]. The objective of fault-tolerant computing is to achieve satisfactory performance in the presence of faults [297].

Achieving fault tolerance requires redundancy, here broadly defined as anything that would not be needed if faults would never happen. Redundancy may be embodied in some combination of hardware, software, and time (to retry the erroneous operation) [354]. Three common redundancy schemes are: triplication and voting, duplication and comparison (with later identification of faulty module), and standby replacement [297].

An important concept in fault-tolerant computing is that of **coverage** [20, 77, 78], defined as the conditional probability that, given the existence of a fault, the system will recover properly. Coverage is a measure of the capability of a system to cope with faults. Coverage is also used informally to describe the classes of faults that a system can tolerate [254]. System reliability is shown by Bouricius, Carter, and Schneider in their original paper, which introduces the coverage concept, to be extremely sensitive to small variations in the coverage; in their own words, "[Coverage is] the single most important parameter in high-reliability system design." [78]. Coverage, however, is difficult to quantify.

Fault tolerance techniques can also be divided into three major groups (here we follow Elkind's exposition [112, 241]): **fault detection**, **static redundancy**, and **dynamic redundancy**. Fault detection actually gives warning only when faults occur without tolerating them. Static redundancy (also called **masking redundancy**), on the other hand, tolerates failures by masking them but gives no warning. Dynamic redundancy can change configuration dynamically in response to a fault.

Duplication, where the hardware is double that of the simplex system plus extra elements for comparison, is the simplest fault detection technique. Its time redundancy version performs the same operation twice on the same hardware and compares, thus reducing the hardware cost by half at the expense of doubling the execution time. Error-detecting codes are another example of fault detection techniques. Fault detection, by definition, does not improve reliability, defined as the probability that a system survives until a given time $t$.

The classic **Triple Modular Redundancy** (TMR) of von Neumann [375] is one example of static redundancy. TMR can be naturally extended to $N$**-Modular Redundancy** (NMR) with voting. The hardware voters, however, may become the single points of failure in such schemes. Voting can also be done in software. $N$**-version programming** [28, 29, 85], which uses different algorithms for each execution and votes, and error-correcting codes provide two more examples of static redundancy techniques.

Although static redundancy techniques can improve system reliability, they can only hide, but not heal, failures; hence, they conceal the fact that malfunction has happened and reduce the system's tolerance to future malfunctions [158]. For example, injured triads in TMR are not reconfigured back to a state where they can once again mask faults [158]. The ability to fault masking also deteriorates as more copies in NMR fail. These shortcomings of static redundancy are addressed by the next redundancy technique.

Dynamic redundancy generally involves three steps: fault detection, fault isolation, and finally recovery. Once faults are located, they can be contained to control damages. Rapid fault detection and good fault containment are important to the success of later fault recovery [354]. Sparing redundancy is one example of dynamic redundancy techniques. In it, spares are used to replace faulty components through reconfiguration [254]. Graceful degradation techniques, on the other hand, allow surviving hardware to take up the work of faulty and disconnected components [158]. Reconfiguration used in dynamic redundancy techniques prevents failures from affecting the system. Dynamic software redundancy is often employed together with dynamic hardware redundancy. In rollback and retry operation, the computation is retreated to a checkpoint, where the states are error-free and have been saved, and retried [354]. Rollback is generally reserved as the last resort [158].

The advantages of dynamic redundancy over static redundancy include [30]: longer life, greater isolation of catastrophic (non-independent) faults, survival of system until all spares of one type are exhausted, ability to eliminate errors which are caused by transient faults, etc. Hybrid redundancy that employs both masking (to minimize the expensive rollback and retry) and reconfiguration (to achieve high coverage and long life) is also popular [254, 297]. The classic example is TMR with a pool of spares. In comparison, although pure NMR can mask faults without the need for reconfiguration, its extra hardware reduces the long-term reliability of the system [254].

## 9.2.2  Samples

Many techniques of the previous subsection have been applied to real systems. In the Illiac IV computer system, a precursor in supercomputing, each of the 64 processing units is subject to automatic tests. A unit that fails one of the tests is replaced by a spare [325]. In the STAR ("Self-Testing And Repair") computer checkpoint and rollback is used [30]. Transient faults are corrected by retry, and permanent faults are eliminated by replacement. There is evidence that transient faults are more prevalent than permanent ones [241, p. 480].

Two major projects in fault-tolerant computing in the 70s are the FTMP [158] and the SIFT [377] computers. In both, processors are dynamically allocated to triads with multiple triads running concurrently. Any processor can be a member of any triad, and healthy processors may leave their injured triad to join the pool of spares. The number of triads depends on the number of non-faulty processors, and performance degrades gracefully as processors are used up [254, Chapter 3]. Both use TMR with spares, that is, hybrid redundancy. But they adopt different philosophy as to how fault tolerance is to be achieved: in the FTMP voting is done by hardware, while in the SIFT system by software.[1] Therefore, in the SIFT, the triad is defined by program, and each processor typically uses a majority vote on data from other processors executing the same task by message passing. The hardware approach is more efficient, but the software one is more flexible.

There have been many commercial fault-tolerant computers since the 70s. Detailed treatments of the field of fault-tolerant computing can be found in many excellent papers and books [133, 140, 165, 189, 241, 254, 326, 354, 356].

## 9.3   HPC: **Approach and Building Blocks**

It is true that parallel computer architecture is the most efficient and an increasingly economically feasible way to supply multiple fault tolerance and concurrent testing [158]. It is also true that the value of each PE to a parallel computer is proportionally small. However, each PE bears disproportionally large responsibility for guaranteeing correct execution [188], for a single fault not only invalidates its own execution but also affects others' *via* bad messages [377].

Several questions immediately arise if the results covered in the previous chapters are to be used in designing a parallel computer. Although FSRA is fault-tolerant, it only tolerates loss of messages due to link failures. Link failures of this kind are relatively easy to handle as long as their number lies within a reasonable range; at worst, we ask for re-routing. Node (such as processor, switching element, and memory module) failures are altogether different, as they make data unavailable, thus rendering re-routing no solution. Data can also be polluted by node and link failures.

There is also the issue of fault containment. A fault not contained within a well-defined region will propagate to pollute the whole system by supplying invalid data to otherwise innocent nodes [84], making the reliability of the whole system no better than that of its weakest processor. An efficient scheme for fault containment not only detects faults faster, thus making expensive rollback less likely, but also prevents the state saved at the checkpoint from being already polluted by a previous, undetected error [292]. It is desirable that each region of fault containment is composed of physically near processors to minimize the interprocessor communication time and

---

[1]We comment that the experience of the C.mmp/Hydra was claimed to support software-implemented reliability [382].

effects of link failures. Finally, messages used to ensure computational integrity should be *short*, to minimize the propagation delay and buffer space.

The preference for detecting and locating faults on-line suggests replication of program execution and voting. As the SIFT lets each iteration of a task be independently executed by a number of processors to produce results for later voting [377], so the HPC will require that each program be executed at physically near processors — by all members of a cluster, to be precise. Furthermore, incoming packets will be reconstructible at all members of a cluster so that replication of execution can go on. In short, each cluster will form a region of fault containment.

## 9.3.1 Cluster: fault containment and communication

The discussions to follow assume permutation routing, although the basic ideas are general and, for example, can be applied to the PRAM simulation schemes in Chapter 6. The non-destructive model is assumed to simplify the presentation.

Let $N = 2^n$, where $n = k + 2^k$. Below is the definition of cluster.

**Definition 9.1** *A* **cluster at** $x \in V(C_n)$ *is the node set*

$$\mathcal{C}(x) = \{\, y \in V(C_n) \mid y = x//i \quad \text{where} \quad k \leq i < n \,\}.$$

We recall the following abbreviation on page 63.

**Definition 9.2** *Let* $x \in V(C_n)$ *and* $0 \leq i < 2^k$. *Then,* $x^{(i)} \stackrel{\text{def}}{=} x//(k+i)$.

Hence, cluster $\mathcal{C}(x)$ can be equivalently defined as $\{\, x^{(i)} \mid 0 \leq i < 2^k \,\}$. Observe also that each cluster contains $n - k = 2^k$ nodes, each hypercube $C_n$ has $N = 2^n$ clusters, and each node $x$ participates in $2^k$ clusters: $\mathcal{C}\left(x^{(0)}\right)$, $\mathcal{C}\left(x^{(1)}\right)$, ..., $\mathcal{C}\left(x^{(2^k-1)}\right)$, i.e., those clusters at each of its neighbors across dimensions $k, k + 1, \ldots, n - 1$; see Figure 9.1.

Let $\mathcal{I}_x$ be the **instruction** originally designed to run at node $x$ to produce packet $P_x$, which needs to be routed to $\pi(x)$. A **program** is simply a sequence of instructions. In the HPC, $\mathcal{I}_x$ is executed at each node of $\mathcal{C}(x)$, that is, $x^{(i)}$ for $0 \leq i < 2^k$ (note that $x \notin \mathcal{C}(x)$). Or, to view it from another angle, node $x$ executes instructions $\mathcal{I}_{x^{(0)}}, \mathcal{I}_{x^{(1)}}, \ldots, \mathcal{I}_{x^{(2^k-1)}}$ and produces $P_{x^{(0)}}, P_{x^{(1)}}, \ldots, P_{x^{(2^k-1)}}$, respectively.[2] Members of each cluster $\mathcal{C}(x)$ then run FILTERING on $P_x$ to ensure that packets to be sent out are not polluted. That is, node $x$ runs FILTERING together with members of $\mathcal{C}\left(x^{(i)}\right)$ on $P_{x^{(i)}}$ for $0 \leq i < 2^k$.

---

[2]Even though $P_x$ may be unavailable or polluted, we preserve the notations to stress the connection with FSRA.

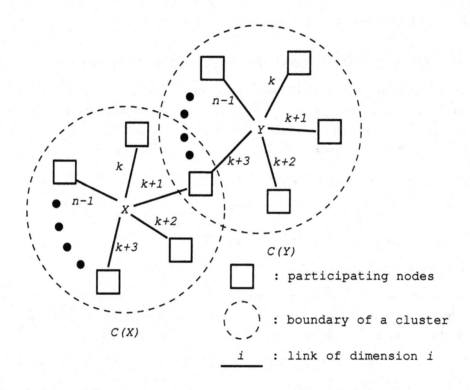

$\square$ : participating nodes

$\bigcirc$ : boundary of a cluster

$\underline{\quad i \quad}$ : link of dimension $i$

Figure 9.1: THE CLUSTERS. The set of nodes (indicated by squares) within each dotted circle forms a cluster. Two clusters, $\mathcal{C}(X)$ and $\mathcal{C}(Y)$, are shown. In the above example, node $A$ participates in both $\mathcal{C}(X)$ and $\mathcal{C}(Y)$, where $X = A^{(1)}$ and $Y = A^{(3)}$. $X$'s program is executed by, and its incoming packets reconstructed at, each member of $\mathcal{C}(X)$.

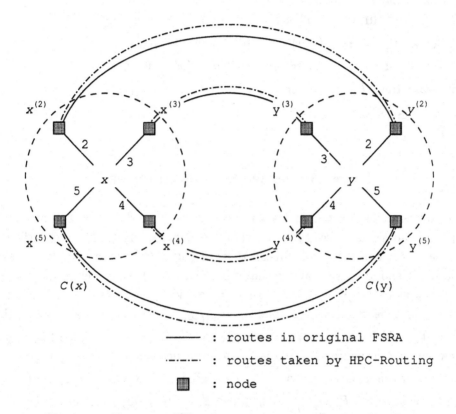

——— : routes in original FSRA

·—·—· : routes taken by HPC-Routing

▣ : node

Figure 9.2: HOW HPC-ROUTING WORKS. Assume $x$ is to send packet $P_x$ to $y = \pi(x)$ under FSRA. Now, under HPC-Routing, $x$'s computation is replicated at $x^{(i)}$ for $0 \le i < 2^k$, i.e., every member of $\mathcal{C}(x)$. Each $x^{(i)}$ produces packet $P_x$, runs IDA on it, and sends the $i^{\text{th}}$ piece, $P_x(i)$, to $y^{(i)}$.

**Algorithm HPC-Routing**
**For** $x \in V(C_n)$:
**Cobegin**

    1. **For** $0 \leq i < 2^k$:

        1.1. Simulate node $x^{(i)}$ and produces packet $P_{x^{(i)}}$;

        1.2. Apply $IDA(2^k, m_0)$ to $P_{x^{(i)}}$;

    2. Run FILTERING with all nodes in $C\left(x^{(i)}\right)$ on $P_{x^{(i)}}$ for $0 \leq i < 2^k$;

    3. Route $P_{x^{(i)}}(i)$ to $\pi\left(x^{(i)}\right)^{(i)}$ for $0 \leq i < 2^k$ in parallel;

    4. Broadcast $P_{\pi^{-1}\left(x^{(i)}\right)}(i)$ to every node in $C\left(x^{(i)}\right)$ for $0 \leq i < 2^k$;

    5. Reconstruct $P_{\pi^{-1}\left(x^{(i)}\right)}$ from $P_{\pi^{-1}\left(x^{(i)}\right)}(0), \ldots, P_{\pi^{-1}\left(x^{(i)}\right)}(2^k - 1)$

        for $0 \leq i < 2^k$;

**Coend.**

Figure 9.3: THE HPC-ROUTING ALGORITHM.

We now come to the communication part. Each $x^{(i)} \in C(x)$ uses IDA to split $P_x$ into pieces and sends piece $P_x(i)$ to $\pi(x)^{(i)} \in C(\pi(x))$. But, this is exactly what Subphases 1.2–2.2 of FSRA do! (Recall that, in FSRA, $P_x(i)$ is at $x^{(i)}$ at the end of Subphase 1.1 and at $\pi(x)^{(i)}$ at the end of Subphase 2.2.) That part of FSRA is used to route $P_x(i)$ to $\pi(x)^{(i)} \in C(\pi(x))$ for each $x \in V(C_n)$ and $0 \leq i < 2^k$. After the routing, each node $x$ receives $2^k$ pieces: $P_{\pi^{-1}\left(x^{(i)}\right)}(i)$ for $0 \leq i < 2^k$, that is, those pieces that would in the original program go to $x^{(i)}$ for $0 \leq i < 2^k$; see Figure 9.2.

Now, node $x$ broadcasts $P_{\pi^{-1}\left(x^{(i)}\right)}(i)$ to each node in $C\left(x^{(i)}\right)$ for $0 \leq i < 2^k$. Finally, each node $x$, after receiving $P_{\pi^{-1}\left(x^{(i)}\right)}(0), P_{\pi^{-1}\left(x^{(i)}\right)}(1), \ldots, P_{\pi^{-1}\left(x^{(i)}\right)}(2^k - 1)$, is able to reconstruct $P_{\pi^{-1}\left(x^{(i)}\right)}$ for $0 \leq i < 2^k$. After every node in the cluster at $x$ reconstructs $P_{\pi^{-1}(x)}$, the next round of replicated computation can continue. In a nutshell, **every member of $C(x)$ in HPC simulates node $x$ of the original program.** The complete scheme, HPC-**Routing**, appears in Figure 9.3 (there, we leave $m_0$ as an adjustable parameter).

We remark that, as we are now allowing the SEs and links to pollute messages, each node would have to employ IDA that can tolerate not only erasures but also errors, such as the Reed-Solomon code discussed in Subsection 2.5.3.

### 9.3.2 HPC-**Routing: analysis of run-time**

We analyze HPC-Routing's run-time with FSRA as the yardstick. There are two components: computation and communication. First, the computation part (Steps 1 and 5). Since each node simulates $x^{(i)}$ for $0 \leq i < 2^k$, the computation part has a uniform slowdown of $2^k$. We ignore the comparisons and summations used in FILTERING of Step 2, as they can only increase the run-time by at most a constant factor.

We now turn to the communication part. Step 3 runs in $2n - 1 = 2\left(2^k + k\right) - 1$ time since it is just FSRA less the first and last epochs. The communication pattern of Step 2 is this: each node has a piece, $P_{x^{(i)}}(i)$, to broadcast to all the other members of its participating cluster, $C\left(x^{(i)}\right)$, for $0 \leq i < 2^k$. If we copy $P_{x^{(i)}}(i)$ $2^k$ times and route its $j^{\text{th}}$ copy to $x^{(j)}$ and then to $\left(x^{(j)}\right)^{(i)}$, its destination, the routing takes 2 epochs without overflow because every node receives exactly $2^k$ pieces in each epoch. Since we have to repeat the above process for each $0 \leq i < 2^k$, Step 2 takes $2 \cdot 2^k$ time. Step 4 has the same communication pattern and, thus, the same time bound. HPC-Routing thus runs in $6\,2^k + 2\,k - 1 < 6 \log N$ time, roughly tripling the run-time of FSRA.

In summary, HPC-Routing has $n$-fold increase in computation tasks but, as FSRA, runs in $O(\log N)$ time. For cases where communication time overwhelms computation time, HPC-Routing can be almost as efficient as FSRA.

## 9.4 Conclusions

Building on results from the previous chapters, we have designed a fault-tolerant parallel computer, HPC. Prominent there is the use of clusters, which form regions of fault containment through IDA-based voting. Its communication is also shown to be efficient. Several directions are possible from here.

First, we have been assuming random and independent faults all along; in fact, the foundation of replication is built upon this assumption [297, 354], and it has been claimed that "[Few] if any existing designs can deal with the occurrence of a fault which affects more than one module simultaneously" [297]. In reality, Byzantine-type faults, though uncommon, have been observed [148]. In the most general fault model, where faulty components can behave maliciously, the reliability problem has been known as the **Byzantine Generals Problem** [197, 358].[3] Hence, one obvious

---

[3]It is known that, for agreement on data to be possible in that setting, the number of faulty nodes must be less than one-third of the total number of nodes [197, 269] and less than one-half of the connectivity of the underlying communication network [105].

direction is to extend the current design to handle efficiently more general faults, especially for critical applications.

Another issue is asynchronism. Tight synchronism has the disadvantage of having the common clock as a single point of failure, allowing less flexibility with speed variations, making simultaneous transient faults more likely, and increasing the correlation of failures [377]. Synchronizer SA introduced in Chapter 7 performs well and can be applied to the HPC to make it run asynchronously. But, the issue becomes complicated when faults are introduced. In fact, it has been shown that the participants must be synchronized to within a known skew of each other in order to agree on a value, as required by Steps 2 and 5 of HPC-Routing, even under the **fail-stop** failure mode [106]. The logical question to ask is: can SA be modified so that it remains efficient and is robust under less general but still realistic fault models?

The number of memory modules may be reduced if processors are asked to share memory modules, using a high-speed optical bus for example. In practice, the degree of replication may also be decreased to be less than $2^k = \Theta(\log N)$ in HPC-Routing.

Fault-tolerant schemes are like automobile engines: although bigger engines may mean more horsepower, they have to be moved with the cars they power. Eventually, it may be the range of applications that determines the best compromises.

# Bibliography

[1] Abolhassan, F., J. Keller, and W.J. Paul. "On the Cost-Effectiveness of PRAMs." In *Proc. 3rd IEEE Symp. on Parallel and Distributed Processing,* 1991, pp. 1–9.

[2] Abraham, S., and K. Padmanabhan. "Performance of the Direct Binary $n$-Cube Network for Multiprocessors." *IEEE Trans. on Computers,* C-38, No. 7 (July 1989), 1000–1011.

[3] Adams, G.B., and H.J. Siegel. "The Extra Stage Cube: a Fault-Tolerant Interconnection Network for Supersystems." *IEEE Trans. on Computers,* C-31, No. 5 (May 1982), 443–454.

[4] Agrawal, D.P., V.K. Janakiram, and G.C. Pathak. "Evaluating the Performance of Multicomputer Configurations." *Computer,* 19, No. 5 (May 1986), 23–37.

[5] Aho, A., J.E. Hopcroft, and J.D. Ullman. *The Design and Analysis of Computer Algorithms.* Reading, Mass.: Addison-Wesley, 1974.

[6] Aiello, B., and T. Leighton. "Coding Theory, Hypercube Embeddings, and Fault Tolerance." In *Proc. 1991 ACM Symp. on Parallel Algorithms and Architectures,* 1991, pp. 125–136.

[7] Ajtai, M., J. Komlós, and E. Szemerédi. "Sorting in $c\log n$ Parallel Steps." *Combinatorica,* 3, No. 1 (1983), 1–19.

[8] Akers, S.B., and B. Krishnamurthy. "A Group-Theoretic Model for Symmetric Interconnection Networks." *IEEE Trans. on Computers,* C-38, No. 4 (April 1989), 555–566.

[9] Akl, S.G. *The Design and Analysis of Parallel Algorithms.* Englewood Cliffs, New Jersey: Prentice-Hall, 1989.

[10] Aleliunas, R. "Randomized Parallel Communication." In *Proc. ACM Symp. on Principles of Distributed Computing,* 1982, pp. 60–72.

[11] Almasi, G.S., and A. Gottlieb. *Highly Parallel Computing.* Redwood City, California: Benjamin/Cummings, 1989.

[12] Alt, H., T. Hagerup, K. Mehlhorn, and F.P. Preparata. "Deterministic Simulation of Idealized Parallel Computers on More Realistic Ones." *SIAM J. Comput.,* 16, No. 5 (October 1987), 808–835.

[13] Amdahl, G.M. "Validity of the Single Processor Approach to Achieving Large Scale Computing Capabilities." *AFIPS Conf. Proc.,* 30 (1967), 483–485.

[14] Annexstein, F. "Fault Tolerance in Hypercube-Derivative Networks." In *Proc. 1989 ACM Symp. on Parallel Algorithms and Architectures,* 1989, pp. 179–188.

[15] Annexstein, F., M. Baumslag, and A.L. Rosenberg. "Group Action Graphs and Parallel Architectures." *SIAM J. Comput.,* 19, No. 3 (June 1990), 544–569.

[16] Apostol, T.M. *Calculus, Vol. I.* 2nd ed. Waltham, Mass.: Blaisdell, 1967.

[17] Apostol, T.M. *Mathematical Analysis.* 2nd ed. Reading, Mass.: Addison-Wesley, 1977.

[18] Arbib, M.A., and J.A. Robinson. (Ed.) *Natural and Artificial Parallel Computation.* Cambridge, Mass.: MIT Press, 1990.

[19] Archibald, J., and J.-L. Baer. "An Economical Solution to the Cache Coherence Problem." In *Proc. 11th Annu. International Symp. on Computer Architecture,* 1984, pp. 355–362.

[20] Arnold, T.F. "The Concept of Coverage and Its Effect on the Reliability Model of a Repairable System." *IEEE Trans. on Computers,* C-22, No. 3 (March 1973), 251–254.

[21] Aspray, W. *John von Neumann and the Origins of Modern Computing.* Cambridge, Mass.: MIT Press, 1990.

[22] August, M.C., G.M. Brost, C.C. Hsiung, and A.J. Schiffleger. "Cray X-MP: The Birth of a Supercomputer." *Computer,* 22, No. 1 (January 1989), 45–52.

[23] Aumann, Y. "PRAM Emulation: Improved Results Using Coding." Technical Report CS-90-23, Hebrew University, December 1990.

[24] Aumann, Y., and M. Ben-Or. "Asymptotically Optimal PRAM Emulation on Faulty Hypercubes." In *Proc. 32nd Annu. IEEE Symp. Found. Comput. Sci.,* 1991, pp. 440–446.

[25] Aumann, Y., and M. Ben-Or. "Computing with Faulty Arrays." In *Proc. 24th Annu. ACM Symp. on Theory of Computing*, 1992, pp. 162–169.

[26] Aumann, Y., and A. Schuster. "Deterministic PRAM Simulation with Constant Memory Blow-Up and No Time-Stamps." In *Proc. 3rd Symp. on the Frontiers of Massively Parallel Computation*, 1990, pp. 22–29.

[27] Aumann, Y., and A. Schuster. "Improved Memory Utilization in Deterministic PRAM Simulation." *J. Parallel and Distributed Computing*, 12, No. 2 (June 1991), 146–151.

[28] Avižienis, A. "The *N*-Version Approach to Fault-Tolerant Software." *IEEE Trans. on Software Engineering*, SE-11, No. 12 (December 1985), 1491–1501.

[29] Avižienis, A., and L. Chen. "On the Implementation of *N*-Version Programming for Software Fault Tolerance during Execution." In *Proc. COMPSAC-77*, 1977, pp. 149–155.

[30] Avižienis, A., G.C. Gilley, F.P. Mathur, D.A. Rennels, J.A. Rohr, and D.K. Rubin. "The STAR (Self-Testing And Repairing) Computer: an Investigation of the Theory and Practice of Fault-Tolerant Computer Design." *IEEE Trans. on Computers*, C-20, No. 11 (November 1971), 1312–1321.

[31] Awerbuch, B. "An Efficient Network Synchronization Protocol." In *Proc. 16th Annu. ACM Symp. on Theory of Computing*, 1984, pp. 522–525.

[32] Awerbuch, B. "Communication-Time Trade-Offs in Network Synchronization." In *Proc. ACM Symp. on Principles of Distributed Computing*, 1985, pp. 272–276.

[33] Awerbuch, B. "Complexity of Network Synchronization." *J. ACM*, 32, No. 4 (October 1985), 804–823.

[34] Awerbuch, B., A. Israeli, and Y. Shiloach. "Efficient Simulation of PRAM by Ultracomputer." Technical Report TR-20, IBM Israel Scientific Center, May 1983.

[35] Axelrod, T.S. "Effects of Synchronization Barriers on Multiprocessor Performance." *Parallel Computing*, 3 (1986), 129–140.

[36] Backus, J. "Can Programming Be Liberated from the von Neumann Style? A Functional Style and Its Algebra of Programs." *Comm. ACM*, 21, No. 8 (August 1978), 613–641.

[37] Baer, J.-L. *Computer Systems Architecture.* Potomac, Maryland: Computer Science Press, 1980.

[38] Barnes, G.H., R.M. Brown, M. Kato, D.J. Kuck, D.L. Slotnick, and R.A. Stokes. "The ILLIAC IV Computer." *IEEE Trans. on Computers,* C-17, No. 8 (August 1968), 746–757.

[39] Batcher, K.E. "Sorting Networks and Their Applications." *AFIPS Conf. Proc.,* 32 (1968), 307–314.

[40] Batcher, K.E. "STARAN Parallel Processor System Hardware." *AFIPS Conf. Proc.,* 43 (1974), 405–410.

[41] Batcher, K.E. "The Flip Network in STARAN." In *Proc. 1976 International Conf. on Parallel Processing,* 1976, pp. 65–71.

[42] Baudet, G.M. "Asynchronous Iterative Methods for Multiprocessors." *J. ACM,* 25, No. 2 (April 1978), 226–244.

[43] Bell, G. "The Future of High Performance Computers in Science and Engineering." *Comm. ACM,* 32, No. 9 (September 1989), 1091–1101.

[44] Bell, G. "Ultracomputers: a Teraflop before Its Time." *Comm. ACM,* 35, No. 8 (August 1992), 27–47.

[45] Beneš, V.E. "On Rearrangeable Three-Stage Connecting Networks." *The Bell System Technical Journal,* 41, No. 5 (September 1962), 1481–1492.

[46] Ben-Or, M., S. Goldwasser, and A. Wigderson. "Completeness Theorems for Non-Cryptographic Fault-Tolerant Distributed Computation." In *Proc. 20th Annu. ACM Symp. on Theory of Computing,* 1988, pp. 1–10.

[47] Bentley, J.L., and H.T. Kung. "A Tree Machine for Searching Problems." In *Proc. 1979 International Conf. on Parallel Processing,* 1979, pp. 257–266.

[48] Berg, C. *Graphs and Hypergraphs.* Amsterdam: North-Holland, 1973.

[49] Berger, B., and J. Rompel. "Simulating $(\log^c n)$-Wise Independence in *NC*." *J. ACM,* 38, No. 4 (October 1991), 1026–1046.

[50] Berlekamp, E.R. *Algebraic Coding Theory.* New York: McGraw-Hill, 1968.

[51] Berman, F., and L. Snyder. "On Mapping Parallel Algorithms into Parallel Architectures." *J. Parallel and Distributed Computing,* 4, No. 5 (October 1987), 439–458.

[52] Bermond, J.-C., C. Delorme, and J.-J. Quisquater. "Strategies for Interconnection Networks: Some Methods from Graph Theory." *J. Parallel and Distributed Computing,* 3, No. 4 (December 1986), 433–449.

[53] Bermond, J.-C., and C. Peyrat. "De Bruijn and Kautz Networks: a Competitor for the Hypercube?" Manuscript, 1989.

[54] Berra, P.B., A. Ghafoor, M Guizani, S.J. Marcinkowski, and P.A. Mitkas. "Optics and Supercomputing." *Proc. of the IEEE,* 77, No. 12 (December 1989), 1797–1815.

[55] Bertsekas, D.P., C. Özveren, G.D. Stamoulis, P. Tseng, and J.N. Tsitsiklis. "Optimal Communication Algorithms for Hypercubes." *J. Parallel and Distributed Computing,* 11, No. 4 (April 1991), 263–275.

[56] Bertsekas, D.P., and J.N. Tsitsiklis. *Parallel and Distributed Computation: Numerical Methods.* Englewood Cliffs, New Jersey: Prentice-Hall, 1989.

[57] Bestavros, A. "SETH: a VLSI Chip for the Real-Time Information Dispersal and Retrieval for Security and Fault-Tolerance." In *Proc. International Conf. on Parallel Processing,* Vol. I, 1990, pp. 457–464.

[58] Bestavros, A. "IDA-Based Disk Arrays." In *Proc. 1st International Conf. on Parallel and Distributed Information Systems,* 1991.

[59] Bhuyan, L.N., and D.P. Agrawal. "Generalized Hypercube and Hyperbus Structures for a Computer Network." *IEEE Trans. on Computers,* C-33, No. 4 (April 1984), 323–333.

[60] Bhuyan, L.N., Q. Yang, and D.P. Agrawal. "Performance of Multiprocessor Interconnection Networks." *Computer,* 22, No. 2 (February 1989), 25–37.

[61] Birkhoff, G., and S. MacLane. *A Survey of Modern Algebra.* 4th ed. New York: Macmillan, 1977.

[62] Blahut, R.E. "Transform Techniques for Error Control Codes." *IBM J. Res. Develop.,* 23, No. 3 (May 1979), 299–315.

[63] Blahut, R.E. *Theory and Practice of Error Control Codes.* Reading, Mass.: Addison-Wesley, 1983.

[64] Blahut, R.E. *Error-Correcting Codes for Digital Signal Processing.* Recorded March 24, 1989. Stanford, California: University Video Communications, Distinguished Lecture Series, Vol. II, 1989 (VHS).

[65] Blakley, G.R. "Safeguarding Cryptographic Keys." *AFIPS Conf. Proc.,* 48 (1979), 313–317.

[66] Blaum, M., and R.M. Roth. "New Array Codes for Multiple Phased Burst Correction." IBM Research Report RJ 8303 (75664), August 21, 1991.

[67] Blelloch, G.E. "Scans as Primitive Parallel Operations." *IEEE Trans. on Computers,* C-38, No. 11 (November 1989), 1526–1538.

[68] Blelloch, G.E. *Vector Models for Data-Parallel Computing.* Cambridge, Mass.: MIT Press, 1990.

[69] Blum, N. "A Note on the 'Parallel Computation Thesis.'" *Information Processing Letters,* 17, No. 4 (November 1983), 203–205.

[70] Boesch, F.T., F. Harary, and J.A. Kabell. "Graphs as Models of Communication Network Vulnerability: Connectivity and Persistence." *Networks,* 11, No. 1 (Spring 1981), 57–63.

[71] Bollobás, B. *Extremal Graphs Theory.* New York: Academic Press, 1978.

[72] Bollobás, B. *Graph Theory: an Introductory Course.* Berlin: Springer-Verlag, 1979.

[73] Borkar, S., R. Cohn, G. Cox, T. Gross, H.T. Kung, M. Lam, M. Levine, B. Moore, W. Moore, C. Peterson, J. Susman, J. Sutton, J. Urbanski, and J. Webb. "Supporting Systolic and Memory Communication in iWarp." In *Proc. 17th Annu. International Symp. on Computer Architecture,* 1990, pp. 70–81.

[74] Borodin, A. "On Relating Time and Space to Size and Depth." *SIAM J. Comput.,* 6, No. 4 (December 1977), 733–744.

[75] Borodin, A., and J.E. Hopcroft. "Routing, Merging, and Sorting on Parallel Models of Computation." In *Proc. 14th Annu. ACM Symp. on Theory of Computing,* 1982, pp. 338–344. Also in *J. Computer and System Sciences,* 30, No. 1 (February 1985), 130–145.

[76] Borodin, A., and I. Munro. *The Computational Complexity of Algebraic and Numeric Problems.* New York: American Elsevier, 1975.

[77] Bouricius, W.G., W.C. Carter, D.C. Jessep, P.R. Schneider, and A.B. Wadia. "Reliability Modeling for Fault-Tolerant Computers." *IEEE Trans. on Computers,* C-20, No. 11 (November 1971), 1306–1311.

[78] Bouricius, W.G., W.C. Carter, and P.R. Schneider. "Reliability Modeling Techniques for Self-Repairing Computer Systems." In *Proc. of ACM Ann. Conference,* 1969, pp. 295–309.

[79] Brassard, G., and P. Bratley. *Algorithmics: Theory and Practice.* Englewood Cliffs, New Jersey: Prentice-Hall, 1988.

[80] Brigham, E.O., Jr. *The Fast Fourier Transform.* Englewood Cliffs, New Jersey: Prentice-Hall, 1974.

[81] Cam, H., and J.A.B. Fortes. "Rearrangeability of Shuffle-Exchange Networks." In *Proc. 3rd Symp. on the Frontiers of Massively Parallel Computation,* 1990, pp. 303–314.

[82] Carter, J.L., and M.N. Wegman. "Universal Classes of Hash Functions." *J. Computer and System Sciences,* 18, No. 2 (April 1979), 143–154.

[83] Chandra, A.K., D.C. Kozen, and L.J. Stockmeyer. "Alternation." *J. ACM,* 28, No. 1 (January 1981), 114–133.

[84] Chandy, K.M. "A Survey of Analytic Models of Rollback and Recovery Strategies." *Computer,* 8, No. 5 (May 1975), 40–47.

[85] Chen, L., and Avižienis, A. "*N*-Version Programming: a Fault-Tolerance Approach to Reliability of Software Operation." In *Proc. International Symp. on Fault-Tolerant Computing,* 1978, pp. 3–9.

[86] Chen, P.-Y., D.H. Lawrie, P.-C. Yew, and D.A. Padua. "Interconnection Networks Using Shuffles." *Computer,* 14, No. 12 (December 1981), 55–63.

[87] Chernoff, H. "A Measure of Asymptotic Efficiency for Tests of a Hypothesis Based on the Sum of Observations." *Ann. Math. Statist.,* 23 (1952), 493–507.

[88] Clos, C. "A Study of Non-Blocking Switching Networks." *The Bell System Technical Journal,* 32 (March 1953), 406–424.

[89] Conte, S.D., and C. de Boor. *Elementary Numerical Analysis: an Algorithmic Approach.* New York: McGraw-Hill, 1980.

[90] Cook, S.A. "A Taxonomy of Problems with Fast Parallel Algorithms." *Information and Control,* 64 (1985), 2–22.

[91] Cragon, H.G., and W.J. Watson. "The TI Advanced Scientific Computer." *Computer,* 22, No. 1 (January 1989), 55–64.

[92] Crowther, W.R., J. Goodhue, E. Starr, R. Thomas, W. Milliken, and T. Blackadar. "Performance Measurements on a 128-Node Butterfly™ Parallel Processor." In *Proc. 1985 International Conf. on Parallel Processing,* 1985, pp. 530–540.

[93] Dally, W.J., and C.L. Seitz. "Deadlock-Free Message Routing in Multiprocessor Interconnection Networks." *IEEE Trans. on Computers,* C-36, No. 5 (May 1987), 547–553.

[94] de Bruijn, N.G. "A Combinatorial Problem." In *Proc. Akademe Van Wetenschappen,* 49, Part 2, 1946, pp. 758–764.

[95] de Carlini, U., and U. Villano. *Transputers and Parallel Architectures: Message-Passing Distributed Systems.* New York: Ellis Horwood, 1991.

[96] Dennis, J.B. "Data Flow Supercomputers." *Computer,* 13, No. 11 (November 1980), 42–56.

[97] Despain, A., and D. Patterson. "X-Tree: a Structured Multiprocessor Computer Architecture." In *Proc. 5th Annu. International Symp. on Computer Architecture,* 1978, pp. 144–151.

[98] Dias, D.M., and J.R. Jump. "Analysis and Simulation of Buffered Delta Networks." *IEEE Trans. on Computers,* C-30, No. 4 (April 1981), 273–282.

[99] Dias, D.M., and J.R. Jump. "Packet Switching Interconnection Networks for Modular Systems." *Computer,* 14, No. 12 (December 1981), 43–53.

[100] Dickey, S.R., and R. Kenner. "Hardware Combining and Scalability." In *Proc. 1992 ACM Symp. on Parallel Algorithms and Architectures,* 1992, pp. 296–305.

[101] Dietzfelbinger, M., S. Madhavapeddy, and I.H. Sudborough. "Three Disjoint Path Paradigms in Star Networks." In *Proc. 3rd IEEE Symp. on Parallel and Distributed Processing,* 1991, pp. 400–406.

[102] Digital Equipment Corporation. *Introduction to Local Area Networks.* Maynard, Mass., 1982.

[103] Dijkstra, E.W. "Solution of a Problem in Concurrent Programming Control." *Comm. ACM,* 8, No. 9 (September 1965), 569.

[104] Dinning, A. "A Survey of Synchronization Methods for Parallel Computers." *Computer,* 22, No. 7 (July 1989), 66–77.

[105] Dolev, D. "The Byzantine Generals Strike Again." *J. Algorithms,* 3, No. 1 (March 1982), 14–30.

[106] Dolev, D., C. Dwork, and L.J. Stockmeyer. "On the Minimal Synchronism Needed for Distributed Consensus." *J. ACM,* 34, No. 1 (January 1987), 77–97.

[107] Dowd, P.W. "High Performance Interprocessor Communication through Optical Wavelength Division Multiple Access Channels." In *Proc. 18th Annu. International Symp. on Computer Architecture,* 1991, pp. 96–105.

[108] D.-Z. Du, Y.-D. Lyuu, and D.F Hsu. "Line Digraph Iterations and the Spread Concept — with Application to Graph Theory, Fault Tolerance, and Routing." In *Proc. Graph-Theoretical Concepts in Computer Science,* 1991. *Lecture Notes in Computer Science,* 570 (1992), 169–179. To appear in *IEEE Trans. on Computers.*

[109] Dubois, M., C. Scheurich, and F. Briggs. "Synchronization, Coherence, and Event Ordering in Multiprocessors." *Computer,* 21, No. 2 (February 1988), 9–21.

[110] Duncan, R. "A Survey of Parallel Computer Architectures." *Computer,* 23, No. 2 (February 1990), 5–16.

[111] Dymond, P.W., and S.A. Cook. "Complexity Theory of Parallel Time and Hardware." *Information and Computation,* 80 (1989), 205–226.

[112] Elkind, S.A. "Reliability and Availability Techniques." In [326, pp. 63–181].

[113] Feitelson, D.G. *Optical Computing: a Survey for Computer Scientists.* Cambridge, Mass.: MIT Press, 1988.

[114] Feldman, C. "The ABC of DCC." *Audio,* January 1992, pp. 42–46.

[115] Feldmann, R., and W. Unger. "The Cube-Connected Cycles Network Is a Subgraph of the Butterfly Network." Submitted to *Parallel Processing Letters.*

[116] Feng, T.-Y. "Data Manipulating Functions in Parallel Processors and Their Implementations." *IEEE Trans. on Computers,* C-23, No. 3 (March 1974), 309–318.

[117] Feng, T.-Y. "A Survey of Interconnection Networks." *Computer,* 14, No. 12 (December 1981), 12–27.

[118] Fiduccia, C.M., and E.M. Jacobson. "Universal Multistage Networks via Linear Permutations." In *Proc. Supercomputing '91,* 1991, pp. 380–389.

[119] Fisher, A.L., and H.T. Kung. "Synchronizing Large VLSI Processor Arrays." *IEEE Trans. on Computers,* C-34, No. 8 (August 1985), 734–740.

[120] Flynn, M.J. "Very High-Speed Computing Systems." *Proc. of the IEEE,* 54, No. 12 (December 1966), 1901–1909.

[121] Flynn, M.J. "Some Computer Organizations and Their Effectiveness." *IEEE Trans. on Computers,* C-21, No. 9 (September 1972), 948–960.

[122] Fortune, S., and J. Wyllie. "Parallelism in Random Access Machines." In *Proc. 10th Annu. ACM Symp. on Theory of Computing,* 1978, pp. 114–118.

[123] Fox, G.C. "Applications of Parallel Supercomputers: Scientific Results and Computer Science Lessons." In [18, pp. 47–90].

[124] Fraigniaud, P., S. Miguet, and Y. Robert. "Scattering on a Ring of Processors." *Parallel Computing,* 13, No. 3 (March 1990), 377–383.

[125] Fuller, E., and B. Krishnamurthy. "Symmetries in Graphs: An Annotated Bibliography." Technical Report CR–86–03, Computer Research Lab., Tektronix Laboratories, January 1986.

[126] Fürer, M. "Generalized Iterative Arrays." Technical Report No. 79-07-03, Department of Computer Science, University of Washington, 1979.

[127] Gajski, D.D., V.M. Milutinović, H.J. Siegel, and B.P. Furht. (Ed.) *Tutorial: Computer Architecture.* Washington D.C.: IEEE Computer Society Press, 1987.

[128] Gajski, D.D., and J. Peir. "Essential Issues in Multiprocessor Systems." *Computer,* 18, No. 6 (June 1985), 9–27.

[129] Gehringer, E.F., J. Abullarade, and M.H. Gulyn. "A Survey of Commercial Parallel Processors." *ACM Computer Architecture News,* 16, No. 4 (September 1988), 75–107.

[130] Gibbons, A., and W. Rytter. *Efficient Parallel Algorithms*. Cambridge: Cambridge University Press, 1988.

[131] Giladi, E. Master's Thesis (manuscript), Hebrew University, Israel, 1989.

[132] Goke, C.R., and G.J. Lipovski. "Banyan Networks for Partitioning Multiprocessor Systems." In *Proc. 1st Annu. International Symp. on Computer Architecture*, 1973, pp. 21–28.

[133] Goldberg, J. "A Survey of the Design and Analysis of Fault-Tolerant Computers." In *Reliability and Fault Tree Analysis*. Edited by R.E. Barlow, J.B. Fussell, and N.D. Singpurwalla. Philadelphia, Penn.: SIAM, 1975, pp. 687–731.

[134] Goldschlager, L.M. "A Unified Approach to Models of Synchronous Parallel Machines." In *Proc. 10th Annu. ACM Symp. on Theory of Computing*, 1978, pp. 89–94.

[135] Goldschlager, L.M. "A Universal Interconnection Pattern for Parallel Computers." *J. ACM*, 29, No. 4 (October 1982), 1073–1086.

[136] Golub, G.H., and C.F. Van Loan. *Matrix Computations*. Baltimore, Maryland: The Johns Hopkins University Press, 1983.

[137] Gottlieb, A., R. Grishman, C.P. Kruskal, K.P. McAuliffe, L. Rudolph, and M. Snir. "The NYU Ultracomputer — Designing an MIMD Shared Memory Parallel Computer." *IEEE Trans. on Computers*, C-32, No. 2 (February 1983), 175–189.

[138] Gottlieb, A., B.D. Lubachevsky, and L. Rudolph. "Basic Techniques for the Efficient Coordination of Very Large Numbers of Cooperating Sequential Processors." *ACM Trans. on Programming Languages and Systems*, 5, No. 2 (April 1983), 164–189.

[139] Gottlieb, A., and J.T. Schwartz. "Networks and Algorithms for Very-Large-Scale Parallel Computation." *Computer*, 5, No. 1 (January 1982), 27–36.

[140] Gray, J., and D.P. Siewiorek. "High-Availability Computer Systems" *Computer*, 24, No. 9 (September 1991), 39–48.

[141] Green, P.E. "The Future of Fiber-Optic Computer Networks." *Computer*, 24, No. 9 (September 1991), 78–87.

[142] Greenberg, D.S., and S.N. Bhatt. "Routing Multiple Paths in Hypercubes." In *Proc. 1990 ACM Symp. on Parallel Algorithms and Architectures,* 1990, pp. 45–54.

[143] Grossman, I., and W. Magnus. *Groups and Their Graphs.* 1964; rpt. Washington, D.C.: The Mathematical Association of America, n.d.

[144] Gustafson, J.L. "Reevaluating Amdahl's Law." *Comm. ACM,* 31, No. 5 (May 1988), 532–533.

[145] Hamming, R.W. *Numerical Methods for Scientists and Engineers.* 2nd ed. New York: McGraw-Hill, 1973.

[146] Harary, F., J.P. Hayes, and H.-J. Wu. "A Survey of the Theory of Hypercube Graphs." *Computers and Mathematics with Applications,* 15, No. 4 (1988), 277–289.

[147] Hardy, G.H., and E.M. Wright. *An Introduction to the Theory of Numbers.* 5th ed. Oxford: Oxford University Press, 1979.

[148] Harper, R.E., J.H. Lala, and J.J. Deyst. "Fault Tolerant Parallel Processor Architecture Overview." In *Proc. International Symp. on Fault-Tolerant Computing,* 1988, pp. 252–257.

[149] Håstad, J., F.T. Leighton, and M. Newman. "Reconfiguring a Hypercube in the Presence of Faults." In *Proc. 19th Annu. ACM Symp. on Theory of Computing,* 1987, pp. 274–284.

[150] Håstad, J., F.T. Leighton, and M. Newman. "Fast Computation Using Faulty Hypercubes." In *Proc. 21st Annu. ACM Symp. on Theory of Computing,* 1989, pp. 251–263.

[151] Haynes, L.S., R.L. Lau, D.P. Siewiorek, and D.W. Mizell. "A Survey of Highly Parallel Computing." *Computer,* 15, No. 1 (January 1982), 9–24.

[152] Hennessy, J.L., and N.P. Jouppi. "Computer Technology and Architecture: an Evolving Interaction." *Computer,* 24, No. 9 (September 1991), 18–29.

[153] Hennessy, J.L., and D.A. Patterson. *Computer Architecture: a Quantitative Approach.* San Mateo, California: Morgan KaufmannWesley, 1990.

[154] Hill, G.R. "Wavelength Domain Optical Network Techniques." *Proc. of the IEEE,* 77, No. 1 (January 1991), 121–132.

[155] Hillis, W.D. *The Connection Machine.* Cambridge, Mass.: MIT Press, 1985.

[156] Hinton, H.S. "Switching to Photonics." *IEEE Spectrum,* February 1992, pp. 42–45.

[157] Ho, C.-T., and M.T. Raghunath. "Efficient Communication Primitives on Circuit-Switched Hypercubes." In *Proc. 6th Distributed Memory Computing Conference,* 1991, pp. 390-397.

[158] Hopkins, A.L., Jr., T.B. Smith, III, and J.H. Lala. "FTMP — a Highly Reliable Fault-Tolerant Multiprocessor for Aircraft." *Proc. of the IEEE,* 66, No. 10 (October 1978), 1221–1239.

[159] Horowitz, E., and S. Sahni. *Fundamentals of Computer Algorithms.* Potomac, Maryland: Computer Science Press, 1978.

[160] Hsu, D.F., and Lyuu, Y.-D. "A Graph-Theoretical Study of Transmission Delay and Fault Tolerance." In *Proc. Fourth ISMM International Conf. on Parallel and Distributed Computing and Systems,* 1991, pp. 20–24.

[161] Hwang, K., and F. Briggs. *Computer Architecture and Parallel Processing.* New York: McGraw-Hill, 1984.

[162] IEEE Scientific Supercomputer Subcommittee. "The Computer Spectrum: a Perspective on the Evolution of Computing." *Computer,* 22, No. 11 (November 1989), 57–63.

[163] IEEE Scientific Supercomputer Subcommittee. "Supercomputer Hardware: an Update of the 1983 Report's Summary and Tables." *Computer,* 22, No. 11 (November 1989), 63–68.

[164] Jayasimha, D.N. "Distributed Synchronizers." In *Proc. 1988 International Conf. on Parallel Processing,* 1988, pp. 23–27.

[165] Johnson, B.W. *Design and Analysis of Fault Tolerant Digital Systems.* Reading, Mass.: Addison-Wesley, 1989.

[166] Johnsson, S.L., and C.-T. Ho. "Optimum Broadcasting and Personalized Communication in Hypercubes." *IEEE Trans. on Computers,* C-38, No. 9 (September 1989), 1249–1268.

[167] Jones, A.K., and P. Schwarz. "Experience Using Multiprocessor Systems — a Status Report." *Computing Surveys,* 12, No. 2 (June 1980), 121–165.

[168] Jones, T. "Engineering Design of the Convex C2." *Computer,* 22, No. 1 (January 1989), 36–44.

[169] Kaklamanis, C., D. Krizanc, and A. Tsantilas. "Tight Bounds for Oblivious Routing in the Hypercube." In *Proc. 1990 ACM Symp. on Parallel Algorithms and Architectures,* 1990, pp. 31–36.

[170] Karchmer, M. *Communication Complexity: a New Approach to Circuit Depth.* Cambridge, Mass.: MIT Press, 1989.

[171] Karlin, A.R., and E. Upfal. "Parallel Hashing — an Efficient Implementation of Shared Memory." In *Proc. 18th Annu. ACM Symp. on Theory of Computing,* 1986, pp. 160–168.

[172] Karp, R.M., and V. Ramachandran. "Parallel Algorithms for Shared-Memory Machines." In *Handbook of Theoretical Computer Science, Vol. A: Algorithms and Complexity.* Edited by J. van Leeuwen. Cambridge, Mass.: MIT Press, 1990, pp. 869–941.

[173] Katzman, J.A. "The Tandem 16: a Fault-Tolerant Computing System." In [325, pp. 470–480].

[174] Kindervater, G.A.P., and J.K. Lenstra. "An Introduction to Parallelism in Combinatorial Optimization." *Discrete Applied Mathematics,* 14 (1986), 135–156.

[175] Knuth, D.E. *The Art of Computer Programming, Vol. I: Fundamental Algorithms.* 2nd ed. Reading, Mass.: Addison-Wesley, 1973.

[176] Knuth, D.E. *The Art of Computer Programming, Vol. II: Seminumerical Algorithms.* 2nd ed. Reading, Mass.: Addison-Wesley, 1981.

[177] Koch, R.R. "Increasing the Size of a Network by a Constant Factor Can Increase Performance by More Than a Constant Factor." In *Proc. 29th Annu. IEEE Symp. Found. Comput. Sci.,* 1988, pp. 221–230.

[178] Kothari, S.C. "Multistage Interconnection Networks for Multiprocessor Systems." *Advances in Computers,* 26 (1987), 155–199.

[179] Kruskal, C.P. "Direct Connection Machines," and "Shared Memory Machines." In *Control Flow and Data Flow: Concepts of Distributed Programming.* Edited by M. Broy. Berlin: Springer-Verlag, 1985, pp. 282–297.

[180] Kruskal, C.P., "Performance Bounds on Parallel Processors: an Optimistic View." In *Control Flow and Data Flow: Concepts of Distributed Programming.* Edited by M. Broy. Berlin: Springer-Verlag, 1985, pp. 331–344.

[181] Kruskal, C.P., L. Rudolph, and M. Snir. "A Complexity Theory of Efficient Parallel Algorithms." *Theoretical Computer Science,* 71 (1990), 95–132.

[182] Kruskal, C.P., and M. Snir. "The Performance of Multistage Interconnection Networks for Multiprocessors." *IEEE Trans. on Computers,* C-32, No. 12 (December 1983), 1091–1098.

[183] Kruskal, C.P., and M. Snir. "A Unified Theory of Interconnection Network Structure." *Theoretical Computer Science,* 48 (1986), 75–94.

[184] Kuck, D.J. "A Survey of Parallel Machine Organization and Programming." *Computing Surveys,* 9, No. 1 (March 1977), 29–59.

[185] Kuck, D.J. *The Structure of Computers and Computations,* Vol. I. New York: John Wiley, 1978.

[186] Kuck, D.J. "Keynote Address, 15th Ann. International Symp. on Computer Architecture." *ACM Computer Architecture News,* 17, No. 1 (March 1989), 5–26.

[187] Kuck, D.J., E.S. Davidson, D.H. Lawrie, and A.H. Sameh. "Parallel Supercomputing Today and the Cedar Approach." *Science,* 231 (February 1986), 967–974.

[188] Kuhl, J.G., and S.M. Reddy. "Distributed Fault-Tolerance for Large Multiprocessor Systems." In *Proc. 7th Annu. International Symp. on Computer Architecture,* 1980, pp. 23–30.

[189] Kuhl, J.G., and S.M. Reddy. "Fault-Tolerance Considerations in Large, Multiple-Processor Systems." *Computer,* 19, No. 3 (March 1986), 56–67.

[190] Kumar, M., and G.F. Pfister. "The Onset of Hot Spot Contention." In *Proc. 1986 International Conf. on Parallel Processing,* 1986, pp. 28–34.

[191] Kunde, M., and T. Tensi. "Multi-Packet-Routing on Mesh Connected Arrays." In *Proc. 1989 ACM Symp. on Parallel Algorithms and Architectures,* 1989, pp. 336–343.

[192] Kung, H.T. "Synchronized and Asynchronous Parallel Algorithms for Multiprocessors." In *Algorithms and Complexity: New Directions and Recent Results.* Edited by J.F. Traub. New York: Academic Press, 1976, pp. 153–200.

[193] Kung, H.T. "Computational Models for Parallel Computers." *Phil. Trans. R. Soc. Lond.,* A 326, No. 1591 (September 1988), 357–371.

[194] Kung, H.T., and C.E. Leiserson. "Systolic Arrays." In [245, pp. 271–292].

[195] Lakshmivarahan, S., and S.K. Dhall. *Analysis and Design of Parallel Algorithms: Arithmetic and Matrix Problems.* New York: McGraw-Hill, 1990.

[196] Lamport, L. "How to Make a Multiprocessor Computer That Correctly Executes Multiprocess Programs." *IEEE Trans. on Computers,* C-28, No. 9 (September 1979), 690–691.

[197] Lamport, L., R. Shostak, and M. Pease. "The Byzantine Generals Problem." *ACM Trans. on Programming Languages and Systems,* 4, No. 3 (July 1982), 382–401.

[198] Lang, S. *Algebra.* 2nd ed. Reading, Mass.: Addison-Wesley, 1984.

[199] Lang, T. "Interconnections between Processors and Memory Modules Using the Shuffle-Exchange Network." *IEEE Trans. on Computers,* C-25, No. 5 (May 1976), 496–503.

[200] Lang, T., and L. Kurisaki. "Nonuniform Traffic Spots (NUTS) in Multistage Interconnection Networks." In *Proc. 1988 International Conf. on Parallel Processing,* 1988, pp. 191–195.

[201] Lang, T., and H.S. Stone. "A Shuffle-Exchange Network with Simplified Control." *IEEE Trans. on Computers,* C-25, No. 1 (January 1976), 55–65.

[202] Lauer, H.C., and R.M. Needham. "On the Duality of Operating System Structures." *ACM Operating Systems Review,* 13, No. 2 (April 1979), 3–19.

[203] Lawrie, D.H. "Access and Alignment of Data in an Array Processor." *IEEE Trans. on Computers,* C-24, No. 12 (December 1975), 1145–1155.

[204] Lazowska, E.D., J. Zahorjan, G.S. Graham, and K.C. Sevcik. *Quantitative System Performance: Computer System Analysis Using Queueing Network Models.* Englewood Cliffs, New Jersey: Prentice-Hall, 1984.

[205] LeBlanc, T.J. "Shared Memory versus Message Passing in a Tightly Coupled Multiprocessor: a Case Study." In *Proc. 1986 International Conf. on Parallel Processing*, 1986, pp. 463–466.

[206] Lee, G. "Another Combining Scheme to Reduce Hot Spot Contention in Large Scale Memory Parallel Computers." In *Proc. 1987 International Conf. on Supercomputing*, 1987. *Lecture Notes in Computer Science*, 297 (1988), 68–79.

[207] Lee, G. "A Performance Bound of Multistage Combining Networks." *IEEE Trans. on Computers*, C-38, No. 10 (October 1989), 1387–1395.

[208] Lee, G., C.P. Kruskal, and D.J. Kuck. "The Effectiveness of Combining in Shared Memory Parallel Computers in the Presence of 'Hot Spots.'" In *Proc. 1986 International Conf. on Parallel Processing*, 1986, pp. 35-41.

[209] Lee, R. "On 'Hot Spot' Contention." *ACM Computer Architecture News*, 13, No. 5 (December 1985), 15–20.

[210] Leighton, F.T. *Complexity Issues in VLSI*. Cambridge, Mass.: MIT Press, 1983.

[211] Leighton, F.T. "Parallel Computation Using Meshes of Trees." In *Proc. 1983 Workshop on Graph-Theoretic Concepts in Computer Science*. Osnabruck, West Germany: Trauner Verlag, pp. 200–218.

[212] Leighton, F.T. "Tight Bounds on the Complexity of Parallel Sorting." *IEEE Trans. on Computers*, C-34, No. 4 (April 1985), 344–354.

[213] Leighton, F.T. *Introduction to Parallel Algorithms and Architectures: Arrays, Trees, Hypercubes*. San Mateo, California: Morgan Kaufmann, 1992.

[214] Leighton, F.T. "Methods for Message Routing in Parallel Machines." In *Proc. 24th Annu. ACM Symp. on Theory of Computing*, 1992, pp. 77–96.

[215] Leighton, T., Y. Ma, and C.G. Plaxton. "Highly Fault-Tolerant Sorting Circuits." In *Proc. 32nd Annu. IEEE Symp. Found. Comput. Sci.*, 1991, pp. 458–469.

[216] Leighton, F.T., and B.M. Maggs. "Expanders Might Be Practical: Fast Algorithms for Routing around Faults on Multibutterflies." In *Proc. 30th Annu. IEEE Symp. Found. Comput. Sci.*, 1989, 384–389.

[217] Leighton, F.T., B.M. Maggs, and S. Rao. "Universal Packet Routing Algorithms." In *Proc. 29th Annu. IEEE Symp. Found. Comput. Sci.*, 1988, pp. 256–269.

[218] Leighton, F.T., B.M. Maggs, and R. Sitaraman. "On the Unexpected Fault-Tolerance of Some Popular Bounded-Degree Networks." Technical Report TR-92-034-3-0053-4, NEC Research Institute, May 1992.

[219] Leighton, F.T., F. Makedon, and I.G. Tollis. "An $2n - 2$ Step Algorithm for Routing in an $n \times n$ Array with Constant Size Queues." In *Proc. 1989 ACM Symp. on Parallel Algorithms and Architectures,* 1989, pp. 328–335.

[220] Leighton, F.T., and C.G. Plaxton "A (Fairly) Simple Circuit That (Usually) Sorts." In *Proc. 31st Annu. IEEE Symp. Found. Comput. Sci.,* 1990, 264–274.

[221] Leiserson, C.E. *Area-Efficient VLSI Computation.* Cambridge, Mass.: MIT Press, 1983.

[222] Leiserson, C.E. "Fat-Trees: Universal Networks for Hardware-Efficient Super-computing." *IEEE Trans. on Computers,* C-34, No. 5 (May 1985), 892–901.

[223] Leiserson, C.E. "The Network Architecture of the Connection Machine CM-5." In *Proc. 4th ACM Symp. on Parallel Algorithms and Architectures,* 1992, pp. 272–285.

[224] Lenoski, D., J. Laudon, K. Gharachorloo, W.-D. Weber, A. Gupta, J. Hennessy, M. Horowitz, and M.S. Lam. "The Stanford Dash Multiprocessor." *Computer,* 25, No. 3 (March 1992), 63–79.

[225] Lev, G., N. Pippenger, and L.G. Valiant. "A Fast Parallel Algorithm for Routing in Permutation Networks." *IEEE Trans. on Computers,* C-30, No. 2 (February 1981), 93–100.

[226] Lilienkamp, J.E., D.H. Lawrie, and P.-C. Yew. "A Fault Tolerant Interconnection Network Using Error Correcting Codes." In *Proc. 1982 International Conf. on Parallel Processing,* 1982, pp. 123–125.

[227] Lillevik, S.L. "The Touchstone 30 Gigaflop DELTA Prototype." In *Proc. 6th Distributed Memory Computing Conference,* 1991, pp. 671–677.

[228] Lin, S., and D.J. Costello, Jr. *Error Control Coding: Fundamentals and Applications.* Englewood Cliffs, New Jersey: Prentice-Hall, 1983.

[229] Lipovski, G.J., and P. Vaughan. "A Fetch-and-Op Implementation for Parallel Computers." In *Proc. 15th Annu. International Symp. on Computer Architecture,* 1988, pp. 384–392.

[230] Lipson, J.D. *Elements of Algebra and Algebraic Computing.* Reading, Mass.: Addison-Wesley, 1981.

[231] Liu, Z. "Optimal Routing in the De Bruijn Networks." In *Proc. 10th International Conf. on Distributed Computing Systems,* 1990, pp. 537–544.

[232] Lubiw, A. "Counterexample to a Conjecture of Szymanski on Hypercube Routing." *Information Processing Letters,* 35, No. 2 (29 June 1990), 57–61.

[233] Lyuu, Y.-D. "Fast Fault-Tolerant Parallel Communication with Low Congestion and On-Line Maintenance Using Information Dispersal." Technical Report TR-19-89, Aiken Computation Lab., Harvard University, 1989.

[234] Lyuu, Y.-D. "Fast Fault-Tolerant Parallel Communication and On-Line Maintenance Using Information Dispersal." In *Proc. 2nd ACM Symp. on Parallel Algorithms and Architectures,* 1990, pp. 378–387. Also in *Mathematical Systems Theory,* 24 (1991), 273–294.

[235] Lyuu, Y.-D. *An Information Dispersal Approach to Issues in Parallel Processing.* Ph.D. Dissertation, Aiken Computation Lab., Harvard University, Cambridge, Mass., 1990.

[236] Lyuu, Y.-D. "Fast Fault-Tolerant Parallel Communication for de Bruijn Networks Using Information Dispersal." In *Proc. 3rd IEEE Symp. on Parallel and Distributed Processing,* 1991, pp. 466–473.

[237] Lyuu, Y.-D. "Fast Fault-Tolerant Parallel Communication for de Bruijn and Digit-Exchange Networks Using Information Dispersal." To appear in *Networks.*

[238] MacWilliams, F.J., and N.J.A. Sloane. *The Theory of Error-Correcting Codes.* Amsterdam: North-Holland, 1977.

[239] Martin, J. *Telecommunications and the Computer.* 2nd ed. Englewood Cliffs, New Jersey: Prentice-Hall, 1976.

[240] Masson, G.M., G.C. Gingher, and S. Nakamura. "A Sampler of Circuit Switching Networks." *Computer,* 12, No. 6 (June 1979), 32–48.

[241] Maxion, R.A., D.P. Siewiorek, and S.A. Elkind. "Techniques and Architectures for Fault-Tolerant Computing." *Ann. Review of Computer Science,* 2 (1987), 469–520.

[242] May, D. "Towards General-Purpose Parallel Computers." In [18, pp. 91–121].

[243] McColl, W.F. "General Purpose Parallel Computing." Technical Report TR-92-032-3-9025-1, NEC Research Institute, April 1992.

[244] McEliece, R.J., and D.V. Sarwate. "On Sharing Secrets and Reed-Solomon Codes." *Comm. ACM,* 24, No. 9 (September 1981), 583–584.

[245] Mead, C., and L. Conway. *Introduction to VLSI Systems.* Reading, Mass.: Addison-Wesley, 1980.

[246] Mehlhorn, K., and U. Vishkin. "Randomized and Deterministic Simulations of PRAMs by Parallel Machines with Restricted Granularity of Parallel Memories." *Acta Informatica,* 21 (1984), 339–374.

[247] Messina, P., and A. Murli (Ed.) *Practical Parallel Computing: Status and Prospects.* New York: John Wiley, 1991.

[248] Mirsky, L. *An Introduction to Linear Algebra.* Oxford, 1955; rpt. New York: Dover, 1990.

[249] Moitra, A. "Parallel Algorithms for Some Computational Problems." *Advances in Computers,* 26 (1987), 93–153.

[250] Monien, B., and H. Sudborough. "Comparing Interconnection Networks." In *Proc. Symp. Mathematical Foundations of Computer Science. Lecture Notes in Computer Science,* 324 (1988), 138–153.

[251] Myers, W. "High-Performance Computing Is 'Window into Future,' Says President's Science Advisor." *Computer,* 25, No. 1 (January 1992), 87–90.

[252] Nassimi, D., and S. Sahni. "Data Broadcasting in SIMD Computers." *IEEE Trans. on Computers,* C-30, No. 2 (February 1981), 101–107.

[253] Nassimi, D., and S. Sahni. "A Self-Routing Benes Network and Parallel Permutation Algorithms." *IEEE Trans. on Computers,* C-30, No. 5 (May 1981), 332–340.

[254] Nelson, V.P., and B.D. Carroll. *Tutorial: Fault-Tolerant Computing.* Washington D.C.: IEEE Computer Society Press, 1987.

[255] Norton, T.J. "Industry Update: Japan." *Stereophile,* February 1992, pp. 39–47.

[256] Norton, V.A., and G.F. Pfister. "A Methodology for Predicting Multiprocessor Performance." In *Proc. 1985 International Conf. on Parallel Processing,* 1985, pp. 772–781.

[257] Owens, H.D. "Computer Memory: Abacus to DRAM." *IEEE Potentials*, December 1989, pp. 32–35.

[258] Padmanabhan, K. "Cube Structures for Multiprocessors." *Comm. ACM*, 33, No. 1 (January 1990), 43–52.

[259] Padmanabhan, K., and D.H. Lawrie. "A Class of Redundant Path Multistage Interconnection Networks." *IEEE Trans. on Computers*, C-32, No. 12 (December 1983), 1099–1108.

[260] Pakzad, S. "Fault Tolerance Analysis of the Class of Rearrangeable Interconnection Networks." *J. Parallel and Distributed Computing*, 7, No. 1 (August 1989), 148–164.

[261] Parberry, I. *Parallel Complexity Theory*. New York: John Wiley, 1987.

[262] Parker, D.S., Jr. "Notes on Shuffle/Exchange-Type Switching Networks." *IEEE Trans. on Computers*, C-29, No. 3 (March 1980), 213–222.

[263] Parker, D.S. "The Gamma Network: a Multiprocessor Interconnection Network with Redundant Paths." In *Proc. 9th Annu. International Symp. on Computer Architecture*, 1982, pp. 73–80.

[264] Patel, J.A. "Performance of Processor-Memory Interconnections for Multiprocessors." *IEEE Trans. on Computers*, C-30, No. 10 (October 1981), 771–780.

[265] Patterson, D.A., G. Gibson, and R.H. Katz. "A Case for Redundant Arrays of Inexpensive Disks (RAID)." In *Proc. 1988 ACM SIGMOD*, 1988, pp. 109–116.

[266] Paturi, R., D.-T. Lu, J.E. Ford, S.C. Esener, and S.H. Lee. "Parallel Algorithms Based on Expander Graphs for Optical Computing." *Applied Optics*, 30, No. 8 (10 March 1991), 917–927.

[267] Pease, M.C., III. "An Adaptation of the Fast Fourier Transform for Parallel Processing." *J. ACM*, 15, No. 2 (April 1968), 252–264.

[268] Pease, M.C., III. "The Indirect Binary $n$-Cube Microprocessor Array." *IEEE Trans. on Computers*, C-26, No. 5 (May 1977), 458–473.

[269] Pease, M., R. Shostak, and L. Lamport. "Reaching Agreement in the Presence of Faults." *J. ACM*, 27, No. 2 (April 1980), 228–234.

[270] Peleg, D., and J.D. Ullman. "An Optimal Synchronizer for the Hypercube." *SIAM J. Comput.*, 18, No. 4 (August 1989), 740–747.

[271] Perry, T.S., and G. Zorpette. "Supercomputer Experts Predict Expansive Growth." *IEEE Spectrum,* February 1989, pp. 26–33.

[272] Peterson, W.W., and E.J. Weldon, Jr. *Error-Correcting Codes.* 2nd ed. Cambridge, Mass.: MIT Press, 1972.

[273] Pfister, G.F., W.C. Brantley, D.A. George, S.L. Harvey, W.J. Kleinfelder, K.P. McAuliffe, E.A. Melton, V.A. Norton, and J. Weiss. "The IBM Research Parallel Processor Prototype (RP3): Introduction and Architecture." In *Proc. 1985 International Conf. on Parallel Processing,* 1985, pp. 764–771.

[274] Pfister, G.F., and V.A. Norton. "'Hot Spot' Contention and Combining in Multistage Interconnection Networks." *IEEE Trans. on Computers,* C-34, No. 10 (October 1985), 943–948.

[275] Pippenger, N. "On Simultaneous Resource Bounds." In *Proc. 20th Annu. IEEE Symp. Found. Comput. Sci.,* 1979, pp. 307–311.

[276] Pippenger, N. "Parallel Communication with Limited Buffers." In *Proc. 25th Annu. IEEE Symp. Found. Comput. Sci.,* 1984, pp. 127–136.

[277] Pippenger, N. "Communication Networks." In *Handbook of Theoretical Computer Science, Vol. A: Algorithms and Complexity.* Edited by J. van Leeuwen. Cambridge, Mass.: MIT Press, 1990, pp. 805–833.

[278] Pollard, J.M. "The Fast Fourier Transform in a Finite Field." *Mathematics of Computation,* 25, No. 114 (April 1971), 365–374.

[279] Pradhan, D.K., and S.M. Reddy. "A Fault-Tolerant Communication Architecture for Distributed Systems." *IEEE Trans. on Computers,* C-31, No. 9 (September 1982), 863–870.

[280] Preparata, F.P. "Holographic Dispersal and Recovery of Information." *IEEE Trans. on Information Theory,* IT-35, No. 5 (September 1989), 1123–1124.

[281] Preparata, F.P., and J.E. Vuillemin. "The Cube-Connected Cycles: a Versatile Network for Parallel Computation." *Comm. ACM,* 24, No. 5 (May 1981), 300–309.

[282] Quinn, M.J., and N. Deo. "Parallel Graph Algorithms." *Computing Surveys,* 6, No. 3 (September 1984), 319–348.

[283] Rabin, M.O. "Probabilistic Algorithms." In *Algorithms and Complexity: New Directions and Recent Results.* Edited by J.F. Traub. New York: Academic Press, 1976, pp. 21–39.

[284] Rabin, M.O. "Probabilistic Algorithms in Finite Fields." *SIAM J. Comput.,* 9, No. 2 (May 1980), 273–280.

[285] Rabin, M.O. "Efficient Dispersal of Information for Security, Load Balancing, and Fault Tolerance." *J. ACM,* 36, No. 2 (April 1989), 335–348.

[286] Rabin, M.O. "The Information Dispersal Algorithm and Its Applications." In *Sequences: Combinatorics, Compression, Security and Transmission.* Edited by R.M. Capocelli. Berlin: Springer-Verlag, 1990, pp. 406–419.

[287] Raghavan, P. "Probabilistic Construction of Deterministic Algorithms: Approximating Packing Integer Programs." In *Proc. 27th Annu. IEEE Symp. Found. Comput. Sci.,* 1986, pp. 10–18.

[288] Raghavendra, C.S., and A. Varma. "Fault-Tolerant Multiprocessors with Redundant-Path Interconnection Networks." *IEEE Trans. on Computers,* C-35, No. 4 (April 1986), 307–316.

[289] Ralston, A. "De Bruijn Sequences — a Model Example of the Interaction of Discrete Mathematics and Computer Science." *Mathematics Magazine,* 55, No. 3 (May 1982), 131–143.

[290] Ranade, A.G. "Equivalence of Message Scheduling Algorithms for Parallel Communication." Technical Report YALEU/DCS/TR-512, Yale University, 1987.

[291] Ranade, A.G. "How to Emulate Shared Memory." In *Proc. 28th Annu. IEEE Symp. Found. Comput. Sci.,* 1987, pp. 185–194.

[292] Randell, B. "System Structure for Software Fault Tolerance." *IEEE Trans. on Software Engineering,* SE-1, No. 2 (June 1975), 220–232.

[293] Raynal, M. *Algorithms for Mutual Exclusion.* Cambridge, Mass.: MIT Press, 1986.

[294] Reddy, A.L.N., and P. Banerjee. "Gracefully Degradable Disk Arrays." In *Proc. International Symp. on Fault-Tolerant Computing,* 1991, pp. 401–408.

[295] Reed, D.A., and R.M. Fujimoto. *Multicomputer Networks: Message-Based Parallel Processing.* Cambridge, Mass.: MIT Press, 1987.

[296] Reed, I.S., and G. Solomon. "Polynomial Codes over Certain Finite Fields." *J. Soc. Ind. Appl. Math.*, 8 (June 1960), 300–304.

[297] Rennels, D.A. "Fault-Tolerant Computing — Concepts and Examples." *IEEE Trans. on Computers*, C-33, No. 12 (December 1984), 1116–1129.

[298] Rennels, D.A. "On Implementing Fault-Tolerance in Binary Hypercubes." In *Proc. Ann. International Symp. on Fault-Tolerant Computing Systems*, 1986, pp. 344–349.

[299] Rettberg, R.D., W.R. Crowther, P.P. Carvey, and R.S. Tomlinson. "The Monarch Parallel Processor Hardware Design." *Computer*, 23, No. 4 (April 1990), 18–30.

[300] Rettberg, R.D., and R. Thomas. "Contention Is No Obstacle to Shared-Memory Multiprocessing." *Comm. ACM*, 29, No. 12 (December 1986), 1202–1212.

[301] Rosenberg, A.L. "Graph Embeddings 1988: Recent Breakthroughs, New Directions." In *Proc. 3rd Aegean Workshop on Computing*, 1988. *Lecture Notes in Computer Science*, 319 (1988), 160–169.

[302] Rosenfeld, A. (Ed.) *Multiresolution Image Processing and Analysis*. Berlin: Springer-Verlag, 1984.

[303] Rudolph, L.S. *Software Structures for Ultraparallel Computing*. Ph.D. Dissertation, Computer Science Dept., New York University, New York, 1981.

[304] Ruzzo, W.L. "On Uniform Circuit Complexity." *J. Computer and System Sciences*, 22, No. 3 (June 1981), 365–383.

[305] Saad, Y., and M.H. Schultz. "Topological Properties of Hypercubes." *IEEE Trans. on Computers*, C-37, No. 7 (July 1988), 867-872.

[306] Saad, Y., and M.H. Schultz. "Data Communication in Hypercubes." *J. Parallel and Distributed Computing*, 6, No. 1 (February 1989), 115–135.

[307] Saad, Y., and M.H. Schultz. "Data Communication in Parallel Architectures." *Parallel Computing*, 11, No. 2 (August 1989), 131–150.

[308] Samatham, M.R., and D.K. Pradhan. "The De Bruijn Multiprocessor Network: a Versatile Parallel Processing and Sorting Network for VLSI." *IEEE Trans. on Computers*, C-38, No. 4 (April 1989), 567–581.

[309] Santz, J.L.C. (Ed.) *Opportunities and Constraints of Parallel Computing.* Berlin: Springer-Verlag, 1989.

[310] Sarwate, D.V. "On the Complexity of Decoding Goppa Codes." *IEEE Trans. on Information Theory,* IT-23, No. 4 (July 1977), 515–516.

[311] Sauer, C.H., and K.M. Chandy. *Computer Systems Performance Modeling.* Englewood Cliffs, New Jersey: Prentice-Hall, 1981.

[312] Schneck, P.B. "Supercomputers." *Ann. Review of Computer Science,* 4 (1990), 13–36.

[313] Schwartz, J.T. "Ultracomputers." *ACM Trans. on Programming Languages and Systems,* 2, No. 4 (October 1980), 484–521.

[314] Seitz, C.L. "Concurrent VLSI Architectures." *IEEE Trans. on Computers,* C-33, No. 12 (December 1984), 1247–1265.

[315] Seitz, C.L. "The Cosmic Cube." *Comm. ACM,* 28, No. 1 (January 1985), 22–33.

[316] Seitz, C.L., and J. Matisoo. "Engineering Limits on Computer Performance." *Physics Today,* 37, No. 5 (May 1984), 38–45.

[317] Serlin, O. "Fault-Tolerant Systems in Commercial Applications." *Computer,* 17, No. 8 (August 1984), 19–30.

[318] Shamir, E. "How To Share a Secret." *Comm. ACM,* 22, No. 11 (November 1979), 612–613.

[319] Shiloach, Y., and U. Vishkin. "Finding the Maximum, Merging, and Sorting in a Parallel Computation Model." *J. Algorithms,* 2, No. 1 (March 1981), 88–102.

[320] Siegel, H.J. "Partitionable SIMD Computer System Interconnection Network Universality." In *Proc. 16th Ann. Allerton Conf. on Communication, Control, and Computing,* 1978, pp. 586–595.

[321] Siegel, H.J. "Interconnection Networks for SIMD Machines." *Computer,* 12, No. 6 (June 1979), 57–65.

[322] Siegel, H.J. *Interconnection Networks for Large-Scale Parallel Processing: Theory and Case Studies.* Lexington, Mass.: Lexington Books, 1984.

[323] Siegel, H.J., and R.J. McMillen. "The Multistage Cube: a Versatile Interconnection Network." *Computer,* 14, No. 12 (December 1981), 65–76.

[324] Siegel, H.J., and S.D. Smith. "Study of Multistage SIMD Interconnection Networks." In *Proc. 5th Annu. International Symp. on Computer Architecture*, 1978, pp. 223–239.

[325] Siewiorek, D.P., C.G. Bell, and A. Newell. *Computer Structures: Principles and Examples*. New York: McGraw-Hill, 1982.

[326] Siewiorek, D.P., and R.S. Swarz. *The Theory and Practice of Reliable System Design*. Bedford, Mass.: Digital, 1982.

[327] Simmons, M.L., H.J. Wasserman, O.M. Lubeck, C. Eoyang, R. Mendez, H. Harada, and M. Ishiguro. "A Performance Comparison of Four Supercomputers." *Comm. ACM*, 35, No. 8 (August 1992), 116–124.

[328] Singleton, R.C. "On Computing the Fast Fourier Transform." *Comm. ACM*, 10, No. 10 (October 1967), 647–654.

[329] Sivarajan, K.N., and R. Ramaswami. "Multihop Lightwave Networks Based on de Bruijn Graphs." In *Proc. 1991 IEEE INFOCOM*, 1991.

[330] Snir, M. "On Parallel Searching." In *Proc. ACM Symp. on Principles of Distributed Computing*, 1982, pp. 242–253.

[331] Snyder, L. "Supercomputers and VLSI: The Effect of Large-Scale Integration on Computer Architecture." *Advances in Computers*, 23 (1984), 1–33.

[332] Snyder, L. "Type Architectures, Shared Memory, and the Corollary of Modest Potential." *Ann. Review of Computer Science*, 1 (1986), 289–317.

[333] Somani, A.K., and S.B. Choi. "On Embedding Permutations in Hypercubes." In *Proc. 6th Distributed Memory Computing Conference*, 1991, pp. 622–629.

[334] Spectrum. Special Issue: Supercomputers. *IEEE Spectrum*, September 1992, pp. 26–76.

[335] Squire, J.S., and S.M. Palais. "Programming and Design Considerations of a Highly Parallel Computer." *AFIPS Conf. Proc.*, 23 (1963), 395–400.

[336] Stallings, W. *Data and Computer Communications*. New York: Macmillan, 1988.

[337] Stockmeyer, L.J. "Classifying the Computational Complexity of Problems." *J. Symbolic Logic*, 52, No. 1 (March 1987), 1–43.

[338] Stockmeyer, L.J., and U. Vishkin. "Simulation of Parallel Random Access Machines by Circuits." *SIAM J. Comput.,* 13, No. 2 (May 1984), 409–422.

[339] Stone, H.S. "Parallel Processing with the Perfect Shuffle." *IEEE Trans. on Computers,* C-20, No. 2 (February 1971), 153–161.

[340] Stone, H.S. "Parallel Computers." In *Introduction to Computer Architecture.* 2nd ed. Edited by H.S. Stone. Chicago: Science Research Associates, 1980, pp. 363–425.

[341] Stone, H.S. *High-Performance Computer Architecture.* Reading, Mass.: Addison-Wesley, 1987.

[342] Stone, H.S., and J. Cocke. "Computer Architecture in the 1990s." *Computer,* 24, No. 9 (September 1991), 30–38.

[343] Sullivan, H., T. Bashkov, and D. Klappholz. "A Large Scale, Homogeneous, Fully Distributed Parallel Machine." In *Proc. 4th Annu. International Symp. on Computer Architecture,* 1977, pp. 105–124.

[344] Swan, R.J., S.H. Fuller, and D.P. Siewiorek. "Cm*: a Modular Multi-Microprocessor." *AFIPS Conf. Proc.,* 46 (1977), 637–644.

[345] Szymanski, T.H., and C. Hamacher. "On the Permutation Capability of Multistage Interconnection Networks." *IEEE Trans. on Computers,* C-36, No. 7 (July 1987), 810–822.

[346] Tanenbaum, A.S. *Computer Networks.* Englewood Cliffs, New Jersey: Prentice-Hall, 1981.

[347] Tanenbaum, A.S. *Structured Computer Organization.* Englewood Cliffs, New Jersey: Prentice-Hall, 1984.

[348] Tanimoto, S., and T. Pavlidis. "A Hierarchical Data Structure for Picture Processing." *Computer Graphics and Image Processing,* 4 (1975), 104–119.

[349] Thinking Machines Corp. "Connection Machine Model CM-2 Technical Summary." Thinking Machines Technical Report HA87-4, Cambridge, Mass., April 1987.

[350] Thinking Machines Corp. "CM-5 Technical Summary." Cambridge, Mass., October 1991.

[351] Thomas, R. "Behavior of the Butterfly™ Parallel Processor in the Presence of Memory Hot Spots." In *Proc. 1986 International Conf. on Parallel Processing*, 1986, pp. 46–50.

[352] Thompson, C.D. "Area-Time Complexity for VLSI." In *Proc. 11th Annu. ACM Symp. on Theory of Computing*, 1979, pp. 81–88.

[353] Thompson, C.D. "Fourier Transforms in VLSI." *IEEE Trans. on Computers*, C-32, No. 11 (November 1983), 1047–1057.

[354] Toy, W.N. "Fault-Tolerant Computing." *Advances in Computers*, 26 (1987), 201–279.

[355] Trew, A., and G. Wilson. (Ed.) *Past, Present, Parallel: a Survey of Available Parallel Computing Systems.* Berlin: Springer-Verlag, 1991.

[356] Trivedi, K.S. *Probability and Statistics with Reliability, Queueing, and Computer Science Applications.* Englewood Cliffs, New Jersey: Prentice-Hall, 1982.

[357] Tsantilas, A.M. "A Refined Analysis of the Valiant-Brebner Algorithm." Technical Report TR-22-89, Aiken Computation Lab., Harvard University, 1989.

[358] Turek, J., and D. Shasha. "The Many Faces of Consensus iin Distributed Systems." *Computer*, 25, No. 6 (June 1992), 8–17.

[359] Tzeng, N.-F. "Design of a Novel Combining Structure for Shared-Memory Multiprocessors." In *Proc. 1989 International Conf. on Parallel Processing*, 1989, pp. 1–8.

[360] Ullman, J.D. *Computational Aspects of VLSI.* Rockville, Maryland: Computer Science Press, 1983.

[361] Upfal, E. "Efficient Schemes for Parallel Communication." In *Proc. ACM Symp. on Principles of Distributed Computing*, 1982, pp. 55–59.

[362] Upfal, E. "A Probabilistic Relation between Desirable and Feasible Models of Parallel Computation." In *Proc. 16th Annu. ACM Symp. on Theory of Computing*, 1984, pp. 258–264.

[363] Upfal, E. "An $O(\log N)$ Deterministic Packet Routing Scheme." In *Proc. 21st Annu. ACM Symp. on Theory of Computing*, 1989, pp. 241–250.

[364] Upfal, E., and A. Wigderson. "How to Share Memory in a Distributed System." *J. ACM*, 34, No. 1 (January 1987), 116–127.

[365] Valiant, L.G. "A Scheme for Fast Parallel Communication." *SIAM J. Comput.,* 11, No. 2 (May 1982), 350–361.

[366] Valiant, L.G. "Optimality of a Two-Phase Strategy for Routing in Interconnection Networks." *IEEE Trans. on Computers,* C-32, No. 9 (September 1983), 861–863.

[367] Valiant, L.G. "Optimally Universal Parallel Computers." *Phil. Trans. R. Soc. Lond.,* A 326, No. 1591 (September 1988), 373–376.

[368] Valiant, L.G. "General Purpose Parallel Architectures." Technical Report TR-07-89, Aiken Computation Lab., Harvard University, 1989.

[369] Valiant, L.G. "A Bridging Model for Parallel Computation." *Comm. ACM,* 33, No. 8 (August 1990), 103–111.

[370] Valiant, L.G. "General Purpose Parallel Architectures." In *Handbook of Theoretical Computer Science, Vol. A: Algorithms and Complexity.* Edited by J. van Leeuwen. Cambridge, Mass.: MIT Press, 1990, pp. 943–971.

[371] Valiant, L.G., and G.J. Brebner. "Universal Schemes for Parallel Communication." In *Proc. 13th Annu. ACM Symp. on Theory of Computing,* 1981, pp. 263–277.

[372] Varhol, P.D. "Gigabytes Online: Disk Arrays Offer High Performance." *Personal Workstation,* June 1991, pp. 44–49.

[373] Varma, A., and C.S. Raghavendra. "Fault-Tolerant Routing in Multistage Interconnection Networks." *IEEE Trans. on Computers,* C-38, No. 3 (March 1989), 385–393.

[374] Vishkin, U. "A Parallel-Design Distributed-Implementation (PDDI) General-Purpose Computer." *Theoretical Computer Science,* 32 (1984), 157–172.

[375] Von Neumann, J. "Probabilistic Logics and the Synthesis of Reliable Organisms from Unreliable Components." In *Automata Studies.* Edited by C.E. Shannon and J. McCarthy. Princeton: Princeton University Press, 1956, pp. 43–98.

[376] M. Wegman, and J.L. Carter. "New Hash Functions and Their Use in Authentication and Set Equality." *J. Computer and System Sciences,* 22, No. 3 (June 1981), 265–279.

[377] Wensley, J.H., L. Lamport, J. Goldberg, M.W. Green, K.N. Levitt, P.M. Melliar-Smith, R.E. Shostak, and C.B. Weinstock. "SIFT: Design and Analysis of a Fault-Tolerant Computer for Aircraft Control." *Proc. of the IEEE,* 66, No. 10 (October 1978), 1240–1255.

[378] Wittie, L.D. "Communication Structures for Large Networks of Microcomputers." *Computer,* 30, No. 4 (April 1981), 264–273.

[379] Wu., C.-L., and T.-Y. Feng. "On a Class of Multistage Interconnection Networks." *IEEE Trans. on Computers,* C-29, No. 8 (August 1980), 694–702.

[380] Wu., C.-L., and T.-Y. Feng. "The Universality of the Shuffle-Exchange Network." *IEEE Trans. on Computers,* C-30, No. 5 (May 1981), 324–332.

[381] Wulf, W.A., and C.G. Bell. "C.mmp — a Multi-Mini-Processor." *AFIPS Conf. Proc.,* 41 (1972), 765–777.

[382] Wulf, W.A., and S.P. Harbison. "Reflections in a Pool of Processors — an Experience Report on C.mmp/Hydra." *AFIPS Conf. Proc.,* 47 (1978), 939–951.

[383] Yen, W.C., D.W.L. Yen, and K.-S. Fu. "Data Coherence Problem in a Multi-cache System." *IEEE Trans. on Computers,* C-34, No. 1 (January 1985), 56–65.

[384] Yew, P.-C., N.-F. Tzeng, and D.H. Lawrie. "Distributing Hot-Spot Addressing in Large-Scale Multiprocessors." *IEEE Trans. on Computers,* C-36, No. 4 (April 1987), 388–395.

[385] Zhu, C.-Q., and P.-C. Yew. "A Synchronization Scheme and Its Applications for Large Multiprocessor Systems." In *Proc. 4th International Conf. on Distributed Computing Systems,* 1984, pp. 486–491.

[386] Zorpette, G. "Large Computers." *IEEE Spectrum,* January 1992, pp. 33–35.

# Index

1ESS, 131

access pattern, 95, 96, 99
Ajtai, M., 48
Aleliunas, R., 47
alternating Turing machine, 89
ancestor, 96
Arimoto, 21
asymptotically optimal network, 72, 72n
asynchronism, 3, 5, 7, 110, 111, 140
    algorithm, 112
    network, 5, 112
    sensitivity, 116
Atanasoff, J., 7
Aumann, Y., 47, 84, 90, 91
availability, 124

background traffic, 92, 94
Backus, J., 2
banyan network, 34
baseline network, 34
    illustration, 39
Batcher, K.E., 48
BCH codes, 21
Bell, G., 30n
Beneš network, 31, 35
    illustration, 37
Ben-Or, M., 22, 47, 84, 91
Bertsekas, D.P., 82, 111
Blakley, G.R., 22
blocking, 45
Borodin, A., 44

"boudoir," 29
Bouricius, W.G., 132
Brebner, G.J., 47, 78
Brigham, E.O., Jr., 14
buffer overflow, see overflow
bus, 30n, 45
bus network
    illustration, 37
Butterfly™, 29, 34
butterfly network, 33–34, 46–48, 108
    embedding, 107
    illustration, 38
Byzantine Generals Problem, 139

C104, 47
cache coherence, 7
Caley graph, 35
canonical path, 71
capacity, 54
Carrol, Lewis, 1
Carter, W.C., 132
Cauchy matrix, 19
CCC network, see cube-connected-cycles
        network
Cedar, 34, 92, 131
cell, 88
checkpoint, 133, 134
Chernoff's bound, 54
CHoPP, 92
chordal ring network, 33, 35
    illustration, 37
Churchill, Winston, 50

circuit, 89
circuit switching, 30
clock, 111, 111n, 140
    global, 5, 110, 111, 113
        failure, 111
        fault tolerance, 111n
    skew, 5
Clos network, 31
cluster, 131, 135–138
Cm$^*$, 131
C.mmp, 29, 131, 134n
combining, 47, 91–95, 100, 109
    k-way, 92, 96
    pairwise, 92, 94, 96
    software, 94, 100
combining tree, 92
communication, 3, 5, 9
    PRAM, 88
    all-to-all personalized, 81
    all-to-one, 99
    bottleneck, 5
    complexity, *see* complexity, communication
    relative uniformity, 99
    store-and-forward, 30
    total exchange, *see* total exchange problem
compact disc, 21
complete disablement set, 125
completely connected network, 35, 90
    illustration, 37
complexity
    communication, 5, 121
    time, 112
computation model, 5
computational integrity, 135
concurrency control, 111
Connection Machine, 4, 29, 32, 35, 45

contention, 91, 92, 94
Cosmic Cube, 29, 32
coverage, 132, 133
Cray Y-MP, 3n
crossbar network, 35, 36
crossbar switch, 49
cube-connected-cycles network, 33, 35
    illustration, 38

d-way digit-exchange network, 34, 46, 47
"dance hall," 29
Dash computer, 30n, 35
DAT, 21
data alignment, 94
data scattering, 94
database, 111
DCC, 21
de Bruijn network, 4, 33–34, 44, 46–48, 50, 71–80, 83
    illustration, 38
    shortest path, 33
    symmetry, 83
deadlock, 45, 47, 48
delta network, 34, 36
determinant, 11
digit, 71
digraph, 32, 52
dimension, 55
divided-differences table, 13, 17, 20
"domino effect," 4, 10
double rooted tree network
    illustration, 37
Du, D.-Z., 33
duplication, 132
    packet, 45, 48

Eckert, P., 7
ECS, 51, 117, 119

asynchronism, 111, 113
global clock, 111
packet, 117, 119
Elkind, S.A., 132
embedding, 36, 48
butterfly network, *see* butterfly network, embedding
emulation, 47
epoch, 51, 53, 111
epoched communication scheme, *see* ECS
erasure, 10, 20, 21
error propagation, 10, 24, 134
error-correcting codes, 6, 10, 44, 132
complexity, 21
routing, 44
error-detecting codes, 132

failure, 5, 36
fail-stop, 140
link, 10, 48, 53, 83, 134, 135
node, 4, 70, 134
Fast Fourier Transform, 6, 8, 10, 13–14, 16–19
VLSI complexity, 14
parallel, 14
fat-tree network, 35
fault
Byzantine, 139
containment, 4, 10, 131, 133–138
correlation, 140
dynamic, 48, 91, 132
independence, 139
model, 25
permanent, 133
transient, 4, 24n, 133, 140
fault detection, 132, 133, 135
fault isolation, 133
fault tolerance, 3, 4, 36, 42, 44, 48, 49, 131–134, 140

connectivity, 44
responsibility of individuals, 134
feature size, 2
Feng, T.-Y, 34
Fermat-Euler Theorem, 19n
fetch-and-add, 89, 94
**Fetch-and-Add**, 89n
FFT, *see* Fast Fourier Transform
FILTERING, 10, 22–24, 131, 135, 138, 139
finite field, 11, 14
flip network, 34
flooding, 113
Fortune, S., 88
forward phase, 95
Foucault, Michel, 26
Fourier transform, 13–14, 16
Fourier transform matrix, 13
FSRA, 4–7, 45–47, 63–65, 67–70, 72, 81, 82, 82n, 83, 84, 87, 95, 107–109, 115, 121–125, 128, 129, 131, 134, 135n, 137–139
description, 63
h-relation, 81
sensitivity, 110, 112, 119–122
FTMP, 45, 111n, 133, 134
FTPP, 131

Galois field, 11
generator, 21
GF-11, 31
ghost piece, 96
Giladi, E., 45
Goldwasser, S., 22
graceful degradation, 133, 134
graph, 6, 32
connectivity, 6, 32, 33, 36, 44n, 45, 82, 83, 139n
degree, 36, 37

diameter, 32, 36, 37, 72n, 113, 115
edge-disjoint paths, 32
in-degree, 32
incidence, 32
node-disjoint paths, 6, 44n, 83
node-symmetric, 6, 35, 82, 83
out-degree, 32
path, 32
  length, 32
spanner, 122
spread, 33, 36, 44n
symmetry, 35
group-based graph, 35

Hamiltonian path, 115
hashing, 5, 87, 91, 94
  r-wise independence, 109
  universal, 91, 108
Håstad, J., 47
Hennessy, J.L., 7
heterogeneous system, 5
Hopcroft, J.E., 44
Horner's rule, 17, 19, 20
Horowitz, E., 13
"hot spot," 92–94
HPC, 6, 130, 131, 134, 135, 138–140
HPC-Routing, 137–140
Hsu, D.F., 33
hypercube network, 4–6, 32–33, 35, 36,
    44–48, 50, 54–70, 72, 83, 91,
    94, 95, 107–109, 115, 119, 121,
    123–125, 129
  generalized, 33, 83
  illustration, 38
  rearrangeability, 33
  universality, 31, 33
hypercube parallel computer, *see* HPC

IDA, 5, 6, 8–10, 14, 16, 18–20, 20n, 21–

24, 44–47, 60, 78, 81, 82, 87, 90,
    91, 108, 129, 131, 137–139
Illiac IV, 29, 34, 133
indirect binary cube network, 32, 34
  illustration, 38
inefficiency, 90n
information dispersal, 6, 9, 10, 22, 42
information dispersal algorithm, *see* IDA
interpolation, 10
  polynomial, *see* polynomial, inter-
    polation
inverse, 11
invertibility, 11
iPSC/860, 30, 32
iWarp, 35

Joel network, 35

Kaklamanis, C., 44
Karlin, A.R., 90
Kautz network, 33, 83
  illustration, 38
Komlós, J., 48
Krizanc, D., 44
Kruskal, C.P., 109
KSR 1, 30n

Lawrie, D.H., 34n
Leibniz's rule, 104
Leighton, F.T., 35, 47, 48
Leiserson, C.E., 35
l-graph, 117
linear array network, 35
  illustration, 37
link delay, 116, 117, 119
Lipson, J.D., 18
Liu, Z., 33
locality, 29, 36
lock, 92
loop network, 33, 83

*l*-path, 117
Lyuu, Y.-D., 33

Ma, Y., 49
Maggs, B.M., 48, 49
maintenance, 5, 83, 123
    on-line, 3, 5, 7, 123–129
Makedon, F., 49
masking, 132, 133
masking redundancy, 132
Mauchly, J., 7
maximum distance separable, 21
McEliece, R.J., 22
Mehlhorn, K., 91
memory hierarchy, 7
memory module, 27, 29, 89, 90
Menger's theorem, 44n
Menger, Karl, 6
mesh network, 34, 35, 47, 49
    illustration, 39
mesh-of-trees network, 35
    illustration, 37
message passing, 30, 51, 110, 111, 134
message switching, 30
MIN, *see* multistage interconnection net-
    work
modified data manipulator network, 34
    illustration, 38
Monarch, 30n, 92
Moore bound, 36
multi-butterfly network, 34, 49
multiplexing, 108
multipoint link, 30n
multistage interconnection network, 33,
    34, 34n, 45, 92

$\mathcal{NC}$, *see* "Nick's class"
*n*-cube, 55
NCUBE, 32

neighborhood, 30
network, 3, 6, 27, 52
    communication, 27
    diameter, *see* graph, diameter
    direct, 27, 29, 30, 42, 48, 89, 112
    indirect, 27, 29–31
    non-blocking, 31
    partition, 45
    point-to-point, 30
    simulation, 90
    store-and-forward, 30, 112
    strictly non-blocking, 31
    switching, 27
    synchronous, 112
    topology, 3, 32, 36, 42
Newman, M., 47
"Nick's class," 89
*N*-Modular Redundancy, 132, 133
$(N, M)$-PRAM, 89
NMR, *see* *N*-Modular Redundancy
non-destructive model, 51, 54
Norton, V.A., 92
*N*-Ultracomputer, 89
*N*-version programming, 132
NYU Ultracomputer, 29, 34, 92, 94

offset routing, *see* routing, offset
omega network, 31, 34n, 34, 44
    illustration, 38
on-line maintenance, *see* maintenance,
    on-line
    simulation, *see* PRAM, simulation
optical network, 31, 34
optical technology, 7
order, 19n
overflow, 10, 54
Özveren, C., 82

packet, 42

packet switching, 30

pancake network, 35

Parallel Computation Thesis, 89

parallel processing, 2, 3, 5, 7, 92, 131
    experiences, 7
    general-purpose, 87

parallel slackness, 90n, 91

parallelism, 2

partition, 124, 125

Patel, J.A., 34

Patterson, D.A., 7

PE, *see* processing element

PE-to-PE organization, 28, 29, 31

peak performance, 3n

Pease, M.C., III, 32

Peleg, D., 122

performance analysis, 7

permutation, *see* routing, permutation

permutation routing, *see* routing, per-
    mutation

Pfister, G.F., 92

"piece," 96

piece, 9
    bundling, 46, 53, 96
    concatenation, 53

piece-set, 72, 73

pipelining, 2, 49, 107, 108

Pippenger, N., 47

Plaxton, C.G., 49

Pollard, J.M., 14

polynomial, 11
    evaluation, 8–10, 13
    interpolation, 8, 10, 12–13, 17
    irreducible, 11

PRAC, 88

PRAM, 5–7, 86–91, 94–96, 100, 106, 107,
    109, 111
    CREW, 88

EREW, 88

CRCW, 48n, 48, 88, 90, 91, 94, 95,
    99, 107–109
    priority, 89, 91, 92
    simulation, 5–7, 47, 86, 87, 89–109,
    135
        fault tolerance, *see* simulation, fault
        tolerance
        non-uniform, 90
        on-line maintenance, 129

preconditioning, 13

Preparata, F.P., 22, 33

primitive root of unity, 21

principal root of unity, 13

processing element, 28–32, 35, 89, 134

processor-to-memory organization, 29

program transformation, 7

propagation delay, 112, 135

PSC/2, 30, 32

pyramid network, 35
    illustration, 39

queueing delay, 4, 10, 45, 57, 60

RA, 47

Rabin's conjecture, 4, 45, 58

Rabin's paradigm, 82, 83

Rabin, M.O., 6, 9, 10, 14, 20, 44, 47, 82

RABN, 46, 72–75, 77–79, 115
    description, 72

RAM, 111

Ranade, A.G., 47, 48, 87, 91, 107–109

Randell, B., 4

Rao, S., 48

rearrangeable network, 31–33

"reasonable" length, 53

reconfiguration, 48

reconstruction, 17
    operation, 10, 14, 15, 17

reconstructibility, 53

recovery, 133

redundancy, 5, 131, 132

    dynamic, 132, 133

      hardware, 133

      software, 133

    hardware, 132

    hybrid, 133, 134

    software, 132

    sparing, 133

    static, 132, 133

    time, 132

Redundant Array of Inexpensive Disks
    (RAID), 10

Reed, I.S., 21

Reed-Solomon codes, 6, 21, 22, 138

    applications, 21

    complexity, 21

    decoding, 21

    generalized, 21

region of fault containment, *see* fault,
    containment

reliability, 4, 132, 134

    data, 9

Rennels, D.A., 56

replace-add, 89

**Replace-Add**, 89n

replacement

    on-line, 124

    wire, 6

replication, 84, 131, 135, 139

retry, 132, 133

return phase, 95

reverse baseline network, 34

    illustration, 39

ring, 11

ring network, 35

    illustration, 37

rollback, 133, 134

routing, 3–7, 10, 27, 34, 36, 42, 44, 53,
    90, 91

    deterministic, 48

    distributed, 42, 44

    framework using IDA, 46

    global, 42

    h-relation, 42, 81

    oblivious, 42, 44

    offset, 48

    permutation, 31–33, 42, 49, 99

    randomized, 47n, 47

    successful, 53

    two-phase, 47

RP3, 34, 92, 94

Rudolph, L., 109

Russell, Bertrand, 41

SA, 112–115, 117, 119, 121, 122, 140

same cell condition, 94–96, 99

sample point, 12

sample value, 12

Sarwate, D.V., 22

SC, *see* same cell condition

scalability, 42, 92, 116

scans, 87

scheduling, 42

Schiller, Friedrich, 123

Schneider, P.R., 132

Schumpeter, Joseph Alois, 86

Schuster, A., 90

SE, *see* switching element

secret sharing, 22

self-timing, 112

sensitivity, 3, 5, 112, 116, 121, 122

    link, 116, 119, 121

    low, 110, 112, 116, 119

    processor, 116, 119, 121

serialization, 89

Shakespeare, 8

Shamir, A., 22

shared memory, 30

shuffle, 34n, 34

shuffle-exchange network, 34, 42, 44

    illustration, 39

    subgraph of de Bruijn network, 34

SIFT, 45, 111n, 133–135

sim-FSRA, 95, 96, 99, 100, 105, 107

simplex system, 132

simulation, 3

    fault tolerance, 91, 95, 108

    PRAM, *see* PRAM, simulation

Sitaraman, R., 48

slackness, *see* parallel slackness

slowdown, 5, 48, 90, 106–107

Snir, M., 109

Solomon, G., 21

sorting, 48, 49, 87, 90, 91

sorting network, 48

spanner, *see* graph, spanner

spanning tree, 113

spare, 133, 134

SPCS, *see* symmetric parallel communication scheme

speedup, 7

splitting operation, 9, 14–17, 22

spread, *see* graph, spread

SRA, 45–47, 57–60, 62, 64, 81, 82, 82n, 95, 113

   description, 56

   h-relation, 58, 81

   sensitivity, 119, 121, 122

Stamoulis, G.D., 82

"standard method," 15

standby replacement, 132

STAR, 133

star network, 33, 35, 83

illustration, 37

start node, 112, 113

Stone, H.S., 34

storage allocation, 90, 94, 100

STRETCH, 92n

subcube, 47, 56, 61, 63, 72, 82n, 129

subnetwork, 72

subpacket, 45

superpipeline, 2

superscalar, 2

suspect, 10, 23

switching, 30

switching element, 27, 29–32, 35, 36, 42, 45, 138

symmetric parallel communication scheme, 51, 52, 60, 66, 76, 82, 83

synchronism, 111, 140

synchronization, 7, 92, 111, 112

   global, 51, 111

   local, 51, 110, 111

   rollback, 111

synchronization message, 5, 111, 113, 117n, 119, 121, 122

synchronizer, 112, 122

   acknowledgment, 112, 121–122

Szemerédi, E., 48

Szymanski conjecture, 33

Tandem/16, 124

testability, 56

testing, 134

   wire, 6

Thucydides, 110

TMR, *see* Triple Modular Redundancy

Tollis, I.G., 49

torus network, 35

total exchange problem, 81

Touchstone, 35

transient fault, *see* fault, transient

transpose, 11
tree network, 35
tree saturation, 92
tree-of-meshes network, 35
Triple Modular Redundancy, 132–134
triplication, 132
Tsantilas, A., 44
Tseng, P., 82
Tsitsiklis, J.N., 82, 111
Turing machine, 89
Tzeng, N.-F., 92

Ullman, J.D., 122
Ultracomputer, 89, 90, 94, 95
unique path property, 34, 45
universality, 31
Upfal, E., 34, 47, 49, 90
UPP, *see* unique path property

Valiant, L.G., 47, 60, 78, 81, 87, 90n, 91
Vandermonde matrix, 9, 12, 14, 16, 17
    inverse, 12
Vinci, Leonardo da, 130
Vishkin, U., 91
VLIW, 2
VLSI, 2, 7, 112
von Neumann bottleneck, 2
    history, 7
von Neumann machine, 2, 7, 87
    controversy, 7
von Neumann, J., 7, 132
    parallel processing, 7
voting, 4, 6, 8, 10, 21, 22, 132, 134, 135
    software, 132
Voyager, 21
Vuillemin, J.E., 33

wait buffer, 91, 95, 100–106
wake-up message, 113

Waksman network, 35
Wigderson, A., 22
wire
    disablement, 123
    replacement, *see* replacement, wire
    testing, *see* testing, wire
work, 90n
work-preserving, 90n
Wu, C.-L., 34
Wyllie, J., 88

x-tree network, 35
    illustration, 39